Penguin B

THE LAW
OF THE LAND

Henry Reynolds is the author of twelve books, including *An Indelible Stain?*, *The Other Side of the Frontier*, *Black Pioneers*, *Fate of a Free People*, *This Whispering in Our Hearts* and the award-winning *Why Weren't We Told?* Born in Hobart, Tasmania, in 1938, Henry taught in secondary schools in Australia and England after receiving a Master of Arts from the University of Tasmania, and for many years was on the teaching staff in the history department of James Cook University in Townsville. He is currently Research Professor at the University of Tasmania and is the recipient of an Australian Research Council Senior Research Fellowship.

WHAT THE REVIEWERS HAVE SAID ABOUT HENRY REYNOLDS AND *THE LAW OF THE LAND*

'Reynolds' is a project concerned with nothing less than the revision of our interpretations of ourselves as a people.'
Veronica Brady, *Australian Book Review*

'Propositions advanced in . . . *The Law of the Land* . . . overturn 200 years of white assumptions in Australia over who owns the land.'
Michael Davie, *London Observer*

'The duplicity of white Australia's reasoning is laid bare in a meticulous history with a strong moral purpose.'
Cassandra Pybus, *Top Shelf*

'Henry Reynolds's books have remade the way in which European conquest and racial contacts are understood . . . [they] are among the most theoretically informed to be published about Australia's past.'
Humphrey McQueen, *Independent Monthly*

'lucid, original and forcefully argued'
Gordon Hawkins, *Weekend Australian*

'an absorbing story going to the very heart of the dilemma of modern Australia'
Judith White, *Sun-Herald*

'The most important influence on the way many of us view the history of relations between black and white Australians has been the work of Henry Reynolds.'
Michael Duffy, *The Australian*

'Henry Reynolds is that rare kind of academic, a public intellectual prepared to engage forcefully with the main ethical, political and social issues that trouble our tentative nation . . . [he] has refashioned the way we regard our tenure on this land we call home, and our relationship to those original Australians dispossessed by European settlement.'
Cassandra Pybus, *The Weekend Australian*

'indispensable to anyone wanting to know more about the legal doctrines used in Australia's colonisation, and the history of agitation for Aboriginal rights'
Madeleine Smith, *Australian Left Review*

'a challenge to all Australians . . . cannot be ignored'
Peter Hennessy, *Legal Service Bulletin*

'wide-ranging in its political significance. Those who do not read *The Law of the Land* will disqualify themselves from commenting on the legalities of land rights or sovereignty during the Bicentennial year.'
Humphrey McQueen, *Sydney Morning Herald*

'a radical revision of conventional acceptances . . . epoch-making – or ending'
Judith Wright, *The Age*

'Henry Reynolds's books have invited a nation to change the way it thinks about the past. His careful research unravels the myths and half-truths that have characterised our stories of white settlement.'
Suzy Freeman-Greene, *The Age*

ALSO BY HENRY REYNOLDS

Aborigines and Settlers
Race Relations in North Queensland
The Other Side of the Frontier
Frontier
Dispossession
Black Pioneers
Fate of a Free People
Aboriginal Sovereignty
This Whispering in Our Hearts
Why Weren't We Told?
An Indelible Stain?

HENRY REYNOLDS

The Law of the Land

PENGUIN BOOKS

Penguin Books

Published by the Penguin Group
Penguin Books Australia Ltd
250 Camberwell Road, Camberwell, Victoria 3124, Australia
Penguin Books Ltd
80 Strand, London WC2R 0RL, England
Penguin Putnam Inc.
375 Hudson Street, New York, New York 10014, USA
Penguin Books, a division of Pearson Canada
10 Alcorn Avenue, Toronto, Ontario, Canada M4V 3B2
Penguin Books (NZ) Ltd
Cnr Rosedale and Airborne Roads, Albany, Auckland, New Zealand
Penguin Books (South Africa) (Pty) Ltd
24 Sturdee Avenue, Rosebank, Johannesburg 2196, South Africa
Penguin Books India (P) Ltd
11, Community Centre, Panchsheel Park, New Delhi 110 017, India

First published by Penguin Books Australia Ltd 1987
Second edition published 1992
This revised and updated third edition published 2003

1 3 5 7 9 10 8 6 4 2

Copyright © Henry Reynolds 1987, 1992, 2003

The moral right of the author has been asserted

All rights reserved. Without limiting the rights under copyright reserved above,
no part of this publication may be reproduced, stored in or introduced into a retrieval
system, or transmitted, in any form or by any means (electronic,
mechanical, photocopying, recording or otherwise), without the prior written
permission of both the copyright owner and the above publisher of this book.

Design by Cathy Larsen, Penguin Design Studio
Typeset in 12.5/15pt Perpetua by Midland Typesetters, Maryborough, Victoria
Printed and bound in Australia by McPherson's Printing Group, Maryborough, Victoria

National Library of Australia
Cataloguing-in-Publication data:

Reynolds, Henry, 1938– .
The law of the land.

3rd edition.
Bibliography.
Includes index.
ISBN 0 14 100642 0.

1. Land tenure – Law and legislation – Australia.
2. Aborigines, Australian – Land tenure – History.
3. Land settlement – Australia – History. I. Title.

346.940432

www.penguin.com.au

*For John, Anna, Rebecca
in whom the passion for justice lives on*

Contents

ACKNOWLEDGEMENTS	xi
PREFACE TO THE THIRD EDITION	xiii
PREFACE TO THE SECOND EDITION	xv
PREFACE TO THE FIRST EDITION	xvii
INTRODUCTION	1
1. WHO WAS IN POSSESSION?	9
2. BY WHAT TENURE?	37
3. RECONNAISSANCE AND REASSESSMENT	67
4. THE FIRST LAND RIGHTS MOVEMENT	99
5. LAND RIGHTS FRUSTRATED, 1834–38	127
6. LAND RIGHTS RECOGNISED, 1838–48	153

7. PASTORAL LEASES	179
8. A FORGOTTEN LEGACY	191
9. MABO AND WIK REMAKE THE LAW OF THE LAND	205
10. THE AFTERMATH OF MABO	221
CONCLUSION	245
ABBREVIATIONS	249
NOTES	250
BIBLIOGRAPHY	269
INDEX	289

Acknowledgements

Two grants made research for this book possible – one from the Australian Research Grants Committee that enabled me to spend several valuable weeks in Britain, and a Harold White Fellowship at the National Library in Canberra.

Over the past decade I have worked in many libraries and archives, but the bulk of the work for this book was done in only three: the Australian National Library, the Practitioners Library of the High Court of Australia and the British Library in London. I received help and encouragement in each place.

My colleagues at James Cook University have, as always, been supportive, encouraging and understanding. Val Hicks has been a prompt and efficient typist.

1987

While preparing a new edition of *The Law of the Land* I have been supported by an Australian Research Council Senior Research Fellowship held at the University of Tasmania in Launceston. I have had the advantage of having access to the work of a great many scholars in law, history and other disciplines who have contributed to the intense national debate about Indigenous land rights since the second edition was published in 1992.

2003

Preface to the Third Edition

In the eleven years since the publication of the second edition of this book in 1992, the Mabo decision and the affirmation of native title have become central – and controversial – questions in Australian national life, impacting on law, politics, scholarship and the arts. The Wik decision of the High Court was so closely related to themes that had been discussed in *The Law of the Land* that it was necessary to greatly expand the material on the origin of the pastoral leases and to treat the case itself in some detail. The principal native title cases dealt with by the High Court between 1996 and 2002 also provided apt illustrations of the way the principles of native title were evolving in Australia.

Preface to the Second Edition

Readers and reviewers responded very favourably to the first edition. Given the continuing importance of the issues with which it was concerned, *The Law of the Land* remains highly relevant to contemporary debate. Some critics felt that, given the illustration on the front cover, much greater attention should have been paid to John Batman's treaty with the Aborigines. It was suggested that the rejection of the treaty was proof of the government's acceptance of *terra nullius* and was, by implication, a major challenge to the interpretation advanced in *The Law of the Land*. Although I had dealt with the Batman treaty in an earlier book (*Frontier*, 1987), I decided to re-examine the whole issue. The new material has been added to the beginning of Chapter 6.

The decision of the High Court in *Mabo v. Queensland* in June 1992 was of such direct relevance to the book that I decided to add a new chapter concerned with the judgement.

Preface to the First Edition

This book grew out of two previous works: *The Other Side of the Frontier* and *Frontier*. Both were about white–Aboriginal relations. Both dealt in part with the land question. But it was only in the last two chapters of *Frontier* that I began to investigate the complex political, legal and moral questions involved in the first and second land rights movements.

This was a very belated development for someone who had been studying the history of Australian race relations for fifteen years. There were two reasons for this. Unlike historians of an earlier generation who began the study of colonial society with the official British records and moved thematically in the same direction as the settlers – from England to Australia – I began at the frontier, with the experience of white and black at the point of contact in those districts furthest removed from the colonial towns and from London.

The first book to emerge from this work, *The Other Side of the Frontier*, was much more about the Aborigines than the settlers. *Frontier* was concerned with frontier conflict and racial ideology as much as it was with the land question. It had taken a long time to get to what had always been the central issue. But the question appeared to be settled. There was little disagreement from any point of the political or intellectual spectrum. Discovery, it was generally agreed, had delivered to the Europeans not just sovereignty over Australia but ownership of every inch of land as well; Australia was a colony of settlement, not conquest; there had never been any recognition of native title; what ameliorative measures were taken did not imply any acceptance of Aboriginal land rights.

It was only after a great deal of research into the legal aspects of settlement that I began to appreciate the complexity of the issues involved, the ramification, the overlapping. It gradually became clear that the conventional view was in need of major correction. I realised that I had gone on for years accepting at face value ideas and interpretations that were wrong, that I had taught them over and over to students, never doubting their accuracy. My conviction strengthened as my research progressed and by the time I came to plan this book I believed that the conventional view of Australian settlement, seen from both a legal and a historical point of view, had to be significantly reassessed. This in turn had important implications for the way Australians see their past, the way they assess present problems, the way they plan for the future.

Once begun, the book was written very quickly. Perhaps some of the excitement of the search will be passed on to the reader. The complexity of some of the themes created problems of presentation. Hopefully the balance between detailed explanation and clarity of expression has been struck sufficiently well to enable the reader to understand issues which have for too long been left in obscurity and to ask questions left unanswered for 200 years.

Introduction

Numerous problems arise when updating a book, especially when the bulk of it was written fifteen years ago. The problems are more apparent when the subject of the study has changed so quickly and so broadly, as has this one.

There are strong differences of opinion about the impact of the Mabo judgement in 1992, but few people would now contest the view that it represented a watershed in the relations between Australia's Indigenous population and the wider society. It also brought about dramatic changes in both the letter and the spirit of Australian jurisprudence, guiding it towards the mainstream traditions of common law native title, now almost 200 years old.

The judgement itself, and the Wik case of 1996, were also about history and the way the past has been interpreted – even to the question of what actually happened when British law was brought into the fledgling colonial societies. In the long run, these things will matter more than the strong current of moral concern that ran through some of the judgements. While debate will persist and fluctuate about the question of whether Indigenous Australians on the whole benefited from Mabo and Wik, there can be no doubt about the enhancement of their status. They are now either actual or potential landowners or dispossessed landowners. And the Mabo judgement suggested that the loss of property was, if not illegal, then certainly morally wrong, although the High Court has been careful to shut the jurisprudential door on the question of compensation for expropriated land.

These changes may not seem to be all that significant but the symbolic importance was profound, given that the doctrine of *terra nullius* had been premised on the assumption that the Aborigines and Torres Strait Islanders were uniquely primitive, having no traditional system of land ownership at all.

Another problem that arose when updating *The Law of the Land* was the intellectual and cultural impact of Mabo and Wik, and the way in which their content – once seen as being radical, surprising and even shocking – has now come to be seen as commonplace, axiomatic, and taken for granted. In 1987 the major task of this book was to explain what native title was, where it had come from, and how it had taken root in Canada and New Zealand but not in Australia. At the time it was a foreign, exotic concept, little known or understood, even in the legal profession.

As Australian law accommodates native title, what needs to be explained is the idea of *terra nullius* that was taken for granted until so recently. I would like to think that *The Law of the Land* does explain this and can be appreciated by a new generation of readers who accept the Mabo judgement and wonder what all the fuss was about when it was handed down.

On re-reading the Introduction to the first edition I was immediately struck by how dated it now was, and the question arose as to whether it should be preserved as a historic document; radically rewritten; or deleted altogether. I decided to preserve the original piece, and to add this preamble to the third edition.

In 1937 R. T. E. Latham, a prominent legal scholar, remarked that when the first settlers reached Australia,

> their invisible and inescapable cargo of English law fell from their shoulders and attached itself to the soil on which they stood. Their personal law became the territorial law of the Colony.[1]

It is a graphic image. What was not mentioned was that in transit from shoulder to soil the inescapable cargo struck the Aborigines such a severe blow that they have still not recovered from it.

The legal profession as a whole has been remarkably reluctant to admit the role of the law in the dispossession of the Aborigines and the ongoing injustices that they have been subjected to during the last 200 years. The claim has always been that English law was blind to racial differences and that the Aborigines became subjects of the Crown from the first instance of settlement. But the facts speak for themselves. Despite coming under the protection of the common law, it is my belief that as many as 20 000 Aborigines were killed in the course of Australian settlement. They were not, in a legal sense, foreign enemies struck down in war, although a few were shot down during periods of martial law. Most were murdered – nothing more nor less. Yet the law was powerless to staunch the flow of blood – and neither lawyers nor judges appear to have done much to bring the killing to an end. It is not an honourable record.

There was another, even more profound, failure of trust that still deeply influences relations between whites and

Aborigines. It concerns the question of land. At the time of Australian settlement, English law protected property more than it protected life itself. Private property was vigorously defended against thieves and trespassers, as well as against the prerogative power of the Crown. How, then, could Aboriginal rights be totally ignored? English law, like most other legal systems in Europe, paid great respect to possession: it was 'nine points of the law', as the old legal maxim ran, or, as the most widely used nineteenth-century legal dictionary observed, *beati possidentis*, 'blessed are those in possession'.[2]

'It hath been truly a custom of old,' wrote John Selden, the father of international law in England,

> and which holds to this daie in the more eminent Nations, that Vacancies are his who apprehends them first by occupation; as we used to saie of those wee call no man's Goods. This appears plain in the Imperial Law, nor do wee know of any Nation where it is not received.[3]

The truly amazing achievement of Australian jurisprudence was to deny that the Aborigines were ever in possession of their own land, robbing them of the great legal strength of that position, and of compensation which should have been paid following resumption by the Crown. South Australia's second governor, George Gawler, put his finger on the fundamental issue in 1840 when he observed that 'if the claims of the natives are not void before all, they are preliminary to all. They cannot occupy a middle station'.[4]

The official view has always been that Aboriginal claims were always 'void before all'. The intellectual and moral gymnastics required to sustain that position have been quite extraordinary. Before the settlers arrived in Australia there was some reason to suppose that the continent was largely uninhabited and that the Europeans would actually be the first occupants. But that idea was known to be erroneous within a few years of arrival of the First Fleet and certainly by 1800. Despite all the evidence to the contrary, the law continued to insist that Australia was uninhabited, that no one was in possession. Various jurists described the country as being 'waste and uninhabited', 'waste and unoccupied', 'desert and uninhabited', 'unpeopled'. This assessment was given even greater status by the Privy Council in a case in 1889, when it determined that at the time of settlement Australia was 'practically unoccupied without settled inhabitants'.[5]

What was even more extraordinary than this judgement by an English law lord who knew little about Australia or the Aborigines was that it was binding on Australian courts as late as the 1970s and even now its status is not finally determined. In the only detailed treatment of the question in an Australian court (the so-called Gove Land Rights Case in 1971) it was determined that the Aborigines in question had a feeling of obligation towards the land but not the actual ownership of it.[6] The local clans belonged to the land, but the land didn't belong to them and hadn't done so since 1788.

It was an amazing dismissal of Aboriginal tenure that would have been seen as extraordinary by well-informed colonists and by Imperial government officials in the 1830s, as the discussion following will show. In a 1985 High Court judgement, Justice Deane dealt with the legal position of Aborigines who were still living on their own country and whose relationship to it remained unobliterated,

> yet almost two centuries on, the generally accepted view remains that the common law is ignorant of any communal

native title or other legal claims of the Aboriginal clans or peoples even to the ancestral lands on which they still live.[7]

This was surely the distinctive and unenviable contribution of Australian jurisprudence to the history of relations between Europeans and the Indigenous people of the non-European world. It was not to provide justification for conquest or cession of land or assumption of sovereignty – others had done that before Australia was settled – but to deny the right – even the fact – of possession to people who had lived on their land for 40 000 years. Settlers in comparable countries (New Zealand, United States, Canada, South Africa) did not deny that the indigenes were the original owners of the soil, whatever else they may have done in the course of colonisation.

The common law was corrupted in Australia by the nature of the relationship between settlers and Aborigines in the same way in which it was corrupted in Britain's slave colonies. In the West Indies, the law accommodated the bondage of the slave and the vast power of the master. In Australia, it accommodated the dispossession of the owners of the land without payment of any compensation at all. Slavery was abolished in 1833 by Imperial legislation and the law was eventually purged of the relics of the system. Forced and uncompensated dispossession was frowned on by the Imperial government but in one way or another the colonists continued to take Aboriginal land and convince themselves that it was not theft. Justice Deane correctly observed that Australian law 'has still not reached the stage of retreat from injustice'[8] that American law had attained by 1823 with the famous judgement of Chief Justice John Marshall in *Johnson v. MacIntosh* and the enunciation of the doctrine of native title, which will be discussed in the following pages.

The inability of Australian law to retreat from historical injustice has had major implications for relations between white Australians and Aborigines. No matter what governments have done or said over the last 200 years, they have not been able to convince Aboriginal communities of their *bona fides* or to expunge that deeply ingrained sense of injustice. This is scarcely surprising. Many Europeans – though probably always a minority – have been equally unconvinced. So, too, have most outsiders who have looked at the Australian scene – and their critical scrutiny may increase in importance in years to come. Outwardly a majority of white Australians has rejected the claims of historic injustice. But there has always been a sense of uneasiness, a lurking shadow of guilt, a 'whisper in the heart'[9] that encouraged a tendency to explain the problem away by blaming the Aborigines themselves and to argue that they lost their land because they were too primitive, or too passive or too savage or too unproductive. It eased the conscience but did nothing for the moral health of the nation.

ONE

Who Was in Possession?

WHAT HAPPENED IN 1788?

What happened on 7 February 1788 when the officials of the First Fleet raised the British flag over the motley collection of convicts and jailers at Sydney Cove and took 'possession of the colony in form'?[1] What did Australians celebrate 200 years later?

For 200 years before the Mabo judgement the official view was clear. The British claimed not only *sovereignty* over New South Wales — then comprising the whole eastern half of Australia — but also *ownership* of all the 400 million hectares contained therein. In a major judgement in the Supreme Court of the Northern Territory in 1971, Justice Blackburn declared that 'on the foundation of New South Wales . . . and of South Australia, every square inch of territory in the colony became the property of the Crown'.[2] In a High Court case in 1913 Justice Isaacs had pushed the date of the expropriation back even further. 'So we start,' he declared,

> with the unquestionable position that, when Governor Phillip received his first Commission from King George III on 12th October 1786 the whole of the lands of Australia were already in law the property of the King of England.[3]

Australians were so familiar with the events of January and February 1788 that they have lost the ability to see how extraordinary the claim was. This is not true of outsiders. The leading modern authority on the law of the British Commonwealth, Sir Kenneth Roberts-Wray, found Isaacs's view 'startling' and 'incredible'. The first settlement in Australia, he observed,

> was founded in 1788; but even if it had been in 1786, could a foothold in a small area on the east side of a sub-continent 2000 miles wide be sufficient in English law (as it certainly would not be in international law) to confer sovereignty but also title to the soil throughout the hinterland of nearly three million square miles?[4]

If the extravagance of the British claim impressed an eminent twentieth-century jurist, it would have seemed even more extraordinary to the resident Aborigines had they known of the proceedings. As many as half a million people, living in several hundred tribal groupings and in occupation of even the most inhospitable corners of the continent, had, in a single instant, been dispossessed. From that apocalyptic moment forward, they were technically trespassers on crown land even though many of them would not see a white person for another thirty or fifty years. Even the sons and daughters of those dispossessed might not meet their expropriators until middle age. English legal witchcraft was so powerful that it had wiped out all tenure and all rights to land that had been occupied for 40 000 years, for 1600 generations and more. The white man's technology had brought him to the southern continent. His jurisprudence delivered the ownership of four million square kilometres of someone else's land. That land could be received with a clear conscience in the belief that the dispossessed would respond to the 'amity and kindness' of the first settlers.

It was a stunning takeover. It would have dazzled even the lions of the modern business world, their financial power and electronic wizardry notwithstanding. How did it happen? The generally accepted view is that Australia became British by 'discovery' as a result of Captain James Cook's voyage along the east coast in 1770.[5] Cook did, in fact, claim eastern Australia for the Crown. By relating the dispossession of the Aborigines to that act, many moral and legal difficulties appear to have been resolved. Discovery was achieved by heroism, endurance and skill. It gave Australians the impression that Cook and the later explorers had 'earned' the country for the British. And discovery could only be performed by Europeans. Aborigines might be in possession, which was open to debate, but they couldn't, after tens of thousands of years of occupation, discover themselves. That gave the European side an enormous advantage in any debate about land rights.

The situation was never as simple as that. The case in favour of acquisition by discovery is not nearly as strong as it appears.

Discovery

The fundamental problem with discovery as a base for possession is that one can only discover that which is ownerless, that which doesn't belong to anyone. This principle was enshrined in European international law and in the Roman law on which it was based. The great seventeenth-century Dutch jurist Hugo Grotius warned his contemporaries about this problem. 'Equally shameless is it,' he wrote, to claim for oneself by right of discovery what is held by another, even though the occupant may be wicked, may hold wrong views about God, or may be dull of wit. For discovery applies to those things which belong to no one.[6]

We know now that Cook didn't really 'discover' eastern Australia. It was doubtful if he did even as that term was understood in the international law of the time. But the question of whether New South Wales belonged to anyone will be addressed later.

What discovery actually involved was clearly defined by European and American international lawyers by the late eighteenth and early nineteenth centuries. It was above all else a means of adjudicating between competing European powers, allowing them to define spheres of influence while avoiding perpetual conflict over competing claims in the non-European world. Cook's claim was, therefore, important in respect of other European powers but not in relation to the Aborigines. The issue is an important one, so reference will be made to those authorities from the early nineteenth to the early twentieth centuries who took it up. The eminent American jurist Joseph Story observed that, as a conventional rule, discovery might

> properly govern all the nations which recognised its obligation, but it could have no authority over the Aborigines of America, whether gathered into civilised communities or scattered in hunting tribes of the wilderness.[7]

Chief Justice Marshall of the American Supreme Court argued in 1832 that claims of discovery 'asserted a title against Europeans only and were considered as blank pages so far as the rights of the natives were concerned'.[8] M.F. Lindley summed up the accepted view of the issue in his authoritative 1928 study, *The Acquisition and Government of Backward Territory in International Law*. Discovery, he explained,

> was adapted to regulate the competition between European Powers themselves, and it had no bearing upon the relations between those Powers and the natives. What the discoverer's State gained was the right, as against other European powers, to take steps which were appropriate to the acquisition of the territory in question. What those steps were would depend on whether there was already a native population in possession of the territory.[9]

Discovery alone did not amount to much. It gave what was termed an 'inchoate title', which could only be developed further by actual occupation. This had been established well before 1788, Grotius remarking that an act of discovery was sufficient to give a clear title to sovereignty 'only when it is accompanied by actual possession'.[10] The individual or nation, J.G. Heineccius had observed in 1743, who only 'seized a thing with his eyes, but does not take hold of it, cannot be said to occupy'.[11] The settlement of 1788 was, then, more significant than the discovery of eighteen years before. It converted an inchoate title into an actual one. But how good was the claim to the whole of eastern Australia?

WHOSE HINTERLAND?

Had the British really taken hold of New South Wales? They had, after all, not even seized most of it 'with their eyes' and were only in occupation of a tiny part of the land in question.

For a generation most settlers were within a day's ride of Sydney. The majority could probably smell the sea. The area that could be legitimately claimed following the planting of a colony on coastline unclaimed by other Europeans was, of necessity, clearly defined in the work of international lawyers. The area claimed could only stretch inland as far as the crest of the watershed of rivers flowing into the ocean on the line of coast actually occupied. The length of coastline that could be legitimately annexed was harder to define, although the general view was that it 'must bear some reasonable proportion to the territory claimed in virtue of possession'.[12]

The British claim to the whole of New South Wales was, as a consequence, weak in international law,[13] a point illustrated by the reaction to possible threats of rival colonies that sparked the extension of settlement in outlying areas of the continent. The British claim survived less because of its intrinsic strength, or as a result of a rapid spread of settlement, than because no European power was in a position, or had the inclination, to challenge it.

But while rival powers could theoretically have challenged British sovereignty over the whole of New South Wales, the official view has been that the claim of ownership as against the Aborigines was unassailable from the first day of settlement.

TERRA NULLIUS

The doctrine underlying the traditional view of settlement was that before 1788 Australia was *terra nullius,* a land belonging to no one. We need to ask what this obscure Latin concept actually means and if it was legitimately applied to Australia in the late eighteenth century. Confusion has abounded because *terra nullius* has two different meanings, usually conflated. It means both a country without a sovereign recognised by European authorities[14] and a territory where nobody owns any land at all, where no tenure of any sort exists. 'In things properly no ones,' Grotius observed, 'two things are occupable, the lordship and the ownership'.[15]

European powers adopted the view that countries without political organisation, recognisable systems of authority or legal codes could legitimately be annexed. It was a case of supplying sovereignty where none existed. Writing in the early nineteenth century, the American jurist James Kent summed up several hundred years of colonial practice in North America where 'an ascendancy' was asserted over the Indians 'in consequence of the superior genius of the Europeans, founded on civilization and Christianity, and of their superiority in the means and the act of war'.[16]

The rights of European powers to carve out spheres of influence were strongly asserted by international lawyers in the late nineteenth century as competition for colonies intensified. John Westlake argued in 1904 that because Indigenous societies were 'unable to supply a government suited to white men', they could not be 'credited with sovereignty'.[17] In his *Principles of International Law* of 1895, T. J. Lawrence asserted that all territory 'not in the possession of states who are members of the family of nations' must be considered 'as technically [*terra nullius*] and therefore open to occupation'.[18]

The British claim of sovereignty over the whole of Australia between 1788 and 1829 was not surprising given the attitudes of European powers. It would have been unexceptional at any time in the nineteenth century. The claim to the actual ownership of every inch of land was another matter altogether. What was the basis for this extraordinary land grab?

In its simplest form, the British justification was that the Aborigines had never actually been in possession of the land. They ranged over it rather than resided on it. The Europeans, therefore, acquired the unassailable legal position of being the first occupants. Such rights were recognised alike by English and international law and almost any other legal code into the bargain. The rights of the first occupants were considered as part of the natural law. Things belonging to none, wrote J. G. Heineccius in 1743, 'fall to the share and right of the first occupants'.[19] Writing a few years later, the author of the popular *Law of Nations,* Emmerich de Vattel, explained that all people have an equal right to things that 'have not yet come into the possession of anyone and these belong to the person who first takes possession'.[20] In a book with the same title published in an English edition in 1788, G. F. von Martens explained that

> from the moment a nation has taken possession of a territory in right of first occupier, and with the design to establish itself there for the future, it becomes the absolute and sole proprietor of it and all that it contains; and has a right to exclude all other nations from it, to use it and dispose of it as it thinks proper . . . It belongs to the possessors, of course, to make the distribution of their territory, and everything attached to it. What is not, in this distribution, granted to individuals, or what afterwards ceases to belong to them, remains, or falls, to the whole society, or to persons amongst them on whom they have conferred the right of acquiring.[21]

If it had been true that the Aborigines had no property and the settlers were literally the first occupiers, the legal situation would, indeed, have been a simple one. We can see today that neither proposition was correct; both were extraordinary claims given the antiquity of Aboriginal occupation and the people's sophisticated systems of land usage and tenure. What is more to the point, the claims appeared extraordinary to many people in the 1830s and 1840s once knowledge about Australia was broadcast.

What justification was there in the late eighteenth and early nineteenth centuries for believing that the Aborigines were not in possession of their land, that it was doubly a *terra nullius*: a land without a sovereign and a land without tenure? To answer these questions it will be necessary to consider general political views and the nature of possession as defined in both international and English law.

POSSESSION IN INTERNATIONAL LAW

The international law of possession was developed in the seventeenth century by Grotius to augment discovery as a basis for European claims to land in the non-European world. He drew on Roman law, adopting the principles relating to the occupation of things that had no owner, *res nullius*.

In his classic nineteenth-century work, *Ancient Law*, H. J. S. Maine observed that 'the Roman principle of occupancy' was 'the source of all modern international law on the subject', and many other writers confirmed this interpretation.[22] What was the understanding of the Roman law of possession in the late eighteenth and early nineteenth centuries, and how was this understanding reflected in the international law of the time?

The classic study of the relevant law, Friedrich von Savigny's *Treatise on Possession*, was first published within a few years of the settlement of Australia and was republished many times during the nineteenth century. The main principles of the law of possession can be quickly outlined.

1. Possession, independent of all right, is the foundation of property. In any conflict over property the possessor has the benefit of the burden of proof being thrown on his adversary.
2. Possession is achieved by two crucial steps. The first is actual physical presence on the land, although it is not the 'mere act of treading with the feet which gives possession of the land, but the presence upon the spot which enables [the occupant], not merely to walk over every individual portion of it but to deal with it in any way he chooses at pleasure'. Personal presence is then the fundamental first step in acquiring possession; 'the only factum by which the possession of immovables is acquired'. And, crucially, von Savigny insisted that 'in order to acquire Possession it is only necessary to be present on the land, without the performance of any other act thereon'.
3. As well as being present, the possessor must have the desire or the will to have the land as his own, the *animus possidendi*. Presence on the land must, therefore, 'be accompanied by a definite act of mind', consisting in the first place 'in the fact of the possessor dealing with the subject as his own property'.[23]
4. Possession can only be lost when the land is physically abandoned and a determination exists to give it up. Land that is only visited occasionally – like alpine pastures, for instance – would not be considered abandoned because of intermittent use. As von Savigny argued, 'Where the use is of such a nature that it only recurs at

certain periods, the omission to visit the land during the interval is not evidence of any intention to give up possession'.[24]

Possession and tenure were discussed in two of the major works of international law published in the middle of the eighteenth century, both entitled *The Law of Nations,* written respectively by Christian Wolff and Emerich de Vattel. Wolff was the most celebrated international jurist of the time and in the first half of the nineteenth century was 'justly considered as the founder of the science' of international law.[25] He is of particular interest because, as part of a vast work, he considered the question of what rights to land could be claimed by people who, like the Aborigines, lived in small groups and moved regularly over land owned collectively or held under what he called a 'mixed community holding'. Wolff argued that if the families in question had

> no settled abode but wander through the uncultivated wilds . . . they are understood to have tacitly agreed that the lands in that territory in which they change their abodes as they please, are held in common, subject to the use of individuals, and it is not to be doubted but that it is their intention that they should not be deprived of that use by outsiders. Therefore they are supposed to have occupied that territory as far as concerns the lands subject to their use, and consequently to have jointly acquired ownership of those lands, so that the use of them belongs to all without distinction.

Clearly Wolff believed that nomadic people engaged in putting animals to pasture or in hunting and gathering had a form of property in the land they used. Indeed, their constant movement was dictated by their economic life and was, if anything, proof of their exploitation or 'enjoyment' of the land.

'Things are occupied for the sake of their use,' Wolff argued, and

> if indeed, separate families should be accustomed to wander about . . . for the purpose of pasturing cattle or for some other purpose, the intention of wandering, which is governed by that intended use, gives sufficient evidence of the occupation of the lands subject to that use, although they have not established a permanent abode on them.

Nomadic people could not legitimately be dispossessed simply because their pattern of land use differed from that of agriculturists. In Wolff's work, as in von Savigny's, intermittent use was not a reason to argue that nomads were not in actual occupation of the land and could as a result be displaced 'even if at the time those who inhabit the territory are not using those lands'.

'Ownership,' Wolff explained,

> is not lost by non-user. And if separate families wander through uncultivated places, they intend a use of the places only in alternation, a thing which is readily evident, if only you turn your attention to the reason which impels them to wander through uncultivated places.[26]

Wolff was not writing about Australia or the Aborigines. Cook's departure from England was twenty years in the future when his work was first published. But Wolff's work contained arguments of great relevance to the settlement of Australia. For him, nomadic people, wandering over large territories, were not living in a state of nature. They had a form of communal

Who Was in Possession?

ownership and could not legitimately be dispossessed. They did not have to become agriculturalists to establish possession, nor did they have to reside permanently in any one place.

Wolff was not alone in these views. In his *Methodical System of International Law*, published a few years before Wolff's work, Heineccius argued that 'none therefore can deny that hunting, fishing, fowling are a species of occupancy, not only in desert places unpossessed, but likewise in territories already possessed'.[27]

What of Vattel? He too wrote before the 'discovery' of eastern Australia. His book was widely read in the English-speaking world in the late eighteenth and early nineteenth centuries and was well-known and widely quoted in colonial Australia. Indeed, he has always been regarded as the principal apologist of European colonisation. In providing ideological justification for settlement in America he also provided it for British colonisation of Australia. He argued in several passages, quoted many times in 200 years of Australian settlement, that given the Divine injunction to subdue the earth, the Indians could not expect to remain forever in exclusive possession of the whole North American continent. The European powers were, therefore, justified in establishing colonies for their surplus population.[28] This is the well-known Vattel, who was sure of a ready audience in any colonial gathering. But there was another side to him that has been overlooked in Australia and that must be examined.

Vattel was a student, indeed a disciple, of Wolff. His book was written to popularise the work of his master. In his preface he explained that at first he thought he would have nothing further to do than detach his thesis from Wolff's much larger work and clothe it in a 'more agreeable form, more proper to afford it a reception in the polite world'.[29] He followed the main lines of Wolff's argument, including Wolff's defence of the property rights of nomadic people. Thus he argued that

> families wandering in a country, as the nations of shepherds who pass over it, according as their wants require, possess it in common; it belongs to them exclusively of all other nations and we cannot without injustice deprive them of the countries which are appropriated to their use . . . no other nation has a right to reduce the bounds, unless it be under an absolute want of land. For, in fine, they possess their country, they make use of it after their manner, they reap from it an advantage suitable to their manner of life, and in which they receive laws from no one.[30]

How does Vattel reconcile these two contradictory strands of his work: the property rights of nomadic people, and an enthusiasm for colonisation that appeared to place him on the side of the British in Australia? He does so by advocating a limited right of settlement. At no point does he provide justification for the blanket expropriation of a whole continent as occurred in the Antipodes. The colonists were to confine themselves 'within just bounds'; they might lawfully 'take possession of a part of a vast continent', settle 'in a part of this country', 'possess a part', 'settle in some parts of a region'. The Indigenous people were in possession of their land. They could not be simply dispossessed. The settlers might confine the natives 'within narrower limits' or 'reduce their bounds', but even then the whole process was only acceptable if the natives were 'not reduced to want land'.[31]

Clearly the writer who has been seen as providing justification for the settlement of Australia for the last 200 years, who has been quoted to that effect in parliament, from the bench, the pulpit and the rostrum, provides nothing of the sort. Vattel could certainly be used to justify the establishment of a colony on the shores of Sydney Harbour. He could not, without totally distorting his work, be said to justify the claim that in 1788 every inch of territory became the property of the British Crown.

The Aborigines for their part suffered the very fate that Vattel had cautioned against. They were reduced 'to want land' in the first seconds of white settlement. Who can doubt that Vattel's description of 'families wandering in a country' fitted the Australian case? They possessed their country, made use of it after their manner, took from it an 'advantage suitable to their manner of life' and received laws from no one.

POSSESSION IN THE COMMON LAW

What of the common law that determined relations between whites and Aborigines from 1788 onwards? The law of possession as outlined by von Savigny did not apply directly to the situation in Australia. But the common law of possession drew heavily on Roman law.[32] In an English commentary on von Savigny's *Treatise*, published in 1839, L. A. Warkoenig argued that the book would be found useful

> not only to the student of the Roman law, but to the practical lawyer; and to the latter, more especially, for the reason, that most of the principles which relate to possession must necessarily be the same or similar in every system.[33]

Could the Aborigines have proven they were in possession under the common law if circumstances – and attitudes – had been different in early New South Wales? Perhaps more to the point, could the Crown have proven they weren't? The commonly accepted view prior to Mabo was that the Aborigines had no land rights because they were not farmers, did not enclose the land and did not till the soil. Yet common sense, let alone the law itself, should tell us that this argument cannot be justified. Only about half of Britain was farmed, much less of New South Wales. There was much forest, mountain and coastal wetland in England. There was land with very few residents, waste and unfenced. But it was all owned – or open to ownership. Title to wasteland in Britain was as secure as title to the best farmland. There was absolutely no obligation to cultivate.

This fact was aptly illustrated by an editorial comment in the 1834 edition of Vattel's *Law of Nations*. In the section entitled 'Of the cultivation of the soil', Vattel argued that despite the institution of private property the state still had a right 'to take the most effectual measures to cause the aggregate soil of the country to produce the greatest and most advantageous revenue possible'. John Chitty, the editor, noted that in England there were 'few legislative enactments respecting the cultivation of the soil or employment of its produce, each individual being left to their own discretion'.[34] By tradition, English landowners could do what they liked with their own; they had 'the right to commit unlimited waste'[35] if that was their humour. Neglect did not open the way to forfeiture to the Crown. Large tracts were, indeed, deliberately kept in an uncultivated condition to provide hunting, fowling and fishing. English gentlemen may not have had much interest in foraging for food but they would have been amazed that they were not actually in possession of their hunting grounds and trout streams because they weren't using them properly.

English law was flexible enough to recognise very different

forms of land tenure. It had grown over centuries, emerging from a highly diverse, pre-industrial society embracing innumerable local customs and traditions, not only in England but in Wales and Ireland as well. In his classic eighteenth-century history of the common law, Sir Matthew Hale discussed the 'settling' of the law of England in the Celtic Fringe. 'Tis true,' he wrote, 'many ancient Irish customs continued in Ireland, and do continue there'. In Wales there were 'very many laws and customs' that were 'utterly strange' to the law of England.[36] The flexibility of the law was enhanced by the unique position accorded to custom – both 'universal' custom common to the whole realm and purely local custom, the *lex loci* that was specific to a particular place and that had existed 'time out of mind'. Local custom was, by definition, contrary to the law of the nation. It was the 'common law within that place to which it extends, though contrary to the law of the realm'.[37] Custom, the courts determined in 1828, 'is a local law which superseded the general law'.[38]

Such a complex legal system had, of necessity, encompassed many forms of common ownership. In his late nineteenth-century study *The Land Laws*, Sir Frederick Pollock observed that 'almost every possible kind of ownership, and almost every possible relation of owners and occupiers of land to the State and to one another have at one time or another existed in England'.[39]

There were numerous decisions in the English courts of the late eighteenth and nineteenth centuries that suggested that in fact the Aborigines were in possession of their land both in respect of international law, as indicated above, and of the common law. In a case in 1837 the courts determined that possession could be 'shown only by acts of enjoyment of the land itself'.[40] What that enjoyment was depended very much on the nature of the land itself or what the land was capable of yielding.[41]

There was no hard and fast rule about what kind of economic activity was necessary to prove possession. There was certainly no provision in the law which confined ownership to tilled fields. The Privy Council determined in 1887 that 'by possession is meant possession of that character of which the thing is capable'.[42] Where the land was uncultivated and partly forested, 'shooting over it during some months of the shooting season' was considered 'enough to constitute *de facto* possession'.[43] In the 1825 case *Harper v. Charlesworth*, the Kings Bench determined that the plaintiff had proved he was in possession by occasionally hunting on the land. The question was:

> What was the land capable of yielding? It was woodland with rides on it, and there was a considerable quantity of game on it, and therefore, it afforded any person going there an opportunity of killing game. The plaintiff himself did not appear to have any other enjoyment of the land than that of shooting game.[44]

Cases about possession of the seashore provided further support for the view that the Aborigines were in possession of their land. In his 1894 *Treatise on Possession of Land*, J. M. Lightwood noted that 'acts of slight importance, such as the gathering of sea-weed, the taking of shell-fish, and the planting of stakes for fishing nets, are often conclusive in claims founded on the alleged possession of foreshore'.[45] In other cases it was established that acts of possession on one part of a tract of land were sufficient to establish a legitimate claim on the whole. This principle was applied in *Jones v. Williams*, 1837, to establish that the act of taking wood in one part of a forest established claim to the whole forest. The judge argued that 'if you prove the cutting of timber in one part, I take that to be evidence to go to a jury to prove a right in the whole wood, although there be no fence, or distinct boundary, surrounding the whole'.[46]

Clearly a strong case can be argued for the fact that the Aborigines were in possession of their land as that term was understood in both international and English law at the end of the eighteenth century and the early years of the nineteenth century. To prove possession it was not necessary to enclose and farm the land in the way of Europeans, nor was it necessary to live permanently in one place. The fundamental requirements were to be present on the land and to manifest a will to ownership. Aboriginal land use was at least as constant, systematic and widespread on their territory as was that of Europeans over at least some of the lands where ownership and possession were never questioned. In forest, mountain, desert and foreshore it was regular enough to be accepted as proof of possession even in England, let alone in colonial Australia where economic activity was mainly confined to extensive grazing on native pastures. Over much of the continent the Aborigines clearly had possession of a character of which the land was capable.

Aboriginal problems stemmed not so much from what the law actually said as from the fact that in many important respects it did not apply to them. The law provided strong protection for European property and defended it against encroachment by the Crown. None of this applied to the Aborigines because they lost all rights to property at the beginning of settlement. In their case, the property law of centuries was suspended while they were dispossessed.

Their occupation, their possession was overlooked for two distinct reasons: European ignorance and European philosophical and political ideas. Before the settlers actually arrived in Australia they knew little about the Aborigines, believing that the continent was largely uninhabited. Their ideas about the Aborigines, and more particularly about 'savages' in general, helped shape settler attitudes in the first generation of colonial history.

A STATE OF PRIMEVAL SIMPLICITY

When formulating their ideas about Indigenous people in the world outside, European thinkers of the seventeenth and eighteenth centuries drew as much on the writers of classical antiquity and on the Old Testament as they did on actual reports about North America or the Pacific. They referred constantly to the age of innocence so dear to Roman authors: a time when there was no private property, when all was held in common, when men were equal and free from restraint except that supplied by natural reason.

But it is beliefs about property that must concern us here. Their relevance to attitudes adopted towards Indians and Aborigines will immediately be clear. Grotius, the founding figure of modern European international law, observed that 'in those ancient times all things were held in common'.[47] The English jurist Selden wrote in 1652:

> As to the first kinde of Dominion, or that which is common to all, frequent mention is made of it, in relation to that State of Communitie, which was in antient [sic] time.[48]

Selden bolstered his argument with quotations from the Roman authors Virgil, Seneca and Ovid:[49]

> All men might pass what they pleas'd to chuse
> And all things were expos'd for common use.
>
> SENECA

> Nor was it lawful then their lands to bound
> They liv'd in common All upon the Ground.
>
> VIRGIL

> The Earth as common once as light or Air
> They then by Art did measure, bound and share.
>
> OVID

There is no doubt that seventeenth- and eighteenth-century writers concluded that, at least in part, Indians and Aborigines lived in the manner of the mythical figures that had haunted the European imagination since the Greek and Roman times. The age of innocence and common ownership could be seen as a starting point to explain all later developments, a benchmark to use when measuring subsequent progress. It was true in three sets of ideas relating to property that influenced attitudes in early colonial Australia.

Among the most influential writers in the English-speaking world in the second half of the eighteenth century were the so-called moral philosophers of the Scottish enlightenment.[50] Among the vast array of topics that came under their scrutiny was the evolution of ideas about property, the 'gradual progress of that sense [of property], from its infancy among savages to its maturity among polished nations'.[51] Common to numerous scholars was a belief that human development had passed through a series of distinct phases, beginning with the age of hunters or savages that was succeeded by the age of nomadic pastoralists or barbarians. In these two earliest stages there was no idea of property in land. In his essay on the history of property Henry Home explained that

> In the first two stages of social life, while men were hunters and shepherds, there scarce could be any notion of landed property. Men being strangers to agriculture, and also to the art of building, if it was not of huts, which could be raised or demolished in a moment, had no fixed habitation but wandered about in hordes or clans, in order to find pasture for their cattle. In this vagrant life men have scarce any connection with land more than with air or water. A field of grass might be considered to belong to a horde or class, while they were in possession; and so might the air in which they breathed, and the water which they drank: but the moment they removed to another quarter, there no longer subsisted any connection betwixt them and the field that was deserted. It lay open to new-comers, who had the same right as if it had not been formerly occupied. Hence I conclude that while men led the life of shepherds, there was no relation formed betwixt them and land, in any manner so distinct as to obtain the name of Property.[52]

Ideas like these were to be extremely important in shaping attitudes to the Aborigines in the early years of settlement. Not that Home knew anything about them or all that much about the ethnography of the new world. His inspiration and source of information was the classics, above all Herodotus's writing on the Scythians dating from the fifth century before Christ.

Similar ideas were advanced in other works of the period. In his *Remarks on the Influence of Climate etc.*, published in 1781, William Falconer argued that hunters and gatherers were ignorant of the nature of property, and because hunting required 'a large scope of ground, and a frequent change of situation', there was 'but little local attachment' and almost no 'local affection'.[53] His contemporary James Millar had much the same view of hunters and shepherds, arguing in his book *The Origin of the Distinction of Ranks* that

> the different families of a tribe are accustomed to feed their cattle promiscuously, and have no separate possession or enjoyment of the ground employed for that purpose. Having exhausted one field of pasture they proceed to another; and when at length they find it convenient to move their tents, and change the place of their residence, it is of no consequence who shall succeed them, and occupy the spot which they have relinquished.[54]

A second important influence on European attitudes to Indigenous land rights was John Locke's major work *Two Treatises of Government*, first published in the late seventeenth century, republished many times and widely read in the eighteenth century. Like the classical authors, Locke began his discussion of property with the state of nature when men were equal and all property was held in common. But God had commanded man to subdue the earth and in order to achieve this he was forced to labour and in so doing created private property. In a chapter entitled 'Of property', Locke explained that

> Whatsoever, then, he removes out of the state that nature hath provided and left it in, he hath mixed his labour with, and joined to it something that is his own, and thereby makes it his property.[55]

Locke's ideas were used to justify the dispossession of the Aborigines because the people had apparently not mixed their labour with the soil. The argument was simple: if there was no sign of agriculture the natives *must* still be in a state of nature, and in that condition there was no property. These ideas met with increasing difficulty when applied in colonial Australia because they had little relationship with what came to be known about the Aborigines, or with the actual law of possession and property.

The third major work to be considered is William Blackstone's *Commentaries on the Laws of England,* first published in 1765 and republished many times over the following decades – it was in its eighteenth edition in 1823. Blackstone provided arguments that could have been used both to establish Aboriginal possession and to deny it. He followed Roman law in stressing the rights of the first occupier. Occupation was achieved by actual presence on the soil and by manifesting a will to possess as one's own – exactly the same conditions which had led Wolff to support land rights for nomadic people. 'Property both in lands and moveables', Blackstone wrote,

> being thus originally acquired by the first taker, which taking amounts to a declaration that he intends to appropriate the thing to his own use, it remains in him, by the principles of universal law, till such a time as he does some other act which shows his intention to abandon it.[56]

Blackstone took up the same point later:

> But when once it was agreed that everything capable of ownership should have an owner, natural reason suggested, that he who could first declare his intention of appropriating anything to his own use, and, in consequence of such intention, actually took it into possession, should thereby gain the absolute property of it

according to that rule of the law of nations, recognized by the laws of Rome, *quod nullius est, id ratione naturali occupanti conceditur* (= natural reason concedes ownership to the first occupier).[57]

Clearly Blackstone's work could have been used to provide powerful arguments for the contention that the Aborigines were in possession, that they and not the settlers were the first occupants, with all the legal potency surrounding that condition. But that would have made things far too difficult. It was easier and much more advantageous to argue that the Aborigines were living in a state of primeval simplicity, where the soil and pasture of the earth 'remained still common as before, and open to every occupant'.

Blackstone developed this idea in a passage that echoed through colonial debates about Aboriginal land rights for half a century and more. In the state of primeval simplicity, the person who first began to use land

> acquired therein a kind of transient property, that lasted so long as he was using it, and no longer: or, to speak with greater precision, the right of possession continued the same time only that the act of possession lasted. Thus the ground was common, and no part of it was the permanent property of any man in particular; yet whosoever was in the occupation of any determined spot of it, for rest, for shade, or the like, acquired for the time a sort of ownership, from which it would have been unjust and contrary to the law of nature, to have driven him by force; but the instant that he quitted the use or occupation of it, another might seize it, without injustice.[58]

'Might seize it without injustice.' What a potent phrase. What a convenient phrase in a colonial society where encroaching settlers faced Indigenous landowners, even if it actually referred to a cloud-cuckoo land of the Roman imagination rather than to any place that had ever existed in the real world.

Where does the discussion to this point leave us? In terms of European thought, the claim of sovereignty over Australia in 1788 was soundly based. Australia was a land without a sovereign as Europeans understood that term. In that sense it was a *terra nullius*. The European powers would have sanctioned the declaration of a protectorate and the exercise of political power over Australia at any time during the nineteenth century, as the partition of Africa was to show. The assertion that it was also a land without anyone in occupation was an extreme one whether viewed in the light of international law or domestic law, despite whatever justification could be found in political and philosophical works. The claim that the British were the first occupiers was the fundamental moral and legal foundation for the settlement of the continent. Yet it was suspect from the very beginning. Within a few years of 1788, growing knowledge about the Aborigines had seriously undermined the original British premise. Almost everything that was learned about the 'blacks' during the first two generations of settlement bolstered the view that they and not the Europeans were the original occupiers of the continent. Views of Australia and the Aborigines framed in Europe before settlement were fatally flawed, both by too little knowledge about the country and its people and by too great a dependence on classical authors and their half-mythical accounts of Scythians, Helvetians and other peoples on the fringes of the ancient world – peoples that modern Europeans had learnt about in Herodotus, Caesar, Thucydides, Tacitus and Diodorus.

Did it matter all that much? Clearly it did. It fundamentally weakened the legal position of the Aborigines. The weakness was felt for 200 years. Their situation would have been much better if they had, from the very beginning of settlement, been recognised as being in possession of the continent by right of first occupancy, even if British rights of sovereignty and pre-emption had been conceded. Rights based on possession were after all the fundamental cornerstone of almost all European legal systems, a fact clearly recognised by every major legal scholar. 'Possession', wrote von Savigny, 'independent of all right, is the foundation of property itself'.[59] Blackstone argued that 'what is in my present possession and use cannot be invaded',[60] and Grotius asserted that 'all property has arisen from occupation'.[61]

In an article published in 1978 on Aboriginal title and the common law a jurist observed:

> the notion that long occupation is to be deemed lawful in the absence of proof to the contrary, is as ancient as the concept of property itself; indeed, the right to use that which one has created, possessed or occupied without wrongfully taking from another is fundamental to any legal system.[62]

While of great importance, the issue of possession was only one of the legal questions associated with the relations between Aborigines and settlers. While the penal colony at Botany Bay was being planned in Britain, the question of whether the Indigenous people had any property rights was entangled with the problem of determining whether Australia was largely uninhabited and therefore literally a *terra nullius*.

TWO

By What Tenure?

'THINLY INHABITED EVEN TO ADMIRATION'

What was known about the population of Australia in the middle years of the 1780s when the decision to establish a colony was made? Most information came from the members of Cook's expedition, and especially from Sir Joseph Banks, who reported in his journal that eastern Australia was 'thinly inhabited even to admiration'. The expedition had seen no large gatherings and the evidence provided by camp sites and huts 'convinced us of the smallness of their parties'.

Banks and his colleagues had never seen the inland. He admitted that 'what the immense tract of country may produce is to us totally unknown'. But he made the extremely important and erroneous assessment that 'we may have liberty to conjecture that [it is] totally uninhabited'. Why so bold, so inaccurate, so portentous a conclusion? It would be best to let Banks explain in his own words. The sea, he argued,

> has I beleive been universaly found to be the cheif source of supplys to Indians ignorant of the arts of cultivation: the wild produce of the land alone seems scarce able to support them at all seasons at least I do not remember to have read of any inland

nation who did not cultivate the ground more or less, even the North Americans who were so well versed in hunting sowd their Maize. But should a people live inland who supported themselves by cultivation these inhabitants of the sea coast must certainly have learn'd to imitate them in some degree at least, otherwise their reason must he suppos'd to hold a rank little superior to that of monkies.[1]

There was a tortuous logic there. Contemporaries appeared to find it persuasive. Books about New South Wales published before 1788 described it as the 'solitary haunt of a few miserable savages'; the population was 'very small in proportion to its extent' and there was reason to believe that the interior was 'either wholly desolate, or at least still more thinly inhabited than the places which have been visited'.[2]

It all would have been so easy if Banks had been right – that apart from the coastal fringe, Australia was uninhabited, literally a *terra nullius*. But he wasn't. The settlers realised that Banks was wrong after a few years of colonial experience.

The fact that the whole of Australia was occupied has important legal implications. While the settlers and informed observers in Britain came to understand the nature of Aboriginal land use and tenure, the law turned a blind eye to everything that happened after January 1788. The theory of an uninhabited continent was just too convenient to surrender lightly. Consequently the gap between law and reality, law and colonial experience, grew progressively wider. The law retreated farther from the real world and farther into injustice as the nineteenth century progressed. In 1819 the Crown Law Officers determined that New South Wales had been taken possession of as 'desert and uninhabitable';[3] the South Australian Constitution Act (1834) referred to the land of the colony as being 'waste and unoccupied'. In a judgement in 1849 the chief justice of New South Wales referred to the 'circumstances of newly discovered and unpeopled territories'.

Forty years later the Privy Council lent its great authority to the mythology. In the case of *Cooper v. Stuart* it was determined that Australia in 1788 had consisted of 'a tract of territory practically unoccupied without settled inhabitants'.[4] That view would have been difficult to sustain in 1789, let alone in 1889. But such are the ways of the law that *Cooper v. Stuart* was considered as the leading case, binding on Australian courts, and was deemed to be so by Justice Blackburn in the so-called Gove Land Rights case in 1971. In *Coe v. The Commonwealth* in 1975, Justice Murphy concluded that it was not binding on the High Court,[5] but the doctrine of *terra nullius* was not finally overturned until the Mabo decision in the High Court in June 1992.

LANDS 'DESERT AND UNCULTIVATED'

The importance of *Cooper v. Stuart* leads us back to the legal theory of the late eighteenth century and particularly to Blackstone's *Commentaries*, which were quoted by the Privy Council in support of their views about Australian settlement.

The vital passage from Blackstone dealt with the establishment of overseas colonies and the transfer of English law. Blackstone drew a clear distinction between colonies won by conquest or treaty and those where 'lands are claimed by right of occupancy only, by finding them desert and uncultivated, and peopling them from the mother countries'.[6] In such colonies of settlement, English law was 'immediately there in force' on the assumption that no prior legal code or land tenure had ever existed.

Did this apply to Australia? Not directly, of course, Blackstone wrote before Cook had left England, but it could apply to Australia by implication. This needs to be established, however, and not merely asserted, as has been done by the courts since the nineteenth century. The crucial phrase 'desert and uncultivated' is ambiguous and has allowed legal commentators far too much latitude in exegesis. Did 'desert and uncultivated' mean uninhabited? It very likely did. Blackstone did not say desert *or* uncultivated. That would have meant that any uncultivated land — pasture, forest, hunting grounds — could be claimed by right of occupancy. Such a claim had no basis in international or English law. Cultivation was not the only way to establish possession. Blackstone adopted a view of possession, of the rights of the first occupant, that was close to that of the Roman-derived international law. His work could have been used to prove that nomadic people like the Aborigines were in possession of their land, and this is what his continental contemporaries argued. The problem lay with the English, not with the Aborigines or their use of the land. Colonial jurists didn't want to prove that the Indigenous Australians had rights of first possession and so they didn't. They went on pretending that the country was 'unpeopled'.

The balance of evidence suggests that when he referred to desert and uncultivated land Blackstone meant uninhabited land. In such a case the legal situation was clear, uncomplicated and well established. In 1772 the Privy Council determined that 'if there be a new and uninhabited country found out by English subjects, as the law is the birthright of every subject, so wherever they go, they carry their law with them'.[7] Elsewhere in his *Commentaries*, Blackstone refers not to 'desert and uncultivated lands' but follows the Privy Council, writing of the situation when 'an *uninhabited* country (was) discovered and planted by English subjects'. Indeed, it was this passage which was quoted by the Privy Council in 1889 to justify the creation of a colony by settlement.[8]

But Blackstone's meaning can be pursued further by examining other sections of his work where he refers to the general question of colonisation, to the

> right of migration, of sending colonies to find out new habitations, when the mother country was overcharged with inhabitants which was practiced as well by the Phoenicians and Greeks, as the Germans, Scythians, and other northern people. And, so long as it was confined to the stocking and cultivation of desert uninhabited countries, it kept strictly within the limits of the law of nature. But how far the seizing of countries already peopled and driving out or massacring the innocent and defenceless natives, merely because they differed from their invaders in language, in religion, in customs, in government, or in colour; how far such a conduct was consonant to nature, to reason, or to Christianity, deserved well to be considered by those, who have rendered their names immortal by thus civilizing mankind.[9]

Given Blackstone's views on the colonisation of already inhabited lands and his comments on the rights acquired by original occupation, it is clear that it is only by a very selective reading that he can be presented as the de facto apologist for the expropriation of Aboriginal land. The British could only claim sovereignty over New South Wales, as well as proprietorship of every inch of landed property, if indeed it was uninhabited. That is the reason why lawyers continued to babble about a desert and uninhabited land when all informed observers knew it was nonsense. Rather than untie the legal tangle created by settlement of an already inhabited land, they went on ignoring the problem, in supreme indifference to reality. It was not until 1992 that Australian courts came to terms with the question.

'BY WHAT TENURE?'

Within a short time of the initial settlement it was known that the interior was not uninhabited. No matter how far back from the coast the Europeans advanced, they found the Aborigines in occupation of the land. By the 1830s well-informed settlers knew that Australia was a patchwork of clearly defined tribal territories and that local blacks defended their territory against both Europeans and traditional enemies. The question of how the British gained possession of this land was, understandably, a matter which concerned many colonists. They discussed it in books, newspapers, speeches, letters and diaries. Many were like G. A. Robinson, who, in 1832, admitted that he was 'at a loss to conceive by what tenure we hold this country'.[10]

Various solutions were suggested to the problem. Perhaps the most popular view was that the Aborigines were savages and heathens who did not deserve to keep their lands. Although it was a simple and emotionally satisfying argument, it had little standing in law. The traditional legal view that infidels were perpetual enemies who had no legal rights had been decisively rejected in English courts before Australia was settled. The position was even clearer in international law. As early as 1532 the Spanish jurist Francisco de Victoria had declared that the Indians of South America could not be barred from 'being true owners, alike in public and in private law, by reason of the sin of non-belief or any other mortal sin'.[11]

In the seventeenth century Grotius was even more emphatic about the property rights of infidels and savages. 'For the exercise of ownership', he explained, 'neither moral nor religious virtue, nor intellectual excellence, is a requirement'.[12] Surely it is a heresy, he argued further,

> to believe that infidels are not masters of their own property, consequently, to take from them their possessions on account of their religious beliefs is no less theft and robbery than it would be in the case of Christians . . . In fact I know of no law against such unbelievers as regards their temporal possessions. Against them no King, no Emperor, not even the Roman Church, can declare war for the purpose of occupying their lands, or of subjecting them to temporal sway.[13]

Another common answer to the problem of finding a moral and legal basis for the expropriation of the Aborigines was to argue that, despite official pronouncements to the contrary, Australia had been conquered by the British. Many people have adopted this view for more than 200 years. It has appealed at different times, and for different reasons, to both white and black.

Those who argued the case for conquest in the 1830s and 1840s believed that it was the simplest and most realistic explanation for what had happened and for which history offered innumerable precedents. It also provided a far more satisfactory explanation of frontier violence than the one available from official sources. Frontiersmen liked the idea: it justified what they were doing, was straightforward and was free from the cant and hypocrisy of the 'nigger lovers'. The mood of the hard-headed, no-nonsense colonist was captured by E. W. Landor, a Western Australian settler, who wrote in 1847:

> Nothing could be more anomalous and perplexing than the position of the Aborigines as British subjects. Our brave and conscientious Britons, whilst taking possession of their territory, have been most careful and anxious to make it universally known, that Australia is not a conquered country; and successive Secretaries of State . . . have repeatedly commanded that it must never be forgotten 'that our possession of this territory is *based on a right of occupancy*'.
>
> A 'right of occupancy'! Amiable sophistry! Why not say boldly at once, the right of power? We have seized upon the country, and shot down the inhabitants, until the survivors have found it expedient to submit to our rule. We have acted exactly as Julius Caesar did when he took possession of Britain. But Caesar was not so hypocritical as to pretend any moral *right* to possession.[14]

The official view, as the irascible Western Australian said, was that Australia had been settled peacefully by right of occupancy. But even the Crown's legal officers had difficulty in explaining how this had actually happened. At the same time as Landor was advocating acceptance of the realities of conquest, similar issues were raised in the New South Wales Supreme Court in the case *Attorney General v. Brown*. Lawyers for Brown challenged the Crown to explain how it had actually come into possession of the land in dispute. 'There was no law', Richard Windeyer argued for the plaintiff,

> which he could discover that described the mode in which the Sovereign should acquire land in newly discovered territories. He did not see, therefore, how the sovereign could have acquired possession of land here so as to grant it.

In reply the solicitor-general asserted that

the right of the Crown to these lands was acknowledged by the law of nations. At the time of the Norman Conquest the Conquerer took possession of the lands of England, and parcelled them out among his followers: and why might not the same be done here? The right of the Crown here was much the same as a right of conquest; for although there had been no battles, the dominion was held because the aborigines were unable to assert their rights.[15]

Shortly after making these remarks the judge suggested it was unnecessary for the solicitor-general to continue; which was just as well given the difficulties he was getting into.

The fundamental problem for the solicitor-general, and for all those who argued that Australia had been conquered, was that while conquest would certainly explain the imposition of British sovereignty over Australia, it did not account for the acquisition of every inch of property. In the ancient world, conquest delivered everything up to the victor, but it didn't in eighteenth- or nineteenth-century Europe, nor did it lead to the confiscation of private property.

The solicitor-general was wrong. The Crown could not explain the acquisition of Aboriginal land by reference to conquest. The fact that his comparison was with the Norman invasion of Britain 800 years before, and that Landor went back to 55 BC, was an indication of how weak the case was 'by the law of nations'. Emmerich de Vattel outlined the situation as it was in eighteenth-century Europe. The conqueror, he explained, 'takes possession of the property of the State and leaves that of individuals untouched'. The citizens suffer only indirectly by war; conquest 'merely brings them a change of sovereign'.[16]

Chief Justice Marshall of the American Supreme Court

outlined the current position in a judgement delivered in 1833. It was, he argued,

> very unusual, even in cases of conquest, for the conqueror to do more than displace the sovereign and assume dominion over the country. The modern usage of nations, which has become law, would be violated; that sense of justice and of right which is acknowledged and felt by the whole civilized world would be outraged, if private property should be generally confiscated, and private rights annulled. The people change their alliance; their relation to their ancient sovereign is dissolved, but their relations to each other, and their rights of property remain undisturbed.[17]

Prescription and Acquiescence

Many of those who were troubled about the exact legal basis of Australian settlement assumed that while the original expropriation may have been wrong, it could not be reversed and had attained a measure of acceptability through the mere passage of time. It was then, and still is, a moot point. Did the overriding of Aboriginal property rights simply annul them?

Some jurists have argued this way, saying that the original acquisition, however achieved, was an act of state that could not be subsequently challenged. Like acts of God, those of state have been deemed inscrutable. This is a contentious view today and would have been in the past. In the middle of the eighteenth century Wolff discussed the problems that arose when a claim was made for land or other forms of property on the mistaken assumption that it belonged to no one. He reiterated the basic principle that the whole notion of occupation 'assumes that a thing capable of occupation belongs to nobody'. Ignorance of the facts did not alter the situation; it could never create a right where none existed.[18]

But long use of someone else's property does eventually create rights based on occupation, or prescription as it is called in the trade. In domestic law, occupation, undisturbed and peaceful, of twenty years is presumed to create a right to the property in question. The same principles have been applied to international law.[19] But the fundamental problem for the relations of whites and Aborigines is that title by prescription depends on the acquiescence of the original owner. In the leading case, *Dalton v. Angus*, 1881, the Privy Council determined that the crucial question was not the claim to possession by a recent occupant but the acquiescence of the original owner. Mere lapse of time, they determined,

> can never . . . on any intelligible principle, confer a right not previously possessed, though lapse of time accompanied by inaction, where action ought to be taken, may well have such a result.[20]

The same principles applied in international law. Prescription required two things: show of authority by one party, and acquiescence in that show by the other. In his 1965 study, *Historic Titles in International Law*, Yehuda Blum argued that from the legal point of view it was 'not the fact of effective possession, but rather the presumption of acquiescence, that sets the seal of legal validity on the historic claim'.[21]

Given the importance of acquiescence, Aboriginal resistance assumed major legal significance. Although Aborigines reacted in a variety of ways to European incursion, they manifestly did not acquiesce. They proved that with many hundreds falling in frontier conflict. What greater proof could be required of any people?

CROWN PREROGATIVE

How did the Crown acquire every inch of Aboriginal land? The land wasn't uninhabited. The Europeans clearly weren't the first occupants. The 'savagery' and 'heathenism' of the natives gave no charter for expropriation. Conquest did not deliver privately owned land to the conqueror and had not done so for hundreds of years. The question was further complicated by the fact that if indeed Australia was a colony of settlement, then the common law arrived with the first settlers and the Aborigines became subjects of the king at exactly the same moment that sovereignty was extended over the far-flung boundaries of New South Wales.

From 1788 onwards the property relations between Aborigines and the Imperial authorities were those which subsisted between Crown and subject. Early legal and administrative decisions made it clear that the prerogative powers of the Crown were no more extensive in New South Wales than in Britain itself.[22] Against that prerogative the common law had built up, over centuries, powerful barriers around the property of the subject; indeed, it was 'not more solicitous of anything than to preserve the property of the subject from the inundation of the prerogative'.[23] Yelverton, a prominent eighteenth-century jurist, explained

> that no man's property can legally be taken from him or invaded by the direct act or command of the sovereign, without the consent of the subject . . . is *jus indigene*, an old home borne truth, declared to be true by diverse statutes of the realm.[24]

By exercising those sovereign powers known as eminent domain, the Crown could take the land of the subject but it could only do so with the consent of the owner and payment of adequate compensation. The actual transaction would have to be sanctioned by statute because the Crown could not 'take or grant but by record'.[25]

If the Crown's powers were no more extensive in New South Wales than in Britain and if the Aborigines really were subjects protected by the law, how did the Crown get their land? It did not seek the consent of its black subjects, it did not pay them compensation and it did not proceed by way of record. Such expropriation was unthinkable in Britain after 1688 and would have provoked riot and rebellion. And when did the transfer of property take place? Did the Aborigines become subjects at precisely the same moment that the Crown extended its sovereignty and grabbed four million square kilometres? How could two such antithetical actions coincide: to throw the mantle of British justice over black Australian subjects with one hand and pinch their land with the other? Perhaps the land was taken first and only then were the newly landless Aborigines made subjects of the Crown. That might meet some of the legal difficulties but it would suggest a degree of cynicism and turpitude not to be expected of the Crown.

Can we be sure that the Crown claimed both sovereignty over Australia and actual ownership of all the land? Jurists have always assumed that to be the case. They may be right, but there is very little evidence about what was actually intended in 1788. From the act of establishing New South Wales (27 Geo 111 C.2) as well as Governor Arthur Phillip's Commission and Instructions only two things are clear: Phillip was to exercise sovereign authority in and over the defined territory and was given the power to grant land. This might mean that the Aborigines had no property at all, but does not mean so necessarily. It could just as easily indicate that the Crown was to exercise its eminent domain to extinguish native title bit by bit around the settlement as land was needed for the development of the colony, leaving the Aborigines in possession of everything else.

There was no mention of compensation in Phillip's Instructions and that may be significant. He was not to interrupt the Aborigines in their 'several occupations' and he was to open an intercourse with them. A recent article argues plausibly that 'possibly one of the objects of this [was] to ascertain whether payment for land was required, and if so how it might be effected'.[26] Perhaps it was an oversight that no mention was made of compensation. On the other hand, the British may have assumed that they were the first occupants and that the Aborigines had no tenure at all, none which demanded compensation. This has been the prevailing legal view since the early nineteenth century. Its plausibility depends on making a huge conceptual leap – from permission given to Phillip to grant land around Sydney, presumably in very small amounts, to the assertion that what was intended was the actual expropriation of as many as 500 000 Aborigines occupying four million square kilometres.

Statements by British officials in the early decades of the nineteenth century failed to clear up the uncertainty. In 1819 the Crown Law Officers determined that the colony had been annexed as a 'desert and uninhabited' territory but referred to 'that part of New South Wales possessed by His Majesty'.[27] It may have been a slip of the pen. Perhaps it should have read 'that part of New Holland' or 'that part of Australia'. But as written it raises the possibility that while the Crown had sovereignty over the whole of New South Wales it was only in actual possession of a part of it. That of course would have accorded with the political and geographical realities. These same questions arose again in 1835 in negotiations between the Colonial Office and the South Australian Colonization Commission. In a letter to the commission Lord Glenelg said that he was concerned with the extent of the proposed colony because, as planned,

> it would extend very far into the interior of New Holland, and might embrace in its range numerous tribes of People whose Proprietary Title to the Soil we have not the slightest grounds for disputing.[28]

It was an important comment and needs careful examination. We can assume it was a serious analysis of the situation. It was almost certainly drafted, or at least approved, by James Stephen, who worked very closely with Glenelg. The following legal implications would have been apparent to Stephen, as he had been legal advisor to the Colonial Office since 1813:

1. The Aborigines had proprietary rights in the soil.
2. These proprietary rights had not been extinguished by the British claims of sovereignty in 1788 or in 1824.
3. The British government was the sovereign power with the right to extinguish the Aboriginal interest but it did not own every inch of territory in Australia.

FEUDAL TENURE

One major implication of the transfer of English law to Australia was that the Crown brought with it the traditions inherited from the feudal past. This was of major importance for property law. Under feudal tenure all land was, in theory at least, originally in the hands of the monarch, who was, therefore, the only source of legal title. Blackstone explained in his *Commentaries* that the 'grand and fundamental maxim of all feudal tenure' was that all lands were 'originally granted out by the sovereign, and are holdings either mediately or immediately, of the Crown'.[29]

But what did feudal theory of tenure have to do with Australian Aborigines? The answer was provided by Justice Blackburn in his judgement in the Gove Land Rights case of 1971. He argued that 'all titles, rights and interests whatever in land' were of necessity the 'direct consequences of some grant from the Crown'.[30] Unless the Aborigines could show such a grant they had no property rights whatever, certainly not any native title. The Norman kings, it seemed, cast very long shadows indeed, not only across the ages but over half the world as well.

It was a powerful argument which appeared to be based on fundamental constitutional reality. But doubts grow as soon as comparison is made with other countries. New Zealand, Canada and the United States all had similar legal traditions. But the result there in respect of Indigenous land rights was very different. Clearly the British legal tradition was far more flexible than appears at first sight. Blackstone did say that in colonies of settlement all English laws were 'immediately in force', but he added the important qualification that this dictum 'must be understood with very many and very great restrictions'. The colonists, he explained, 'carry with them only so much of the English law as is applicable to their own situation and the condition of the infant colony'.[31]

While discussing the question of the adoption of feudal principles into new world societies, Sir Kenneth Roberts-Wray remarked that reasoning of the kind pursued by Blackburn did not take into account

> the vital rule that when English law is in force in a Colony either because it is imported by settlers or because it is introduced by legislation, it is to be applied subject to local circumstances; and, in consequence, English laws which are to be explained merely by English social or political conditions have no operation in a colony. If it were not for some dicta in reported cases, one might expect that, applying this rule, the Courts would hold that feudal law, as such, has no application in a colony.[32]

Australian jurists didn't have to keep Australian law in the straitjacket forged by the eleventh- and twelfth-century legal armourers. They chose to do so. Whether by design or not, it gave them a powerful weapon to use against the Aborigines.

Clearly one of the most important local conditions influencing the law in colonial societies was the presence of Indigenous people — Indians, Maoris and Aborigines. If colonists were to make use of the flexibility of the common law it might be expected that here was the greatest need and scope for innovation. How could English law deal with such a situation without significant modification? The presence of the natives was an inescapable political, geographic and legal reality. While the settlers could appeal to ancient principles of law and argue that all property rights must emanate from the sovereign, the natives could stand on an even older and much more ubiquitous legal principle: the rights of immemorial possession. The problem in Australia was not that the common law was inflexible, nor that it could not recognise native title, but that, initially at least, the settlers tried to pretend that the Aborigines were not in possession and that, consequently, the Europeans were the first occupants with all the legal strength that such a position implied.

The problem of reconciling rights of possession with the feudal nature of tenure is a familiar one in domestic law. The rules of prescription allowed occupants to claim freehold title after a long period (usually twenty years) of continuous and unchallenged occupation. Where it was obvious that no title had ever existed, the courts invented the doctrine of the lost modern title, a purely fictional device to harmonise the two conflicting principles. It was adopted in Australian colonial courts in the nineteenth century. In a South Australian case in 1890, Mr Justice Boucaut determined that while it had been argued that the presumption of a lost grant could not be applied in the colony because everyone knew to the contrary, 'it must be presumed that, after the lapse of time, there has been a lost grant'.[33] While the rights based on occupation were achieved by prescription in the case of Europeans, the problem of Indigenous rights was resolved by the doctrine of native title. It evolved from American colonial experience in the seventeenth and eighteenth centuries.

NATIVE TITLE

Legal theory suggested that the Crown or those holding crown charters had both sovereignty over the American colonies and ownership of the land. The reality was that the Indians were in possession of their tribal territories and were unwilling to give them up unless the Europeans used force or bought them piecemeal. By the time Australia was first settled the tradition of purchasing Indian land was deeply entrenched in colonial practice and in the common law. Indian rights of occupation were officially recognised by the Imperial proclamation issued at the end of the Seven Years War in 1763. The Indians were not to be molested or disturbed in possession of 'such parts of our dominions and territories as, not having been ceded or purchased by Us, are reserved to them . . . as their hunting grounds'.[34] In 1792, when defining the rights of the United States government over Indian land, Thomas Jefferson referred to

> a right of pre-emption . . . that is to say, the sole and exclusive right of purchasing from them whenever they should be willing to sell . . . We consider it as established by the usage of different nations into a kind of *Jus gentium* [law of nations] for America, that a white nation settling down and declaring that such and such are their limits, makes an invasion by any other white nation an act of war, but gives no right of soil against the native possessors.[35]

Practice stretching back 200 years was swept up into a powerful legal synthesis by Chief Justice Marshall in the American Supreme Court between 1810 and 1835. In a series of famous cases Marshall enunciated the basic principles of native or Indian title.

1. Native title was a legal right based on the fundamental principle of prior possession. The Indians were admitted to be the rightful occupants of the soil, with a legal as well as just claim to retain possession of it.
2. Native title did not depend on any particular land-use or kind of settlement. Agriculture was never regarded as a prerequisite for native title, which was 'considered with reference to their habits and modes of life; their hunting grounds were as much their actual possession as the

cleared fields of the whites; and their rights to its exclusive enjoyment in their own way or for their own purposes'.[36]

3. Native title did not exist in opposition to the 'complete, ultimate title' of the United States (or the Crown). The government had the exclusive right to extinguish native title. But that title had to be considered as a form of property. Indian consent should be sought and compensation paid when the Government exercised its right of pre-emption.

Marshall's definition of native title and his resolution of the problem of harmonising it with the ultimate title of the Crown (or the Republic) were highly influential throughout the English-speaking world. His judgements are still considered to be important landmarks in the history of the legal relationship between settlers and native people.

Marshall's views were taken up by the New Zealand Supreme Court in the case of *Symmonds v. The Crown* in 1847. Justice Chapman defined native title as a qualified dominion which was not inconsistent with the absolute rights of the Crown against its British subjects. It secured to the indigenes 'all the enjoyments from the land' that they had before the intrusion of the Europeans. 'Whatever the opinion of jurists as to the strength or weakness of native title,' Chapman insisted, it was 'entitled to be respected'. It could not be extinguished 'otherwise than by the free consent of the native occupiers'. Like Marshall, Chapman believed that he was defining a legal concept that already had a long history. He explained that

the long intercourse of civilised nations, and especially of Great Britain, with the aboriginal natives of America and other countries, during the last two centuries, has gradually led to the adoption and affirmation by the Colonial Courts, of certain established principles of law, applicable to such intercourse. Although these principles may at times have been lost sight of . . . our Colonial Courts, and the Courts of such of the united States of America as have adopted the common law of England, have invariably affirmed and supported them, so that at this day, a line of judicial decision, the current of legal opinion, and above all, the settled practice of Colonial Governments, have concurred to clothe with certainty and precision that which would otherwise have remained vague and unsettled.[37]

Marshall and Chapman were quite clear that native title existed as part of the common law – that area of English law that did not derive from statutes but from 'general immemorial custom', as defined 'from time to time in the decisions of the courts of justice'. Did it apply to Australia in the 1830s and 1840s? Unfortunately there were no cases which required a definition of Aboriginal rights to land. The assertion of the rights of the Crown as against settlers in a number of cases did not necessarily have any direct bearing on the question of native title. The issue was raised, however, by the attempt of the Port Phillip Association to purchase land from Victorian Aborigines and the rejection by the New South Wales government of that transaction. The association took legal advice in London but decided not to challenge the decision.

The opinions they received were particularly interesting in providing a view of legal doctrine at the time. The three lawyers consulted by the association were the best in their field. Thomas Pemberton was the leader of the Chancery Bar and went on to spend twenty years on the judicial committee of the Privy Council. Sir William Follett had been solicitor-general in the short-lived Peel administration of 1834–35 and was attorney-general ten years later. William Burge had been the attorney-general of Jamaica and was regarded as Britain's leading authority on colonial law. In 1838 he published his *Commentaries on Colonial and Foreign Laws*, which became the standard work throughout the nineteenth century.

In the absence of any conflicting interpretation we must conclude that Burge's views (Pemberton and Follett concurred) represented the mainstream of English legal opinion. He strongly supported Marshall's assessment of native title, assuming that it was part of English law and applied with equal force in Australia. There is no suggestion whatever that the situation of the Aborigines was any different from that of North American Indians. Burge argued that it was a principle

> adopted by Great Britain as well as by the other European states, in relation to their settlements on the continent of America, that the title which discovery conferred on Government by whose authority or by whose subjects the discovery was made, was that of ultimate dominion in and sovereignty over the soil, even whilst it continued in possession of the Aborigines. This principle was reconciled with humanity and justice towards the Aborigines, because the dominion was qualified by allowing them to retain, not only the rights of occupancy, but also a restricted power of alienating those parts of the territory which they occupied.[38]

Governor Gipps discussed the general principles governing the relations of settlers and indigenes in a debate on New Zealand in the New South Wales Legislative Council in 1840. There were, he declared, three principles that were 'fully admitted, and indeed received as political axioms':

1. The native people of any country have qualified dominion over their land or a right of occupancy.
2. The Crown had the sole right of extinguishing the native title.
3. Individual settlers had no right to purchase land from the natives.

Challenged with the assertion that these principles were American rather than English law, Gipps insisted that they were 'also the law of England, and founded both on the law and practice of nations'.[39]

At Common Law

Was there a tradition – strong enough to be recognised by the common law – to respect native rights to land in all parts of the British empire at the time of Australian settlement? This question has been recently discussed in the Canadian courts, because they have had to decide whether the royal proclamation of 1763 had general application and could be considered to apply to areas of the country that were unexplored at the time. The general consensus has been that the proclamation did not create Indian land rights; it merely recognised their existence. In a 1980 case the judgement was that the law of Canada 'recognizes the existence of an aboriginal title independent of the Royal Proclamation or any other prerogative Act or legislation. It arises at common law'.[40]

But if Indian title existed everywhere in Canada as a result not of Government action, but of prior possession, could native title have existed throughout the empire? Did the proclamation of 1763 embody and recognise principles of general application that were relevant to the settlement of Australia a generation later? It may seem an extravagant suggestion, but this view was argued by Justice Hall of the Canadian Supreme Court in the case of *Calder v. the Attorney-General of British Columbia* (1973). 'Its force as a statute,' he asserted,

> is analagous to the status of the Magna Carta which has always been considered to be the law throughout the Empire. It was a law which followed the flag as England assumed jurisdiction over newly discovered or acquired land or territories.[41]

This observation was what lawyers call an *obiter dicta,* an incidental remark. But it was taken up and given enhanced authority in 1982 by Lord Denning in a case in the Privy Council.[42] Denning himself had earlier discussed the principles that had governed the relations between the Imperial government and the native inhabitants of the empire in an African case, *Oyekan v. Adele*, that had come before the Privy Council in 1957. In determining his judgement, he was required to examine transactions between the Crown and local inhabitants stretching back to the middle of the nineteenth century. He addressed himself in the broadest terms to the question of what rights could be assumed to have survived a British claim of sovereignty anywhere in the empire. He argued that

> in enquiring, however, what rights are recognized, there is one guiding principle. It is this: The courts will assume that the British Crown intends that the rights of property of the inhabitants are to be fully respected. Whilst, therefore, the British Crown, as Sovereign can make laws enabling it compulsorily to acquire land for public purposes, it will see that proper compensation is

awarded to everyone of the inhabitants who has by native law an interest in it; and the courts will declare the inhabitants entitled to compensation according to their interests, even though those interests are of a kind unknown to English law.[43]

There is, then, a common thread running through the story of British – and American – relations with Indigenous people and their property, which can be seen in the proclamation of 1763, in judgements in English, American and colonial courts throughout the nineteenth century and in the dictum outlined by Denning in the Privy Council in 1957. It was universally assumed that European governments had a right to settle and in the process extinguish the native title, but this was always to be done by negotiation and purchase. On lands not used by Europeans, native rights continued as they did everywhere until formally extinguished.

Roberts-Wray summed up the situation in his 1966 study *Commonwealth and Colonial Law*. The Crown, he explained, was assumed to intend, when annexing a colonial territory,

> that rights of property are to be respected; with the result that private ownership is unimpaired and the tribal or other rights of the inhabitants (not amounting to private ownership) can be extinguished only by the consent of the occupiers and in accordance with statute, and they continue to exist unless the contrary is established.[44]

'WITH THE CONSENT OF THE NATIVES'

The existence, after 1763, of recognised principles for dealing with native people is clearly open to debate. But the practice of purchasing land from them was well established before 1788 and was acted upon in many parts of the world.

It was common in North America throughout the eighteenth century and continued in the nineteenth century. It was normal practice in Africa and the Pacific, as illustrated by admiralty instructions given to Cook and other mariners in the late eighteenth century. For his expedition of 1776, Cook was instructed that he was

> with the consent of the Natives to take possession, in the name of the King of Great Britain, of convenient situation in such countries as you may discover, that have not already been discovered or visited by any other European Power . . . But if you find the Countries so discovered are uninhabited, you are to take possession of them for His Majesty.[45]

Cook also received instructions from the Royal Society that emphasised that the natives of the 'several lands where the Ship may touch' were the 'natural, and in the strictest sense of the word, the legal possessors of the several Regions they inhabit'. James Douglas, the president of the Society, explained that no European nation had the right 'to occupy any part of their country, or settle among them, without their voluntary consent'. Conquest over such people could 'give no just title'.[46]

It was all there. Discovery gave not land but only the right to negotiate for land. Natives were assumed to be in possession and therefore with property rights. Only uninhabited lands were without owners. Clearly Cook's instructions accorded not only with current practice but with accepted principles of international law.

When in 1785 the British government was considering a penal settlement on the African coast at Das Voltas Bay, the

House of Commons Committee on Transportation reported that it appeared 'highly probable that the Natives would, without Resistance, acquiesce in Ceding as much land as may be necessary, for a stipulated Rent'. The committee went further, observing that all the 'Portuguese and Dutch Possessions on that Coast have been so acquired'.[47] Five years later Britain affirmed the same principles when engaged in diplomatic conflict with Spain over Nootka Sound on the north-west coast of America. British negotiators insisted that Spain accept, as a principle, the right to establish any settlement 'as English subjects should form with the consent of the natives of the country not previously occupied by any of the European nations'. The British had their way and the principle was duly embodied in the Anglo-Spanish Convention of October 1790.[48] It is not known whether the Spaniards asked the British if they had sought the consent of the natives around the shores of Botany Bay and Port Jackson before establishing their colony just two years earlier.

Land rights were respected on the fringes of settlement in Canadian provinces and American colonies (states after Independence), on inhabited Pacific Islands, the north-west coast of America and the south-west coast of Africa – but not on the south-east coast of Australia. They were officially confirmed in 1785 and internationally recognised in 1790 but not in 1788. Why? Perhaps the absence of any European competition made a difference. If other powers had already negotiated for Aboriginal land, as was the case on the African coast, the British would have been forced to follow suit. If a Spanish navigator had sailed along the east coast before Cook and made a claim by discovery, the British may well have appealed over the heads – or was it under the feet? – of their European predecessors to the right of the natives in possession to cede portions of their territory.

We can come close to seeing the way the British regarded the Aborigines when they were planning to settle Australia by looking at an important exchange between Sir Joseph Banks and the Commons Committee on Transportation in May 1785. Both questions and answers need to be considered in detail.

Committee: Is the coast in General or the particular part you have mentioned much inhabited?

Banks: There are very few Inhabitants.

Committee: Are they of peaceable or hostile Disposition?

Banks: Though they seemed inclined to Hostilities they did not appear at all to be feared. We never saw more than 30 or 40 together.

Committee: Do you apprehend, in Case it was resolved to send Convicts there, any District of the Country might be obtained by Cession or purchase?

Banks: There was no probability while we were there of obtaining anything either by Cession or purchase as there was nothing we could offer that they would take except provisions and those we wanted ourselves.

Committee: Have you any idea of the nature of the Government under which they lived?

Banks: None whatever, nor of their Language.

Committee: Do you think that 500 men being put on shore there would meet with that Obstruction from the Natives which might prevent them settling there?

Banks: Certainly not – from the experience I have had of the Natives of another part of the same coast I am inclined to believe that they would speedily abandon the country to the newcomers.

Committee: Were the Natives armed and in what Manner?

Banks: They were armed with spears headed with fish bones but none of them we saw in Botany Bay appeared at all formidable.[49]

The committee clearly thought it appropriate, as with Das Voltas Bay, to acquire land by cession or purchase. In his answers Banks did not suggest that such a proposal was wrong in principle. He said it would be difficult to execute.

The real problem wasn't that the Aborigines had nothing to sell. They were unwilling to sell because the Europeans had nothing to tender that would be considered of value, apart from provisions, which in 1770 had been too valuable to part with. It was the Europeans, not the Aborigines, who had nothing to offer; Banks's words are of great significance, 'there was nothing we could offer that they would take'. But that didn't really matter. The land could be occupied against the will of the owners, and quite against the principles of international law the English forced the Spanish to accept in 1790. The Aborigines were not formidable, their weapons held no fear for Europeans and anyway they would probably abandon their territory. Australia was not a *terra nullius*. There were people in possession. It might become one if they abandoned their lands.[50] They didn't, of course. They resisted the encroachment, thereby emphasising their sense of property and creating legal problems that Australian courts have only recently come to terms with.

THREE

Reconnaissance and Reassessment

What were the relations between whites and Aborigines during the initial settlement at Sydney Cove? As the British sailed into southern waters in 1787 they carried with them many assumptions about the Aborigines whom they hadn't yet met. Two were particularly important for the future development of Australian law:

1. New South Wales was *terra nullius* in the sense of being without any landowners, because apart from the coastal fringe it was uninhabited.

2. The scattered coastal tribes could either be absorbed into colonial society or would abandon their territory without a struggle, thus rendering it *terra nullius* as well.

These were convenient assumptions to carry on a colonising expedition. But they were illfounded, as experience was soon to show.

The first illusion to disappear concerned the size and distribution of the Indigenous population. It disappeared quickly.

The Early Experience, 1788–1807

Even before the expedition moved from Botany Bay to Port Jackson, the assessment of Cook and Banks was challenged by experience. Watkin Tench noted that the British found the local Aborigines 'tolerably numerous' around Botany Bay and 'even at the harbour's mouth [they] had reason to conclude the country was more populous than Mr. Cook had thought it'.[1]

When parties began to explore the reaches of Sydney Harbour, it was realised that though the Aborigines spent much of their time in small hunting and foraging parties, as reported by the visitors of 1770, the total population was quite large. A first-fleeter noted in his journal of 5 February 1788:

> There is something odd in their never being seen but in small [numbers] but by accident, tho' there is every reason to suppose they are numerous. Since our arrival at Port Jackson, during a survey of the harbour a body of near a hundred were seen drawn up with an unexpected degree of regularity.[2]

At much the same time, Captain John Hunter found the Aborigines around the harbour 'very numerous', a circumstance that he was 'a little surprised to find after what had been said in the voyage of the *Endeavour*'.[3] By May the British had come across a party of 300, 'a striking proof of the numerousness of the natives', as Tench observed.[4] Phillip reported to his superiors in Britain that he estimated that there were at least 1500 Aborigines resident within a radius of 16 kilometres from the settlement – that is, there were more Aborigines around Sydney Harbour than there were Europeans on the First Fleet.[5] By the following year the reassessment of the Indigenous population was being reported to the British public. In *An Authentic and Interesting Narrative of the Late Expedition to Botany Bay*, the anonymous author noted that Cook had only seen a few blacks and had 'therefore concluded that the country was thinly inhabited [but] in this manner he was much mistaken, as frequently tribes of three or four hundred came down together'.[6]

There were many more Aborigines in New South Wales apart from those around Sydney Harbour. The settlers were gradually forced to accept their presence as colonial experience overwhelmed their original assumptions. But they took quite a bit of convincing. Although Tench was quickly forced to admit that the country was 'more populous than it was generally believed to be in Europe', this observation, he insisted, was not meant to extend into the interior parts of the continent, 'which there is every reason to conclude from our researches, as well as from the manner of living practiced by the natives, to be uninhabited'.[7] During a journey inland in May 1788 Phillip was 'surprised to find temporary huts made by the natives far inland'. He fossicked round in the ashes of Aboriginal fires but could find neither shells nor fishbones, leading him to the conclusion that the blacks must 'depend solely upon animals for food', a fact which contradicted the settlers' preconceptions.[8] Two months later, Phillip saw smoke on the Blue Mountains and concluded that there could not be 'any doubt of there being inhabitants fifty miles inland'. He determined to travel there in order to clear up what was

> at present a mystery to me, how people who have not the least idea of cultivation can maintain themselves in the interior part of the country.[9]

When the presence of inland Aborigines was impossible to overlook it was assumed they were merely stragglers driven away from coastal fishing grounds by more powerful enemies. But contact with more distant clans increased. In April 1791 Tench spoke to a man who told him that his people depended 'but little on fish' and that their principal support was derived from small animals and yams which they dug 'out of the earth'.[10] Later expeditions gradually increased the Europeans' knowledge of Aboriginal land use. By 1802, Francis Barrallier was able to provide a list of many varieties of food used by inland blacks, who 'appeared to be good hunters'.[11]

A major characteristic that Europeans attributed to hunters and gatherers, and to pastoral nomads as well, was their incessant wandering. Still well stocked with classical allusions, they imagined that the Aborigines were ever on the move, with no sense of property or local 'attachments'. But as with preconceived notions about the size of the Indigenous population, these ideas were soon overthrown by direct experience of Aboriginal society. The settlers quickly realised that the Aborigines lived in clanlike or tribal groups, that each group had a specific district with known boundaries, that they took their name from the district and rarely moved outside it. Within months of arrival, the officers of the First Fleet were able to describe both the various local group locations and their boundaries.[12] Hunter noted the following in his journal a few months after the first settlement:

> We have reason to believe, that the natives associate in tribes of many families together, and it appeared now that they have one fixed residence and the tribe takes its name from the place of general residence. You may often visit the place where the tribe resides, without finding the whole society there; their time is so much occupied in the search for food, that the different families take different routes, but in case of any dispute with a neighbouring tribe, they can be soon assembled.[13]

The settlers soon realised that tribal boundaries were longstanding; differences of dialect were apparent over comparatively short distances; coastal blacks knew little about the hinterland. Those Aborigines who accompanied the earliest expeditions inland saw country as new to them as it was to their European travelling companions.[14]

Aboriginal conflict was often about territorial jurisdiction. 'Their battles,' observed a first-fleeter in July 1789, 'are sometimes concerning the right of fishing or dwelling in some particular cove'.[15] When exploring parties took Aboriginal guides into the interior they witnessed the formal diplomatic exchanges necessary when entering the territory of other tribes. In April 1791 Tench was travelling inland with Boladeree and Colbee when he witnessed the following exchange:

Colbee no longer hesitated, but gave the signal of invitation, in a loud hollow cry. After some whooping, and shouting, on both sides a man, with a lighted stick in his hand, advanced near enough to converse with us. The first words, which we could distinctly understand were, 'I am Colbee, of the tribe of Cad-i-gal'. The stranger replied, 'I am Bèr-ee-wan, of the tribe of Boorooberongal'. Boladeree informed him also of his name, and that we were white men and friends, who would give them something to eat. Still he seemed irresolute. Colbee therefore advanced to him, took him by the hand, and led him to us. By the light of the moon, we were introduced to this gentleman, all our names being repeated in form by our two masters of ceremonies, who said that we were Englishmen, and Bud-yee-yee [good], that we came from the coast, and that we were travelling inland.[16]

The tribes around Sydney did not, as Banks predicted, abandon their country. They were far more attached to their land than European savants supposed. 'Strange as it may appear,' David Collins observed in 1791, 'they have also their real estates'. He explained that Bennelong assured him that an island in the harbour was 'his own property' and had been 'his fathers before him'. 'To this little spot he appeared much attached' and was often seen enjoying himself on it. Bennelong told Collins of 'other people who possessed this kind of hereditary property, which they retained undisturbed'.[17] Collins also realised that a major source of Aboriginal hostility was their resistance to the spread of settlement and the consequent expropriation of their tribal land. 'While they entertained the idea of our having dispossessed them of their residences,' he explained, 'they must always consider us as enemies; and upon this principal they made a point of attacking the white people whenever opportunity and safety concurred'.[18]

THE REAL PROPRIETORS OF THE SOIL

So what had the earliest settlers discovered about Aborigines and their land? The Aborigines lived in relatively small districts with known and recognised boundaries. Although the food quest took them in many directions, they had 'fixed residences'. They defended their territories against trespassers. Movement across boundaries necessitated diplomatic niceties. They 'enjoyed' their land, exploiting a wide range of food sources. They identified with their districts and took their name from them.

Clearly the Aborigines around Sydney were in possession of their land according to both international law and the common law. The Europeans knew enough about the Aborigines by the early 1800s to reach that conclusion. Indeed, that is what Governor King had done by 1807. He had just completed his six years as governor and drew on an experience of the colony that stretched back to 1788. When preparing a memo for Bligh, his successor, he observed of the Aborigines that he had 'ever considered them the real proprietors of the soil'.[19] This comment should not surprise us. It was the logical conclusion to be drawn from the first twenty years' experience of Australian settlement.

King governed New South Wales during a period of intense conflict with the Hawkesbury groups. In seeking to contain the problem, he sought to negotiate with the people in question and met three local men just before Christmas 1804. It was an important occasion, best described in King's own words:

> On questioning the cause of their disagreement with the new settlers they very ingeniously answered that they did not like to be driven from the few places that were left on the banks of the river, where alone they could procure food; that they had gone down the river as the white men took possession of the banks; if they went across white men's grounds the settlers fired upon them and were angry; that if they could retain some places on the lower part of the river they should be satisfied and would not trouble the white men. The observation and request appear to be so just and so equitable that I assured them no more settlements should be made lower down the river. With that assurance they appeared well satisfied and promised to be quiet, in which state they continue.[20]

King's negotiations did not lead to a permanent resolution of the problem on the Hawkesbury, or anywhere else for that matter. But they foreshadowed the policy of establishing reserves. In attempting to reconcile the interests of settlers and indigenes King negotiated with the Aborigines as parties who were actually in possession. He did not propose to give land as a gift to indigenes who had either been totally dispossessed or had never been in possession but to set limits to the spread of white settlement, leaving Aborigines in possession of at least part of their ancestral territories.

Europeans learned a lot about Aborigines between 1788 and 1807. Many of the ideas current when the First Fleet arrived were modified or rejected. The forty years between 1807 and 1848 saw an even greater development of understanding. Settlement swept across much of south-eastern and parts of south-western Australia. Explorers ventured deep into the unknown interior. Missionaries and amateur ethnographers lived in close contact with Aboriginal communities, learning languages and studying customs and beliefs.

POPULATION AND LAND USE

By the 1840s, explorers had pushed out into many of the more remote and inhospitable districts of the continent – and found the Aborigines in occupation. There was no uninhabited land. After long experience of Aboriginal society, Edward Eyre wrote:

> I have myself observed, that no part of the country is so utterly worthless, as not to have attractions sufficient occasionally to tempt the wandering savage into its recesses. In the arid, barren, naked plains of the north, with not a shrub to shelter him from the heat, and not a stick to burn for his fire . . . the native is found, and where, as far as I could ascertain, the whole country around appears equally devoid of either animal or vegetable life.[21]

With over half the continent unexplored, including the tropical north, the settlers were uncertain about the overall size of the Indigenous population. Rough censuses were carried out in particular districts; estimates were made of population densities. Governor Phillip assessed the numbers around Sydney; Governor Stirling did the same around Perth. Estimates made by scholars in Europe between 1804 and 1834 ranged from as low as 100 000 to as high as five million. Most estimates were over one million. The most thorough assessment of the available evidence was made by a subcommittee of London's Aborigines Protection Society in 1838. It concluded, after examining 'every reasonable account and estimate', that the total population could not 'be stated as short of 1,400,000'.[22] This may have been too high, but it was probably closer to present-day assessments than the figure of 300 000 accepted from 1930 until recently.

Europeans gradually realised how extensive and varied were Aboriginal food sources, that almost everything edible was exploited at some time or other during a typical year. 'Prior to our coming among them,' missionary Francis Tuckfield observed, 'every forest . . . every valley . . . every plain and sheet of water furnished its number of repasts at the proper season . . .'[23]

Settlers who sought to understand the traditional economy came to appreciate that it was based on sophisticated bushcraft and a profound understanding of the environment. The explorer and colonial governor George Grey observed that in his own district, the Aborigine 'knows exactly what it produces, the proper time at which the several articles are in season, and the readiest means of procuring them'.[24] Eyre realised that the Aborigines were dependent on 'the intimate knowledge they have of every nook and corner of the country they inhabit'. Of the desert groups he wrote:

does a shower of rain fall, they know the very rock where a little water is most likely to be collected, the very hole where the longest grass grows, from which they may collect the spangles, and water is sometimes procured thus in very great abundance.[25]

Eyre quickly understood the advantages that native had over settler in the arid interior, for from his knowledge of the country, long residence and practical experience the tribesman had 'many resources at his command to supply his wants, where the white man would faint or perish by thirst'. The Aborigine had the advantage over the European 'that a swimmer has in the water over a man who cannot swim, conscious of his own power and resources'.[26]

Aboriginal bushcraft and knowledge of the country were valuable to the settlers. From the very earliest forays out of Sydney, European parties took local people with them to find the way, negotiate geographical obstacles, find water and food, track animals, build bark shelters and construct bark canoes. George Caley wrote to Banks in 1801 informing him that he intended to 'keep a native constant soon, as they can trace anything so well in the bush'.[27] The same lesson was learned during the early years of Western Australian settlement, it being thought 'useless for any party of Europeans to go out without the assistance of a native as a guide'.[28] Explorers were helped by local Aborigines resident in country they passed through who showed them fords over rivers and passes through ranges and were able to give detailed descriptions of terrain, vegetation and water sources within the boundaries of their own country.

The more perceptive colonists realised that the locals were more than skilled hunters and foragers and that they positively managed their environment. Grey observed that the groups of south-west Western Australia had rules of behaviour designed to preserve and perpetuate the supply of food. They included the following:

1. No vegetable production used by the natives as food should be plucked or gathered when bearing seed.
2. Certain classes of natives should not eat particular articles of food; this restriction being 'tantamount to game law which preserve certain choice and scarce articles of food from being so generally destroyed as those which are more abundant'.
3. The application of taboos on killing animals related to one's own totem, a custom which acted as a limitation of the culling of animals.[29]

From the earliest years of settlement, travellers were intrigued by open areas of grassland dispersed among the forests 'as if they had been cleared by manual labour'.[30] By the 1830s the Europeans realised that the Aborigines used fire to open up the country and keep it clear of undergrowth, that indeed the Australian landscape was actually man-made.[31] Ludwig Leichhardt noted that in the interior of Queensland

> the natives seemed to have burned the grass systematically along every water-hole, in order to have them surrounded with young grass as soon as the rain sets in . . . Long strips of lately burnt grass were frequently observed extending for many miles along the creeks. The banks of small isolated water-holes in the forest were equally attended to . . . It is no doubt connected with a systematic management of their runs, to attract game to particular spots, in the same way that stockholders burn parts of theirs in proper seasons.[32]

By the middle of the nineteenth century the consequences of not burning the country regularly were becoming apparent. Thomas Mitchell noted that in the open forest around Sydney where formerly a man could gallop without impediment and see 'whole miles before him', there were now thick forests of young trees.[33]

The settlers were often impressed by the elaborate fish traps constructed by the Aborigines in rivers and around the coast. They came across networks of paths linking man-made wells. In the Western District of Victoria they found villages of stone huts and elaborate earthworks covering 4 hectares and designed to harvest eels as they passed down through inland waterways.

While travelling in Western Australia in the late 1830s, Grey was surprised by the evidence he saw of Aboriginal industry:

> As we wound along the native path my wonder augmented; the path increased in breadth and in its beaten appearance, whilst along the side of it we found frequent wells, some of which were ten or twelve feet deep, and were altogether executed in a superior manner. We now crossed the dry bed of a stream, and from that emerged upon a tract of light fertile soil, quite overrun with [yam] plants . . . and now for three and a half consecutive miles we traversed a fertile piece of land, literally perforated with the holes the natives had made to dig this root; indeed we could with difficulty walk across it on that account, whilst this tract extended east and west as far as we could see. It was now evident that we had entered the most thickly-populated district in Australia that I had yet observed, and morever one which must have been inhabited for a long series of years, for more had been done to secure a provision from the ground by

hard manual labour than I could have believed it in the power of uncivilized man to accomplish.[34]

Aboriginal Land Tenure

Settlers who had spent any time with Aborigines came to appreciate that they had a deep emotional bond with their own country. They missed it when away from it and rejoiced when they returned. They were a 'most bigotted race of people to the ground on which they were born'.[35] They were patriotic, proudly telling Europeans where they came from and of the special virtues of their homeland. The surgeon at the Albany settlement in the late 1820s observed that 'every individual would immediately announce to us his tribal name and country'.[36] A pioneer missionary wrote home to his superiors in Britain in 1821 explaining that the Aborigines

> possess some tract of country which they call their own; but, even on this, although it may afford them animals and fish, they will not be permanent. Yet they are so senselessly bigotted to this particular spot, that when you would persuade them to settle in any place, they will not understand you, no more than if you discoursed to them in Latin or Greek.[37]

It was not merely the knowledge of the country and the obvious emotional attachment to it that impressed European observers. There was also the obvious sense of property they detected in Aboriginal society. 'You may take it as certain,' the Presbyterian clergyman J.D. Lang informed English philanthropists, 'that the Aborigines of Australia have an idea of property in the soil'.[38] After learning all he could about the natives, both by study and direct observation, the Polish expatriate Paul de Strzelecki wrote,

> the foundation of their social edifice may, like that of civilized nations, be said to rest on an inherent sense of property. As strongly attached to that property, and to the rights which it involves, as any European political body, the tribes of Australia resort to precisely similar measures for protecting it, and seek redress and revenge for its violated laws through the same means as an European nation would if similarly situated.[39]

From the 1820s onwards a growing number of settlers reported that, from their own experience, they had concluded that the Aborigines they knew had a strong sense of identity with a specific homeland. The missionary W. Walker noted in 1821 that the locals possessed 'some tract of country which they call their own'.[40] A few years later Robert Dawson, manager of the Australian Agricultural Company, observed that the groups he was familiar with had 'a district of country which they call their own, and in some part of which they were always found'.[41] In 1826 a correspondent of the Methodist Missionary Society reported after travelling throughout New South Wales that he had 'every reason to suppose the Aborigines have each a personal possession'.[42] Anglican Bishop Broughton told a House of Commons committee in 1836 that the Aborigines had 'a notion among themselves of certain portions of the country belonging to their own particular tribe'.[43] Lang believed that every tribe had 'its own district'.[44] Methodist missionary Joseph Orton observed in 1839 that each tribe had 'a particular location and boundaries beyond the limits of which they seldom go except on special occasions'.[45]

Settlers reached much the same conclusion in the other

colonies. Governor Arthur told the Colonial Office that in Tasmania 'each tribe claims some portion of territory which they consider peculiarly their own'.[46] G. A. Robinson, the so-called 'conciliator' of the Tasmanians, knew enough about island land tenure to draw a map 'on Aboriginal principles' incorporating place names and boundaries. After an extensive tour of the island, the Quaker missionary James Backhouse noted that 'though the mode of holding property differed among the Aborigines of Van Diemen's Land from that used among English people, yet they had their property'. Each tribe was 'limited to its own hunting ground; and into such hunting grounds the island was divided'.[47] In South Australia, the German missionary C. G. Teichelmann discovered that each tribe had 'a certain district of the country as a property received by the forefathers'.[48] After extensive colonial experience, both as an explorer and as protector of Aborigines, Eyre reported that particular districts 'having a radius perhaps of from ten to twenty miles [were] considered generally as being the property and hunting grounds of the tribes who frequent them'.[49] In a letter to one of the founders of the colony, Governor George Gawler observed that the local tribes had 'very distinct and well defined proprietary rights' that afforded them

> protection from other tribes and bodily support – they hunt the game upon, take the fish in and eat the roots on their own district just as much as English gentlemen kills the deer and sheep or the fish in his private park. The property is equally positive and well defined.[50]

The officers of the First Fleet had realised that the tribal territories around Sydney had clear and known boundaries. Settlers confirmed this impression when they fanned out into the interior of the continent. John Henderson noted in 1832 that although the Aborigines had no settled place of residence, 'the limits of their respective hunting grounds appear to be distinctly recognized'.[51] The following year William Breton observed that each tribe had 'its own particular boundaries, which are seldom passed'.[52] Grey believed that every Aborigine 'knew the limits of his own land and could point out the various objects which mark his boundaries'.[53] Lang thought likewise that the boundaries of particular districts were 'well known by the different tribes, and generally respected by them'.[54] Writing of the Western Australian Aborigines, Backhouse observed that it was

> quite clear that the natives . . . from Swan River to King George Sound, recognize their distinct hunting grounds as the private property of the different families, and that the boundaries are distinctly defined . . . they have their private property clearly distinguished into hunting grounds, the boundaries of which are definite, trees being often recognized by them as landmarks.[55]

The corollary of known boundaries and a keen sense of property that the colonists detected in Aboriginal society was a ready response to trespass. It was appreciated that tribes visited one another for formal ceremonies but that there was always a protocol involved. After joint corroborees tribes returned to their respective territory, 'to pass which at other times is considered an act of aggression, or a signal of war'.[56] Grey discovered that the punishment for trespass was 'invariably death if taken in the fact, and at the very least an obstinate contest ensues'.[57] Strzelecki similarly found that if trespass had been committed by a neighbouring tribe, 'compensation or a reparation of the insult is asked for'.[58] Henderson was witness to a large gathering of Aborigines to deal with a case of trespass because one tribe had 'in defiance of the national law, audaciously hunted Emus within the territories' of their neighbours and the 'latter came to demand reparation for the insult offered'.[59]

European explorers were often conducted through the country by Aboriginal guides who performed formal ceremonies at tribal boundaries and passed the strangers on to their neighbours. Writing of his journey down the Murray, Charles Sturt observed that the Aborigines 'sent ambassadors forward regularly from one tribe to another, in order to prepare for an approach'. The party, he noted in retrospect, had passed tribe after tribe 'under the protection of envoys'.[60] While describing his journey from Port Phillip to the new colony of South Australia, Joseph Hawdon observed that 'in passing through the tribes of natives we were extremely fortunate in keeping a friendly intercourse with them by means of ambassadors sent from one tribe to another'.[61]

Settlers were often uncertain about the exact nature of Aboriginal tenure, although they knew it existed. One difficult area of understanding was the relationship between individuals and groups, between the common ownership of the tribe and the claims by individuals to particular pieces of territory. There was also uncertainty about the mechanics of inheritance, although there was no doubt amongst informed observers that property passed across the generations. G. F. Moore, Swan River pioneer, believed that the 'hunting ground or landed property descends in the male line'.[62] South Australian Protector of Aborigines Matthew Moorhouse believed that certain districts passed from father to son 'with as much regularity or propriety as in our own country'.[63] A fellow South Australian observed in 1842 that 'something in the nature of hereditary succession obtains among them so that they have in their language a term "pang karra" which signifies "a district or tract of country belonging to an individual which he inherits from his father"'.[64]

Many of the writers who commented on the nature of Aboriginal tenure in the 1830s knew they were doing more than merely observing and reporting interesting ethnographic information, that they were reinterpreting Indigenous society, overthrowing orthodoxy and measuring imported ideology against Australian reality. They appreciated, as well, that their reassessment of Aboriginal property had both political and legal implications. Moorhouse noted in an official report in 1840 that the 'more extended knowledge of the language' had given Europeans a more general acquaintance with Indigenous manners and customs. 'We find,' he concluded, 'what the Europeans thought the Aborigines of Australia did not possess: territorial rights'.[65] In a sermon delivered in Sydney in 1838, the Congregational minister Rev. John Saunders argued that it was neither just nor true to argue that the Aborigines 'had no notion of property'. Indeed, 'accurate information' showed that each tribe 'had its own locality'. The colonists could no longer advance the specious argument that they could not technically rob the locals 'of that which they did not possess'.[66] Orton argued in 1842 that it was

> an important truth which has been designedly or ignorantly over-looked but which demands consideration viz. that the Aborigines of this country though an erratic race of Savages they have decidedly a property in the land of their birth which right is recognized and held sacred by themselves in their respective relations of tribes, families and individuals.[67]

Knowledge of Aboriginal land tenure was widespread among humanitarian circles in Britain. The three great missionary organisations – the Church Missionary Society, the Methodist Missionary Society and the London Missionary Society – as well as the Quakers and Colonial Office officials had all received numerous reports on the subject during the 1820s and 1830s. By far the most significant recognition of Aboriginal property rights was made in a Colonial Office memo of James Stephen, the permanent head of the department, in 1840. In a brief note on a dispatch from South Australia he wrote:

> It is an important and unsuspected fact that these Tribes had Proprietary in the Soil – that is, in particular sections of it which were clearly defined and well understood before the occupation of their country.[68]

This was one of the most important sentences ever written in the history of white–Aboriginal relations. We should consider why. It showed how far the thinking about Aboriginal land rights had gone by 1840. It had reached the centre of the Imperial government. Stephen was perhaps the most able of nineteenth-century Colonial Office officials, with a profound knowledge of colonial law. He had been legal adviser to the Colonial Office from 1813 to 1834. The transformation of his thinking was apparent when his 1840 memo is compared with his legal advice of 1822, that Australia had been acquired 'neither by conquest nor cession, but by the mere occupation of a desert or uninhabited land'.[69] But his 1840 comment was more than an affirmation of a 'proprietary in the soil'. It also contained a definition of what that involved: ownership of 'particular sections' that were 'clearly defined and well understood'.

Using that definition, we know now that Aborigines had 'a

proprietary in the soil'. We also know that this was understood in the 1830s and 1840s both in Britain and in the Australian colonies. Well-informed settlers and Imperial officials knew enough to see that the Aborigines were in possession of their land, in possession as it was understood in both international and common law. The Aborigines met all the criteria to establish, if not their sovereignty, then certainly their native title, which, in the authoritative words of Lord Davey in an important Privy Council decision of 1901, was 'a tenure of land under custom and usage which is either known to lawyers or discoverable by them by evidence'.[70]

Stephen was a lawyer, indeed, the empire's pre-eminent authority on colonial law. From the large amount of evidence that had accumulated during the 1820s and 1830s, he had discerned that the Aborigines had 'a tenure of land under custom and usage'. They had native title.

ORIGINAL PROPRIETORS

If, as many had come to believe by the 1840s, the Aborigines were in possession of their tribal territories, they must have been in possession before 1788, a fact which undermined the credibility of the concept of *terra nullius*. How widespread this view was is difficult to determine with any accuracy. But all the available evidence suggests that such sentiments had become commonplace.

In his book *Latest Information with Regard to Australia Felix*, published in 1840, George Arden observed that the Aborigines' 'priority of proprietorship is on all sides acknowledged'[71] and in the books, newspapers, letters and journals of the period there are innumerable references to original

Aboriginal ownership and subsequent dispossession, to the fact that the settlers had 'plundered them of their property', 'invaded the territory of the New Hollanders', 'taken possession of their native soil', 'usurped their territory', 'usurped the rights of others in possessing ourselves of their land', 'robbed them of their land', 'taken forcible possession of their rightful property', 'despoiled them of their country', 'deprived them of their land', 'taken their rights of birth'.

It would be possible to compile a much longer list of such phrases. When they were expressed by private individuals it was one thing; when they entered official conversations, letters, dispatches and speeches it was quite another. And they did so increasingly after the 1820s. Thus in 1821 Governor Brisbane told a visiting missionary that the British had 'taken the land from the Aborigines of this country'.[72] The Tasmanian Colonial Secretary referred to the island tribes who had been 'removed from their native soil';[73] Governor Arthur spoke of the settlers as 'intruders on their native soil'.[74] Governor Hutt of Western Australia referred to 'our taking possession of their countries'.[75] In New South Wales, Governor Gipps issued an official statement referring to the locals as 'the original possessors of the soil',[76] while his colonial secretary issued another alluding to the 'Aboriginal Possessors of the Soil'.[77] In a dispatch to Governor Bourke in 1837 Lord Glenelg, Secretary of State for the Colonies, observed that the British claimed sovereignty 'over the whole of their Ancient Possessions';[78] his successor, Lord Russell, referred to 'the former occupiers'[79] of Australia. Earl Grey, another incumbent, warned Governor Fitzroy of New South Wales that the colonists had incurred deep responsibilities 'in assuming their territory'.[80] In Colonial Office memos, Stephen observed in 1839 that the Europeans 'take possession of their country' and referred four years later to the 'dispossession of the original inhabitants'.[81]

It was only a small step from admitting that the Aborigines were the original possessors of Australia to accepting that they had 'a birthright in the soil'. South Australia's Governor Gawler informed his superiors in London that the natives had 'very ancient rights of proprietary and hereditary possession';[82] Charles Sturt, his land commissioner, referred to their 'natural indefeasible rights . . . vested in them as a birth right'.[83] Joseph Orton believed the Aborigines had a 'right of property in the lands of their birth right',[84] and G. A. Robinson thought they were 'the legitimate proprietors of the soil' because it was 'the land of their forefathers'.[85] A South Australian pioneer argued that the 'rights of the original possessors' were

> not at all affected by Acts of Parliament or Commissioner's instructions: their right rests upon principles of justice. It is impossible to deny the right which the natives have to the land on which they were born, from which age after age they have derived support and nourishment, and which has received their ashes.[86]

The belief that the Aborigines were the original proprietors of Australia and had an interest in the soil took deep root in colonial society between 1820 and 1850. A minority of settlers took the view that the Aborigines were, therefore, the proper, the legitimate owners of the soil and the British were usurpers and brigands. But the great majority continued to accept that Europeans had a right to colonise the world, to turn 'waste' lands to better use and to subdue and replenish the earth.

The obvious way to reconcile the interests of settlers and

indigenes was to give compensation for lands acquired by the Europeans. The need to provide 'an equivalent' runs through much of the public discussion of the period. There was debate about what sort of compensation, and how much, but very few people opposed the idea itself. The editor of the Sydney paper *The Colonist* argued in 1838 that it was 'now a settled doctrine' with both the Imperial government and parliament, and the 'virtuous portion' of the public, that the right to 'take possession of barbarous countries' rested entirely upon the principle 'of a full equivalent being given by the invaders'.[87] Almost everyone accepted that the Aborigines had lost something as a result of settlement, that they had, therefore, originally owned something as well. At the inaugural meeting of Sydney's Aborigines Protection Society in 1838 a local barrister, Sydney Stephens, remarked that

> the great question was, whether we were to give them no equivalent for that which we had taken from them. Had we deprived them of nothing? Was it nothing that they were driven from the lands where their fathers lived, where they were born, and which were endeared to them by associations equally strong with the associations of more civilized people?[88]

THE PHILOSOPHY OF BRIGANDS

Growing knowledge about traditional society strengthened the land rights cause; arguments used against it were increasingly out of touch with colonial reality, reflecting the eighteenth-century European intellectual climate rather than what had been learned at the Antipodes in the nineteenth century.

The case against native title usually began with reference to the world as it was supposed to have been after the Creation, when all land was held in common. The assumption was that Aboriginal society had remained in that condition and therefore the Europeans were the first real occupiers of Australian land. In a long letter to the *Sydney Gazette* in August 1824 an anonymous correspondent argued:

> Which tribe, or which individual, could with propriety be considered as the proper owner of any particular district? Each tribe wandered about wheresoever inclination prompted, without ever supposing that any one place belonged to it more than to another. They were the *inhabitants,* but not the proprietors of the land. The country then was to be regarded as an unappropriated remnant of the common property; and, in taking possession of it, we did not invade another's right, for we only claimed that which before was unclaimed by any.[89]

A variation of this argument was to insist that, regardless of everything that was known about Aboriginal society and land use, Australia was, in effect, a desert. The editor of the *Sydney Herald* asked rhetorically in 1838: 'what is the difference between taking possession of a desert country without inhabitants', and taking possession of one of which 'comparatively few inhabitants make no use'? Such a country, he argued, 'is a *desert* for every purpose involved in this question, and may be justly occupied by civilized men'.[90]

The most common justification for the dispossession of the Aborigines, however, was that the Europeans made better use of the land and were therefore entitled to expropriate it. The Sydney barrister R. Windeyer argued this case strongly at the first meeting of the local Aborigines Protection Society. Labour, he told the far from enchanted audience, was the sole title to land. Therefore the Aborigines 'had no right to the land', which in fact 'belonged to him who should first cultivate it'.[91]

It was a popular argument throughout colonial Australia. But it was deeply flawed and provided no explanation of how the Aborigines, as British subjects, would actually lose the land they had possessed 'time out of mind'. It was often pointed out in debate that there was no legal obligation to cultivate freehold land. The proprietor did not 'lose his title by his voluntary throwing his land out of cultivation and permitting it to become a waste producing nothing but thistles and weeds'.[92] Another powerful riposte to the Windeyer position was that if land really did belong to the first cultivator then very little of New South Wales was owned at all. It was a strange argument to advance in a pastoral country where only a tiny proportion of the land was under crop. Even in Britain there was much land that had never been farmed and yet was held with complete security against trespassers and usurpers. How, then, was it possible to reconcile 'taking possession of land partially occupied by the uncivilized' with the 'scrupulous care taken to avoid anything like trespass on land equally eligible, and at least as much neglected, if claimed by a civilized owner'?[93]

The arguments of the 'expropriators' had hidden dangers that were gleefully exposed by their opponents. Once the proposition that the Crown could expropriate land judged to be under-utilised was accepted, all property rights were in jeopardy. Windeyer's arguments, the editor of Sydney paper *The Morning Chronicle* asserted, embodied the 'philosophy of brigands, or bucaneers, and would justify the Russian autocrat in the oppression of the Poles, or any oppression whatsoever'.[94] G. A. Robinson also took up the question in his 1849 annual report as Chief Protector of Aborigines at Port Phillip, arguing that if the fact that the Aborigines did not cultivate their land was 'held to justify a compulsory transfer of property then would there soon be an end to the right of all property'.[95]

The whole question was extensively debated at a conference called by the Aborigines Protection Society in London. The report of proceedings is worth considering in detail. It was realised that

> at present there is a disposition to consider that the pressure of a numerous population, in itself, confers the right to enter upon and occupy the lands of the imperfectly civilized man, which, by his questionable possession, are prevented from receiving the improvement of which they are susceptible, and consequently from maintaining the individuals who might advantageously occupy them in far larger numbers. This led to a discussion as to the conditions which constitute absolute possession. Beneficial occupation was proposed as the test; to which it was replied, that large portions of land in most civilized countries are kept unoccupied and out of tillage, and in possession of a very few individuals; that there is, perhaps, no land more securely possessed, or more carefully conveyed, that these very tracts; that if the principle contended for, with reference to uncivilized countries, were to be carried out, many acres of valuable land, now constituting the ornamental parks, the preserves for game, and the retreats of noxious animals, would come into the possession of thousands of individuals, now pressed with hunger, or obliged to emigrate to distant countries. But as such intrusions would be regarded as a gross violation of law, it was replied, that such intrusion in the case of a civilized country would involve the destruction of a social system on which the harmony of society depends . . . and that in the case of uncivilized countries,

present expediency and ulterior benefits sanctioned the adoption of a different course.[96]

ABORIGINAL RESISTANCE

The strength and widespread nature of Aboriginal resistance underlined their sense of property and may have been a more decisive influence on European opinion than growing ethno-graphic information. Settlers often attributed Aboriginal resistance to the desire for plunder, the compulsions of savagery, revenge for insults or competition for women. But many of the more perceptive observers of colonial life realised that land and land usage were the major sources of conflict.

David Collins appreciated this during the first years of settlement. His views were echoed many times over and in all parts of the continent. 'They have a conception of our having excluded them from what was their original property,' Bishop Broughton told a House of Commons committee in 1836. 'Certainly,' he added, 'this idea is very prevalent among them'.[97] His Roman Catholic counterpart, Bishop Polding, gave similar evidence to a select committee of the New South Wales Legislative Council in 1845. He believed the 'leading idea' among the natives was that the Europeans had occupied their territories without invitation or compensation. He was asked by J. D. Lang, 'Do you think they have such an idea of the value of land, as to lead them to view its settlement as an act of aggression?' To which Polding replied, 'I am convinced of it, and that is the root of the evil'.[98]

These home truths were accepted in the Colonial Office from as early as the 1820s. The Secretary of State, Sir George Murray, commiserated with the problems faced by Governor

Arthur in conflict with the Tasmanian Aborigines, who were 'possessed with the idea which they appear to entertain in regard to their own rights over the country, in comparison with those of the colonists'.[99]

Similar views were expressed by settlers who had seen much more of life on the frontiers than British ministers or colonial bishops. Prominent Tasmanian pioneer Roderic O'Connor observed that island Aborigines were 'as tenacious of their hunting grounds' as the Europeans were of their farms and were 'displeased when they found houses built or persons hunting on them'.[100] After experiencing Aboriginal society both as explorer and colonial official, Eyre tried to explain black reactions to his white contemporaries. The Europeans, he insisted, should remember that 'our being in their country at all, is, so far as their ideas of right and wrong are concerned, altogether an act of intrusion and aggression'.[101] An army officer who spent some time with the Tasmanians after they had left the mainland for the islands of Bass Strait reported that they considered that they had been 'engaged in a justifiable war against the invaders of their Country'.[102]

Aborigines overcame their original uncertainty about European objectives, and the difficulties they had with communication, to express their own views on the question. In a raid on a farm on Tasmania's Clyde River the Aborigines shouted 'Go away you white [buggers] what business have you here'.[103] In South Australia a settler was confronted by an angry Aborigine who said to him 'damn your eyes, go to England, this my land'.[104] A party of settlers establishing themselves in the Grampians were ordered to leave by local Aborigines because 'it was their country, the water belonged to them, and if it was taken away they could not get another country for they would be killed'.[105] At much the same time in southern Queensland, a large group of Aborigines appeared on a recently established station and ordered the Europeans to be gone 'as it was their ground'.[106]

Missionaries and protectors who lived close to Aboriginal communities during the 1830s and 1840s and often understood the local dialects reported that the tribes they knew were 'not insensible to their original right to the soil'.[107] Port Phillip Protector E. S. Parker was confronted by a man, when he tried to get Aboriginal children to attend classes, who complained that 'the white fellows had stolen their country' and were now taking the children.[108] His colleague William Thomas had a similar experience a few years later. He reported in his journal: 'the Blacks this morning very dissatisfied & talk much about no good white man take away country'. Thomas added, 'This is not the first time they have reasoned in this manner'.[109] The Methodist missionary at Port Phillip, Francis Tuckfield, wrote in his journal:

> They seem to be acquainted . . . with the relative possessions of the Black and the White populations – They are conscious of what is going on – they are driven from this favoured haunt and from their other favoured haunts and threatened if they do not leave immediately they will be lodged in the gaol or shot. It is to the Missionaries they come with their tales of woe and their language is – 'Will you now select for us also a portion of land? My country all you gone. The white men have stolen it'.[110]

The European who had the most extensive experience with Aborigines during the 1830s and 1840s was George Augustus Robinson, who was variously the 'conciliator' in Tasmania, superintendent of the settlement on Flinders Island and then Chief Protector of Aborigines at Port Phillip. After spending months in the bush with the Tasmanian Aborigines, he summarised the reasons for their hostility and resistance to the Europeans. Ill-treatment was important. But so too was the loss of land. 'They have a tradition amongst them,' he noted in his journal, 'that the white men have usurped their territory, have driven them into the forests, have killed their game and thus robbed them of their chief subsistence'.[111] In 1835 Robinson wrote a 'posthumous testimony' to his friend Mannalargenna who had died on Flinders Island and who had been 'fully sensible of the injustice done to himself and people, in the usurpation of his country by the white intruder'.[112]

When he transferred to Port Phillip, Robinson found that mainland Aborigines had similar grievances. While travelling in the Western District in 1841 he met a party of local Aborigines who took him to see their fish trap and 'emphatically remarked that white men had taken it and their country'. A short time later his camp was approached at dawn by an Aboriginal family. When Robinson asked them where their country was, 'they beat the ground and vociferated "deen! deen!" and then in a dejected tone bewailed the loss of their country'. When he returned from the bush Robinson jotted down in his journal a summary of the complaints he had heard from the Aborigines he had met. 'They were poor now,' they said.

> White man had taken their good country, they said, no ask for it but took it. Black men show white men plenty grass and water and then white men say be off, come be off and drive them away and no let them stop.[113]

Europeans learned a lot about Aborigines between 1788 and 1848, although information and understanding did not necessarily improve their situation. There was as much hostility towards Aborigines in the middle of the nineteenth century as there was at the beginning, and just as much violence on the frontiers of settlement. But the misconceptions of 1788 had been buried. The settlers were unsure about the total Aboriginal population but knew they lived in every part of the continent and that there were many more of them than Cook and Banks had imagined. Ideas about Aboriginal property had been transformed. Well-informed settlers knew that Aborignes had a 'proprietary in the soil' and that they enjoyed the land in a wide variety of ways. There was widespread acceptance that the Aborigines were the original occupants, that they had been dispossessed and should be compensated. Aboriginal resistance emphasised the sense of ownership and the cost of ignoring it.

Many of these developments gave stimulus to the land rights movement of the 1830s and 1840s – the first land rights movement. It was more important in Britain than Australia. Much of its impetus came not from the colonial frontiers but from intellectual and political developments in Europe as a whole. Concern for Aboriginal land rights was part of a much wider movement for the amelioration of conditions of native people in all parts of the empire. That movement itself was a late offshoot of the antislavery crusade the culminated in abolition in 1833.

FOUR

The First Land Rights Movement

The crusade against slavery in the British empire coincided neatly with the first fifty years of European settlement in Australia. In May 1787, the month in which the First Fleet sailed for the Antipodes, a meeting in London founded the Society for the Abolition of the Slave Trade. During the following year, while the expedition was establishing a beachhead at Sydney Cove, one hundred antislavery petitions were presented to parliament and the first legislation regulating the trade (from Africa) was passed.

The Atlantic slave trade was abolished in 1807. Slavery itself was increasingly regulated during the 1820s and brought to an end in the Caribbean, Mauritius and South Africa in 1833. The apprenticeship system, which temporarily replaced slavery, was overthrown in 1838, the year when Australian colonists looked back over their first half-century of development. The crusade was initially restricted to a small group of Quakers and evangelical Anglicans, in the so-called Clapham Sect, but it grew in strength as the nineteenth century progressed and by the early 1830s was the most powerful, and by far the best-organised, popular movement of the era. Its strength was greatly enhanced both in parliament and the electorate by the Great Reform Bill of 1832, which enfranchised both those communities and those individuals most concerned with moral reform. In 1833 over 5000 antislavery petitions were presented to parliament bearing more than 1.3 million signatures.

From Slaves to Aborigines

As they watched their crusade advance towards a successful conclusion, antislavery leaders directed their attention to the position of the Indigenous people of the empire: in the Americas, South Africa, Australia and the Pacific. Writing of the Clapham Sect, James Stephen noted that the interests of members were 'rather cosmopolitan than national'. Every human interest, he wrote,

> had its guardian, every region of the globe its representative. If the African continent and the Caribbean Archipelago were assigned to an indefatigable protectorate, New Holland was not forgotten, nor was British India without a patron.[1]

The shift of interest from slaves to Aborigines can best be traced by examining the career of Thomas Fowell Buxton. Buxton was the political heir of the great humanitarian William Wilberforce, and from 1823 to 1833 was the parliamentary leader of the antislavery cause and one of the most influential figures in British politics – both as the 'liberator' of the slaves and as the spokesman for the religious and humanitarian interest in parliament. It was, a contemporary observed,

> well understood that he was the acknowledged head of all the religious and philanthropic body. It was the mantle which he had received from Mr. Wilberforce. The religious world has greatly

increased in power and influence, as well as in numbers, since the days when the little compact body of 'saints' counted their twenty or thirty votes: perhaps a third part of the House are, at the present time, more or less men of avowed religious principle. This extension of at least the outward profession of religion necessarily gave great weight to the acknowledged Parliamentary exponent of the feelings of religious circles, and especially to a man who so clearly deserved their confidence.[2]

Buxton's transition from antislavery crusader to advocate for Aboriginal land rights was a development that had significance not just in Britain itself but in the far-flung empire as well. Initially his interest focused on the situation of the Hottentots and Bushmen at the Cape in Africa, and in July 1828 he successfully moved a motion in the commons affirming their legal equality with Europeans. On hearing of the successful passage of the motion, the South African missionary Dr Phillip wrote to Buxton exclaiming,

> It is ultimately connected with all the great questions now before the public, which have for their object to ameliorate the condition of the coloured population in every portion of the globe . . .[3]

Buxton wrote to Phillip a few years later explaining that he stayed on in parliament 'very much against my inclination for no other purpose except to watch the West Indies, and to protect the Aborigines – chiefly the latter'.[4] Buxton established two basic principles that were to guide his activities on behalf of the empire's Indigenous people.

1. Because European settlement 'must be attended by some evils to them' it was the duty of the Imperial and

Colonial authorities to 'give them compensation for those evils by imparting the truths of Christianity and the arts of civilized life'.
2. The natives had 'a right to their own land'.[5]

In January 1834 he set down the reasons for his new crusade:

> My attention has been drawn of late to the wickedness of our proceedings as a nation, towards the ignorant and barbarous natives of countries of which we seize. What have we Christians done for them? We have usurped their lands, kidnapped, enslaved and murdered themselves. The greatest of their crimes is that they sometimes trespass into the lands of their forefathers.[6]

'SOME PORTION OF THEIR OWN LAND'

Buxton set himself two objectives: to examine past relations with Aboriginal people and to institute 'certain rules and laws on principles of justice' for all future dealings in order to discover the 'most judicious modes of securing to them some portion of their own land'.[7] His first step was to take his cause to the commons. In July 1834 he moved an address to the king which read, in part,

> that a humble Address be presented to His Majesty, humbly to represent to his Majesty that His Majesty's faithful Commons in Parliament assembled, deeply impressed with the duty of acting upon the principles of justice and humanity in the intercourse and relations of this Country with the native inhabitants of its Colonial Settlements, of affording them protection in the enjoyment of their civil rights, and of imparting to them that degree

of civilization and that religion with which Providence has blessed this nation.[8]

The motion had added significance because it was passed unanimously after being seconded by the Secretary of State for the Colonies and was sent to all colonial governors as an expression of government policy. The Chancellor of the Exchequer observed at the time that 'so far from being the expression of any new principle', Buxton's motion embodied and recognised 'principles on which the British Government [had] for a considerable time been disposed to act'.[9]

The crucial point is that when Buxton referred to the civil rights of native people he was above all talking about their *land* rights. Perhaps more to the point, his colleagues knew that that was what he was talking about.

The motion was put without debate for tactical reasons but Buxton returned to the subject a year later, moving a further successful motion to establish a commons select committee to examine the overall circumstances of the empire's indigenes. While expressing his concern for the lives and wellbeing of the Aborigines he returned to the fundamental question of land rights because 'upon every ground of justice and right' they were 'entitled to protection in the possession of their land'.[10] Buxton had no doubt that this applied to Australia. During the speech he expressed his horror at the unfolding fate of the Tasmanians, explaining that a correspondent had informed him that the remnants of the island tribes 'complained that the white men had rooted them out of the soil'.[11] Some time early in 1835 he received a letter from Hobart written by his Quaker friend James Backhouse, who emphasised that the Tasmanians had proprietary rights to specific and clearly defined hunting grounds. Buxton regarded this as an authoritative statement: he included it in the appendices of the report of the select committee he chaired during 1835–36.

The question of land rights was constantly before the select committee. Buxton asserted the importance of the issue both in his questioning of witnesses and in the final report. When interviewing representatives of the three great missionary organisations, Buxton asked if it were not true 'that we are bound to assume as an incontrovertible fact, that [native people] have an inalienable right to their own soil'. To which the three clerical gentlemen readily assented.

In the final report Buxton was even more emphatic. 'It might be presumed,' he wrote,

> that the native inhabitants of any land have an incontrovertible right to their own soil: a plain and sacred right, however, which seems not to have been understood. Europeans have entered their borders, uninvited, and when there, have not only acted as if they were undoubted lords of the soil, but have punished the natives as aggressors if they have evinced a disposition to live in their own country.[12]

Buxton could hardly have been clearer. From the passage that followed this paragraph, it was clear that he was referring above all to Australia. That was the understanding of those in the colonies who welcomed the report. The editor of the *Colonist* devoted several full pages to it and, after quoting Buxton's commitment to land rights, observed that 'on this fundamental principle the whole question, as a civil one turns. Here they take their stand . . .'[13]

With the winding-up of the select committee, Buxton and other antislavery activists formed the British and Foreign

Aborigines Protection Society, which quickly became the focal point for agitation in favour of Indigenous people throughout the empire (and ultimately all over the world). It had a long and distinguished history until it merged with the Anti-Slavery Society in the early twentieth century.

During the late 1830s the society returned again and again to the question of land rights. In an 1839 address to the Marquis of Normanby, Secretary of State for the Colonies, the society 'particularly' alluded to 'the recognition of the Native's title to the soil and the perfect and unequivocal security of an ample portion of land to them and their descendants'.[14] This was necessary in the case of the Australian Aborigines 'whose territory and means of subsistence [were] wrested from them without treaty or payment'.[15] In 1840 they published a program of legislation drawn up by a London barrister, Standish Motte, which included a strong defence of native property rights. Motte argued that it should henceforth be a 'fundamental principle' that no settlement should be made on any land 'possessed or claimed by its aboriginal inhabitants without their consent, formally obtained by treaty, or otherwise substantially acknowledged by them'.[16] The following year the fourth annual meeting of the society passed a further motion affirming the same principles. The motion read:

> that the native inhabitants of our Colonies, whatever the state of civilization or barbarism in which particular races may be found, are endued with the rights of common humanity, in which they cannot without the most criminal injustice be outraged by a system of colonization not adequately compensating them for their lands, and failing to secure to them the protection and privileges of British subjects.[17]

'Worse Than Slavery Itself'

Humanitarians in both Britain and Australia equated the existing system of colonisation with slavery. The two things were equally abhorrent, equally in need of radical reform. Slaves were denied their liberty, Aborigines their land, often their lives.

'I Protest,' wrote Buxton, 'I hate shooting innocent savages worse than slavery itself'.[18]

In 1833 just under 800 000 slaves were emancipated at a cost of £20 million in compensation. In the colonies of settlement, up to five million natives were suffering dispossession and destruction. The desire to redirect the passion and zeal that had achieved abolition to the reform of colonial practice was clearly expressed in the first report of the Aborigines Protection Society:

> The abhorred and nefarious slave traffic, which has engaged for so long a period the indefatigable labours of a noble band of British philanthropists for its suppression and annihilation, can scarcely be regarded as less atrocious in its character, or destructive in its consequences, than the system of modern colonization as hitherto pursued.

The two questions, the report continued, were 'intimately blended with one another'; the energetic spirit that would 'universally suppress the slave traffic, [could] not rest without a corresponding effort to rescue and elevate the coloured races at large'.[19]

Similar arguments were heard in Australia. Lang told the inaugural meeting of the Sydney branch of the society in October 1838 that the emancipation of the slaves had ushered in a new era in English history and that the progress of the same spirit was forcing government and people alike to adopt measures for the amelioration of the Indigenous people of the empire.[20] Alexander Maconochie, the celebrated penal reformer and secretary to Tasmania's Governor Franklin, believed that the slave trade 'with all its horror' had not been 'such a scourge as the English colonizing system'.[21]

Orton, who had been imprisoned by the West Indian planters in the 1820s, was shocked by the destruction and desolation he witnessed in Australia ten years later. He wrote home to his mission society arguing that the issues involved in the spread of European settlement were 'of vast importance' and in need of the attention of 'the Christian public at home as ever did that of the notable slave question in which they moved with much worth and triumphant success'.[22]

British public opinion turned against slavery as a result of a flood of material exposing the violence and injustice inherent in the system. The evils of colonisation were becoming apparent at much the same time. The fate of the Tasmanians was broadcast when the antislavery crusade reached its climax. Two large collections of official documents about the colony were published in 1831 and 1834. The brutality of the conflict was inescapable; stories of atrocity abounded. It was a case of 'bloodshed, cruelty and oppression'[23] of 'aggression and horrid cruelties on the part of the English'.[24]

Above all else there was the rapid decline of the Indigenous population, the impending extermination of a whole 'race', which was a terrible warning and object lesson for Imperial officials and politicians. As a result of Tasmania, 'an indelible stain had been thrown upon the British Government'.[25] The prominent Quaker and antislavery activist Samuel Gurney told the first meeting of the Aborigines Protection Society that on 'inquiring the other day as to what had become' of the

Tasmanians, he had been informed that they 'had been reduced to 150, and that they had been shot like crows'.[26] Buxton told the commons in 1835 that a correspondent had told him 'that all that remained of a tribe formerly 500 strong, were two or three men, as many women and a few children'.[27] A remorseful Governor Arthur wrote home to the Colonial Office in 1834 lamenting that he had been 'reduced to the necessity of driving a simple but warlike, and, as it now appears, noble-minded race, from their hunting grounds'.[28]

The slave rebellion in Jamaica in 1831–32, and its bloody aftermath, had shocked the British electorate. For many it was the last straw. The Black War in Tasmania played a similar role in convincing people that the method of colonisation needed radical change. It was, Buxton argued, a 'system wholly unworthy of a great nation'.[29]

Tasmanian resistance could not fail to impress dispassionate observers. Rebel slaves in Jamaica had only killed a handful of Europeans; in just a few years the Tasmanians dispatched 150 to 200. Colonel Charles Napier, a prominent military figure and governor-elect of South Australia [he didn't go in the end] observed in 1834 that considering the odds against them in 'numbers, in skill, in firearms, in discipline' they made a 'most courageous resistance against us'.[30] Governor Arthur told the Colonial Office that the continued hostility of island Aborigines had

> operated most injuriously in many ways; great expense has been incurred; dissatisfaction has been induced; improvements have been retarded; and emigration has been checked.[31]

If the Tasmanian experience were to be repeated in the rest of Australia, the prospect was daunting. A few years of conflict had left hundreds dead (200 or so whites and certainly more Aborigines, but the true number will never be known[32]) and caused enormous property loss, insecurity and collapse of investor confidence. The Aborigines Protection Society warned in 1842 that in the destruction of the Tasmanians 'is shown what is to be expected from the like conduct on the extensive and neighbouring continent of New Holland'.[33] Mainland Australia was still largely unsettled. The population was presumed in humanitarian circles to be between 1.5 million, which was the Aborigines Protection Society estimate, and 2–3 million, which was Buxton's. It was 'impossible to conceive how long and how fearful will be the struggle between the European and the Australian'.[34] A simple exercise in arithmetic suggested a death toll running into many tens of thousands. It was a perfectly reasonable and deeply disturbing conclusion to be drawn from the events of the recent past.

The Western Australian settler R. M. Lyon warned his fellow colonists of the prospects in a letter written in the colony in 1833 and republished in London by the Aborigines Protection Society in 1841. It is a document worth considering in detail. There were, he explained to his contemporaries,

> two courses open to you to pursue; either a decidedly peaceful one or a decidedly hostile. [sic] To the adoption of the former I know of no obstacle that may not yet be easily surmounted. They have all along shown themselves ready to be reconciled – desirous to live in amity and kindness with you, and even willing to be taught your manners, laws and polity. It remains for you to consider the consequences of adopting hostile measures. A bad name to the colony, – a stop to emigration, – and a depreciated property, are but minor evils. An exterminating war must be the consequence; the flames of which will spread with increasing

fury among the surrounding tribes, as the settlement extends itself. An exterminating war over a continent as large as Europe, and abounding with tribes unknown and innumerable. The very thought is appalling . . . Who will take upon himself the responsibility to giving such counsel? Who among you will answer for the frightful consequences, to God and to his country, and to the myriads of the slain, whose blood will clamour through the skies for vengeance in both worlds, upon the guilty head of him that advised, and on him that lighted up the inextinguishable flame.[35]

Divine Displeasure

Lyon's concern about the judgement of God is a useful reminder that one of the major driving forces behind the antislavery crusade was the conviction that slavery itself was contrary to the laws of God and that it would ultimately lead to divine vengeance.

In a pamphlet entitled *Dangers of the Country*, published in 1807, the prominent antislavery activist George Stephen warned his readers that nations, like individuals, were punished for transgressing divine laws. But individuals were not punished until after death; nations faced retribution in the here and now. What, he asked, were the causes which were 'most frequently assigned in scripture for the chastisement of sinful nations'? Answering his own question he listed the sins of 'oppression, injustice, and violence towards the poor and helpless; and the shedding of innocent blood'.[36] Many years later his son James, the powerful Colonial Office official who drafted the bill to abolish slavery, concluded that it was this measure that had delivered Britain from 'blood-guiltiness for ever'.[37]

By the 1830s, humanitarian reformers in both Britain and the colonies were convinced that methods pursued in European colonisation were both bad in practice and sinful as well. They were not only wrong; they were wicked. Buxton thought that England was a 'deep offender in the sight of God' as a result of the enormities practised upon 'these poor, ignorant, defenceless creatures'.[38] Backhouse warned Governor Bourke that if the Aborigines were exterminated, as appeared likely, 'the unmitigated guilt before God' would be 'fixed irremediably upon the British nation and its Australian descendants'.[39] Lang told the first meeting of Sydney's Aborigines Protection Society that there was 'much blood on the hands of the European population' of the colony, which, like that on the hands of Cain, 'cried aloud for vengeance'.[40] Missionary Lancelot Threlkeld believed he could hear 'the voice of a brother's blood crying aloud for vengeance unto God';[41] his colleague Tuckfield urged the settlers to 'avert the wrath of that righteous God who most assuredly heareth the voice of our brother's blood'.[42] Aboriginal Protector James Dredge expected the Almighty to strike the Europeans down with the 'righteous retribution of insulted heaven'.[43]

Sydney clergyman John Saunders warned his congregation in 1838 that 'if there be anything which calls for a swifter and a more severe punishment than another it is the shedding of human blood'. Oppression and cruelty towards the blacks would 'gather clouds of vengeance', provoke the 'threatening thunder of the Omnipotent' and attract the 'bolt of wrath'. The colonists, he charged, had been

> eradicating the possessors of the soil, and why, forsooth? Because they were troublesome, because some few resented the injuries they had received, and then how were they destroyed?

by wholesale, in cold blood; let the Hawkesbury and Emu Plains tell their history, let Bathurst give in her account, and the Hunter render her tale, not to mention the South . . . The spot of blood is upon us, the blood of the poor and defenceless, the blood of the men we wronged before we slew, and too, too often, a hundred times too often, innocent blood . . . When he maketh 'inquisition for blood' will he not find it here? And finding it, surely we have reason to dread his visitation. In what way he may chasten us it is not for me to suggest; he is a sovereign, and acteth according to the counsels of his own will; but it is only to glance at his resources, and we can at once discern abundant reason for fear; he could parch us with drought, scatter our commerce, pinch us with penury, and lower us with disease; the plague, the tornado, and famine are all at his back; above all, he could weary us with civil dissension, with the miseries of an overflowing wickedness, or with the power of a hostile sword. These things God in his infinite mercy, has restrained, but how soon could he let loose their malignant influence upon us! We have, therefore, reason to dread the approach of the Lord when he cometh out of his place to punish the inhabitants of the earth for their iniquity; 'for the earth also shall disclose her blood, and shall no more cover her slain'.[44]

SONS OF GOD AND RIGHTS OF MAN

Underpinning the writing and agitation of the antislavery and pro-Aboriginal activists was their belief in the radical equality of all people regardless of differences of race, culture or creed. They took their ideas from several different sources. The one most often used was the Bible and its message that all people were the children of God, all alike descendants of Adam and Eve, all capable of salvation and possessing immortal souls.

Reformers, missionaries and protectors returned constantly to this belief as the fountainhead of their often unpopular views and actions. Africans and Aborigines might appear savage or simple, they argued, but they were brothers under the skin who could not be enslaved or slaughtered or dispossessed any more than could one's neighbour. The Rev. Saunders declaimed:

> the New Hollander is a man and a brother . . . the Saviour died as much for him as he did for you [and so by] every sentiment of humanity and love you are bound to love him, to admit him into your fraternity and to treat him as a fellow man.[45]

Ideas of equality drawn from theology were strengthened by others flowing from enlightenment philosophy and the political manifestos of the French Revolution. Antislavery petitions of the 1820s referred increasingly to the natural rights of humanity, which had been denied to the slaves. In Australia Joseph Orton argued that the 'rights of man' had been ignored in the case of the Aborigines; their right of property 'in the lands of their nativity' had been overridden. Aboriginal Protector Robinson believed likewise that the Aborigines had a natural right to their native soil.[46]

The cause of the slaves and Aborigines drew strength from the major political and intellectual movements of the age. Reform at home encouraged reform abroad. The drive to secure formal legal equality applied not just to non-Europeans in the colonial empire but to all other minorities that had suffered historic disabilities – Catholics, Dissenters, Jews.

The demand for Aboriginal land rights was also linked to larger questions – to the desire to create a society based on formal legal equality within a free market. The Aborigines Protection Society demanded that the 'distinctions which have been drawn between the privileges and immunities of the settler and those of the native must be removed'.[47] While he was planning to go to South Australia as the first governor, Colonel Napier declared that he would not leave England without laws 'that shall give the same protection to the savage as to myself . . . we exclaim against monopolies; we must then not have a monopoly of justice'.[48] Colonial land was to be handled like any other commodity – to be bought from the natives and sold to the settler. Neither the patronage of governors distributing free land nor the persuasion of the settler's gun should provide access to property. There was no place for such irregularities in the ordered and predictable world that was emerging in the 1820s and 1830s.

In demanding that the settlers buy Aboriginal land, the mainly middle-class reformers were merely applying standards they would want to operate everywhere, and land purchased in this way would be cheaper in the long run given the great cost involved in forced dispossession. Kindness, Buxton told the commons, would be 'far safer, far cheaper, and far more profitable than coercion'.[49] The Aborigines Protection Society asserted that the '*purchase* of land is a safer as well as a better title, than the acquisitions thereof by force or fraud and its maintenance by oppression and bloodshed'.[50] The report of the 1837 select committee argued that, 'setting aside all considerations of duty', a more just and friendly policy towards Aboriginal people would 'materially contribute to promote the civil and commercial interests of Great Britain'.[51] Writing of his Tasmanian experience, Governor Arthur told his superior, Lord Glenelg, that a more conciliatory approach would be good for business. 'Even in a pecuniary point of view' the government would be 'amply repaid'. There was clear proof of the 'extraordinary effect of personal security upon the value of land'. Once the Aborigines had been pacified, property 'almost suddenly, rose in value from 50–100 per cent *at least*'.[52]

'DREADFUL BEYOND EXAMPLE'

By the 1830s, humanitarians in both Britain and the colonies were convinced that methods of colonisation were both wrong in principle and pernicious in practice, the cause of brutality, bloodshed and oppression. Like slavery, the methods contravened the laws of God and invited Divine displeasure.

The fate of the Tasmanians was the starkest illustration of the existing system. It presaged future disasters. Governor Arthur warned Lord Glenelg in 1837 that unless some 'enlarged plan of proceeding' was introduced in future settlements there would be 'an enormous sacrifice of life'.[53] Backhouse gave similar advice to Buxton in 1834, arguing that the method of colonisation that up until that time had

> been pursued by the British Government has been upon principles that cannot be too strongly reprobated, and which want radical reformation. Aborigines have had wholesale robbery of territory committed upon them by the Government, and the settlers have become the receivers of stolen property, and have borne the curse of it in the wrath of the Aborigines, who, sooner or later, have become exasperated at being driven off their rightful possessions.[54]

The reformers were not against colonisation. Far from it. They believed that Europeans had a duty to carry Christianity and civilisation into the far corners of the world. But the fundamental problem was land; the refusal to recognise

Indigenous property rights was the original sin that coloured every later development.

When their land was taken without consent or compensation the natives were certain, indeed duty-bound, to resist. The settlers would, with equal certainty, put down the resistance with a strong hand. The experience would brutalise them; they would become guilty, aggressive, in danger of damnation. The Aborigines would, for their part, remain sullen and resentful. John Beecham of the Methodist Missionary Society observed that they had to retire, 'but they retire with irritated feelings, and in the spirit of revenge'; and thus the foundation was laid, 'as the natural consequence of the wrong principle on which our colonization is based of a system of painful and angry intercourse between the colonists and the natives for years to come'.[55]

In his evidence to Buxton's select committee, William Ellis of the London Missionary Society argued that colonisation must be based on justice. He referred

> especially to seizing the land of the people whose country we may colonize, and the expulsion or annihilation of its rightful possessors. It has been our custom to go to a country, and because we were stronger than the inhabitants, to take and retain possession of the country, to which we had no claim, but to which they had the most inalienable right, upon no other principle than that we had power to do so. This is a principle that can never be acted upon without insult and offense to the Almighty, the common parent of the human family, and without exposing ourselves, sooner or later, to the most disastrous calamities and indelible disgrace.[56]

Critics of colonial practice believed that something had gone very wrong in the early settlement of Australia. The result was 'dreadful beyond example'.[57] In a letter to Governor Bourke in 1837, Backhouse argued that it could scarcely be supposed 'that in the present day any persons of reflection will be found who will attempt to justify the measures adopted by the British in taking possession of the territory of this people', who had committed no offence against the British but had 'had their lands usurped, without an attempt at purchase by treaty, or any reasonable offer of compensation'.[58]

Experienced colonial officials agreed with the armchair critics. Reflecting on his term as commandant of the military forces in the infant Swan River colony, F. C. Irwin argued, in a book published in 1835, that all future dealings with the Aborigines should be governed by a treaty negotiated between the two parties.[59] Governor Arthur concluded, after twelve years in Tasmania, that the fundamental problem in relations between settlers and island tribes had been the method of taking possession of the land. This had produced a deep and enduring sense of injustice. 'On the first occupation of the colony', it was 'a great oversight that a treaty was not, at that time, made with the natives, and such compensation given to the chiefs as they would have deemed a fair equivalent for what they surrendered'.[60]

There was a consensus in humanitarian circles about what needed to be done.

1. Above all else there had to be recognition of Indigenous rights to land based on prior possession. 'We shall avoid the most frequent causes of dispute,' Ellis argued, 'by recognizing their inalienable right to the soil they inhabit, and the productions of the soil, whether game or fruits and roots on which they live'.
2. Colonisation should proceed on the basis of negotiation for the purchase of land.

3. Aborigines should receive compensation – an equivalent, as it was called – for the land surrendered and the disruption caused by the settlers. They should not 'want for land' but be provided with reserves resting on secure title.
4. Colonial governments should use some of the money received from the sale of land to the settlers to provide for the education and welfare of the natives.

Reformers at the Helm

The political influence of humanitarian and missionary organisations increased after the reform of the electoral system in 1832. It reached its peak in 1835 with the coming to power of the Melbourne administration, when the Colonial Office came under the control of Charles Grant (who became Lord Glenelg in May 1835) and Sir George Grey, respectively Secretary of State and Parliamentary Under-Secretary, and James Stephen, who became deputy to the permanent head in 1834 and took that office himself two years later.

All three had strong ties with the antislavery and mission organisations. They were all members of the Church Missionary Society. Grey had been one of Buxton's inner circle during the final assault on slavery.[61] Glenelg and Stephen were the children of prominent members of the first generation of reformers. Stephen was related by marriage to William Wilberforce, the spiritual leader of the cause. His brother George was the driving force behind the Agency Committee, the radical extraparliamentary wing of the antislavery movement. James explained in a letter in 1828 that the crusade had 'devolved upon [him] by inheritance'.[62] It was, he observed

The First Land Rights Movement

four years later, a cause of 'extreme importance to the happiness of mankind, for which my father, and my connections and friends have been living almost exclusively'. At the end of the 1830s he wrote to Buxton:

> When I look on the last twenty years of my life, all of which have been passed either in the Colonial Office or in close official connection with it, I cannot but be thankful for the innumerable opportunities which have been afforded me of contributing to the mitigation if not the prevention, of the cruel wrongs which our country has inflicted on so large a portion of the human race.[63]

When the new administration moved into the Colonial Office in April 1835, South Africa and Australia presented the most difficult problems associated with the relations of settlers and aborigines. The South African situation was the most pressing. The expansion of the European frontier into the eastern Cape had touched off a series of bloody conflicts with the Bantu, or Kaffirs, as they were called at the time. The fourth Kaffir War of December 1834 had resulted in the death of the Bantu leader Hintza and the annexation of land between the Keiskamma and the Kei rivers, known as the Queen Adelaide Province. During the final months of 1835, Glenelg was strongly lobbied by Buxton and the South African missionary Dr Phillip, then visiting Britain. Buxton described one of his meetings with Glenelg in a letter to his sister. He explained how he

> gave our new Colonial Secretary a disquisition to my heart's content, on the treatment of savages, the death of Hintza, the atrocities of white men, and above all the responsibilities of

the Secretary of State; and I assured him that I knew there was a corner of the next world hotter than the rest, for such of them as tolerate the abominations we practice abroad. I feel happy that I let loose my mind but I am afraid Ellis of the London Missionary Society was almost shocked at the recklessness of his lordship's feelings, with which I spoke. I believe, however, that Lord Glenelg feels both soundly and warmly on the subject.[64]

Glenelg took decisive action on the problems of the eastern Cape frontier. In a famous dispatch to Governor D'Urban, of 26 December 1835, he announced that the annexation of the Queen Adelaide Province was to be renounced because it rested upon a conquest 'resulting from a war in which . . . the original justice is on the side of the conquered, not the victorious party'.[65] It was a severe blow to the ambitions, morale and self-respect of frontier settlers and was one of the factors that drove the Boers outwards from the Cape into the interior beyond the bounds of British control. It signalled that humanitarian influence was paramount in the Colonial Office.

In circles sympathetic to the Aboriginal cause there was exultation. After hearing the news, Buxton lay awake for much of the night 'from an exuberance of gratification and thankfulness, the image rising before me of the hunted people restored to the land'. It was a 'glorious act . . . which he valued more than the victories of Waterloo or Blenheim'.[66] The first annual report of the Aborigines Protection Society was lyrical in praise. Glenelg's dispatch was the 'most comprehensive, the most statesman-like, the most British, the most Christian document of all on this great subject . . . a just, eloquent, and masterly exposition of the sound principles on which our intercourse with the uncivilized tribes of our colonies must be conducted'.[67]

The First Land Rights Movement

Glenelg and his colleagues were well aware of the problems of Australia's violent frontier. The fate of the Tasmanians haunted them and deeply influenced their attitude to the new settlements in South Australia and New Zealand. A dispatch from Governor Arthur in Tasmania arrived in the Colonial Office soon after Glenelg's assumption of power (it was addressed to his predecessor) warning the government of the need to adopt new policies if the South Australian colony was to avoid the bloodshed experienced in Tasmania. Arthur argued that every effort should be made to reach an understanding with the Aborigines before settlement commenced:

> Otherwise some cause of offence may unfortunately arise not less detrimental to the interests of the latter than subversive of that future goodwill, without which it will be impossible to prevent a long continued warfare, in which the whites as well as the Aborigines, becoming more and more inflamed as their mutual injuries accumulate, will destroy each other in detail.[68]

Arthur strongly urged the government to recognise Aboriginal land rights and purchase property from them as it was required for settlement.

Glenelg was impressed. He sent a copy of the letter to the South Australian Colonization Commission with the warning that the matters discussed could not 'but be regarded as of first importance in the formation of the new settlement'.[69] A few weeks later Glenelg again reminded the South Australian colonists of the 'necessity of averting' from the Aborigines of 'that part of the continent the calamities which that race of men have been overwhelmed by in the other British settlements in Australia'.[70] In 1837 James Stephen explained to Treasury officials that Glenelg was 'deeply impressed with the necessity of adopting every means of preventing' in the new colony 'the occurrence of those acts of violence' that had accompanied European settlement since the late eighteenth century.

Negotiations between the Colonial Office and the South Australian commission reached their climax between December 1835 and January 1836, at exactly the same time that new initiatives were being framed for South Africa. In that period it appears that a number of major policy decisions were made. Buxton was in contact with the Colonial Office at the time. He told the veteran antislavery campaigner Zachary Macaulay that he was 'greatly pleased at finding that the Government had agreed to place protectors of the Aborigines in every colony where the English came into contact with them'.[71]

Buxton's influence on South African policy has long been recognised. He may also have persuaded the Colonial Office to appoint Aboriginal protectors. In a letter to Dr Phillip in September 1834 he had asked for advice on 'the measures which I should aim at for the benefit of countries where we make settlements'. He explained that he had already 'thought of a protector, through whom all bargains shall be made, that they may not be cheated out of their land'.[72] In his letter to Macaulay, Buxton said that the Colonial Office officials had 'agreed' to appoint protectors, suggesting that they were responding to proposals that he had put to them. But it may have been less a matter of Buxton's influence and more one of a concurrence of opinion among like-minded individuals. Glenelg, after all, felt 'both soundly and warmly on the subject'. After mentioning to Macaulay the decision to appoint protectors, Buxton added, significantly, 'Many other things did I hear, equally delightful'.[73] What this meant for Australia was soon apparent.

One week after sending off the famous dispatch to Governor D'Urban, Glenelg called the South Australian commission

The First Land Rights Movement

chairman, Robert Torrens, to the Colonial Office and told him the conditions that were to be imposed on the settlers before final approval was given for the ships to depart for the Antipodes. The commissioners were to

> prepare a plan for securing the rights of the Aborigines which plan should include the appointment of a Colonial Officer to be called Protector of the Aborigines and arrangements for purchasing the lands of the Natives.[74]

Glenelg's statement was of major significance in the history of relations between Australian Aborigines and the British government, even though it has been almost totally overlooked by historians and jurists, receiving none of the attention that African and Imperial scholars have given to the dispatch sent to Governor D'Urban a week earlier. But while neglected, the statement raised a number of important points:[75]

1. Glenelg's demands should not surprise us. They followed logically from developments in Britain and the colonies stretching back to the initial meeting of the antislavery movement fifty years before and the first demands for legal equality for British subjects through the empire.

2. The assertion in the report of the 1837 committee that all people had an incontrovertible right to their own soil was widely accepted in humanitarian and missionary circles. The report, though written by Buxton, was closely scrutinised by his friend and fellow committee member Sir George Grey to see that the text was acceptable to the government.

3. The belief that all Aboriginal people had rights based on long occupancy 'time out of mind' had strengthened during the 1820s and 1830s as a result of intellectual and political developments in Britain, America and the empire.

4. Knowledge about the tenure and land use of Australian Aborigines had grown from the earliest days of settlement. By the 1830s the major missionary and humanitarian organisations, prominent colonists, colonial and Imperial officials all accepted that the Aborigines had 'proprietary in the soil' and should be compensated if that property was taken by the settlers.

5. The belief that the Aborigines were the original occupiers of Australia was widespread. If the British had originally assumed that Australia was *terra nullius* in the sense of being without land tenure, they had overwhelmingly rejected that idea by the 1830s.

6. It was clearly understood that while the British had extended sovereignty over Australia in 1788, 1824 and 1829 and acquired the right to extinguish native tenure, they had not gained the absolute title to every inch of property. How else could settlers buy and Aborigines sell the land?

7. The practice of taking land without permission, negotiation or purchase had proved disastrous. The results were 'dreadful beyond example'. It had led to bloodshed, moral anarchy and social and economic disruption. Glenelg and his colleagues sought to bring Australia

into line with colonial practice in North America, where the purchase of native property was long established. American experience indicated that buying Indian land made good business sense. It greatly eased tension without inhibiting settlement. The same principles of colonisation were reaffirmed shortly after 1836 in the settlement of New Zealand.

But statements of policy in London were one thing; implementing them in the colonies on the other side of the world was another. Australian society already had a history of its own. Attitudes, interests and expectations were entrenched. Imperial authorities had little power to force unpopular measures on unwilling communities. The best they could do was to persuade, cajole and exhort.

Closer to home, there was the problem of the legislation establishing South Australia, which had been passed by the parliament eighteen months before Colonel Torrens took tea with Lord Glenelg at the Colonial Office and learned that Aboriginal land rights had been given official recognition. The relations between the Colonial Office and the South Australian settlers must now be considered.

FIVE

Land Rights Frustrated, 1834–38

The South Australian Constitution Act (4 & 5 WILL: IV C95) was drawn up by the company promoting the venture, not by the British government. Ministers 'sanctioned' the introduction of the bill without giving it 'any undue encouragement'. It was debated and read a second time in an almost empty House of Commons at 2 a.m. during the last days of that session. It had little scrutiny. Indeed, some members were critical of the haste with which the measure was being handled. The bill had only been printed a few days before the debate and speakers complained that they had only had a few hours to examine it before the second reading debate.[1]

The most important aspect of the bill, as far as the present discussion is concerned, was the declaration in the preamble that the large area of southern Australia was 'waste and unoccupied lands which are supposed fit for the purposes of colonisation' and therefore open to sale by the promoters.

That claim was widely challenged. Colonel Napier, writing when he still expected to become the first governor of the new colony, described the legislation as 'an act to seize by force' a territory as large as France and Spain, calling it uninhabited when it was known to be populated. It was, he argued, a means to deprive 'an inoffensive race of people of their property, without giving them the slightest remuneration'.[2]

It was a damaging admission from the man chosen by the promoters to be the pioneer governor. In an article on the projected colony in the July 1835 edition of the influential *Westminster Review*, the anonymous author noted that there had been nothing in any of the promotional literature 'respecting payment to the native inhabitants, the owners of the soil'. The claim that the land in question was waste and unoccupied was simply 'not true'. As far as was known at the time, the area was 'better peopled' than any other part of the Australian continent. The hunting grounds, the author concluded, would be

> found there as everywhere else, to be the property of particular tribes. If the natives, therefore, who occupy the lands of the new colony are not to be hunted down like wild beasts, a troublesome and expensive process . . . they must be paid for their lands.[3]

There was concern about the South Australian Act in humanitarian circles as well. It clearly conflicted with the spirit of the Address to the King moved by Buxton in the commons only a few days before the Act was passed. John Beecham, the secretary of the Methodist Mission Society, thought the bill was 'essentially and morally wrong'. As a result of it the colonists and the natives would be 'necessarily brought into painful collision at the very outset'; the settler would seek to 'obtain possession of the lands secured to him by Act of Parliament'; and the Aborigines would try to 'keep possession of those very lands which are theirs by prior right'.[4] In his report of the proceedings of the 1837 committee, Buxton observed that while in some measures parliament had 'laid down the general principles of equity', the South Australian legislation had disposed of lands 'without any reference to the possessors and actual occupants, and without making any reserve of the proceeds of the property of the natives for their benefit'.[5]

The select committee took the view that the Act was anomalous and out of step with the long-term thrust of government policy. It was a 'remarkable exception'. The lack of any reference to compensation or reserves 'must surely be attributed to oversight', because it could not be assumed that Britain had 'any disposition to sanction unfair dealing'.[6]

Even the South Australian commission had doubts about the extravagance of the claim. When pressed by the Colonial Office, the chairman, Robert Torrens, admitted that although the Act referred to waste and unoccupied land, the commission did not wish 'to put forward this declaration of the legislature as absolutely rebutting, the title of any aboriginal inhabitants of the proposed Colony to the occupation of the *Soil*'.[7]

The Act presented considerable difficulties to Colonial Office officials over the six- to seven-month period from the middle of 1835 to early 1836 as they tried to find ways to defend the Aboriginal interest while still sanctioning the establishment of a new colony. And all the while, frustrated colonists, investors and publicists were clamouring for the decision, which would allow emigrant ships to sail the southern ocean.

The correspondence between the Colonial Office and the commission is important and will be considered in detail.

'No Earlier and Preferable Title'

In July 1835, Sir George Grey wrote to the commissioners raising for the first time the question of Aboriginal rights – reminding them of the 1834 Address to the King and enclosing a copy of Governor Arthur's letter, which stressed how important it would be for the new colonists to respect Aboriginal land rights. Grey warned the commissioners that too much care could not be taken to avoid 'those petty encroachments on the aboriginal inhabitants' which would 'engender a distrust of the Settlers, and lead to contentions and conflicts destructive alike of the peace and welfare of the Settlements'.[8]

In December, Lord Glenelg raised the question of the huge size of the proposed colony and the fact that the Act presumed the existence of a vacant territory and therefore gave no recognition at all to the rights of the resident tribes. He remarked that

> before His Majesty can be advised to transfer to his subjects the Property in any part of the land of Australia, he must have at least some reasonable assurance that he is not about to sanction any act of injustice toward the Aboriginal natives of that part of the Globe. In drawing the lines of demarcation for the New Province . . . the Commissioners therefore must not proceed any further than those limits within which they can show, by some sufficient evidence, that the land is unoccupied and that no earlier and preferable title exists.[9]

Remarks made in private a few days earlier by James Stephen were even more interesting. In an intra-office memo he commented on the problems of drawing the boundaries of the new colony. 'How this is to be done in a Terra incognito I cannot imagine,' he wrote, 'nor how it can be done at all with any due regard to the rights of the present Proprietors of the Soil or rulers of the country'.[10]

Taken together, these two views – one public, the other

private — were highly significant, coming as they did from the Secretary of State and the deputy head of the Colonial Office who had been the department's legal adviser since 1813. They strongly reinforce earlier observations. The Colonial Office clearly did not think that the claims of sovereignty of 1788 and 1824 had wiped out all pre-existing rights. The Crown might extinguish them but it did not own, free of encumbrance, every square inch of territory. The commission had to *prove* that no earlier and preferable title existed. The matter could not be taken for granted. There were, very likely, 'present proprietors' who had rights that had to be accorded some respect.

In reply to Glenelg's demands, Torrens adopted two lines of argument — one historical, one practical. He observed that hitherto in the colonisation of Australia it had 'invariably been assumed as an established fact that the unlocated tribes' had not arrived at 'that stage of social improvement in which a proprietary right to the soil exists'.[11]

The new team at the Colonial Office would not have disagreed with that assessment of the situation. Indeed, that was the whole point. They had set their minds firmly against past colonial practice and were determined to bring it to an end, the complaints of would-be colonists notwithstanding. There was more sympathy for the commissioner's argument that the long delay that would be caused by the attempt to prove that the land was vacant, would seriously jeopardise the whole operation. Glenelg's response had been to call Torrens to the Colonial Office and insist that the venture could proceed but only on his conditions, which were that Aboriginal land rights be respected, that the settlers purchase the land, and that all such transactions should be supervised by a protector appointed by the government.

The Protector of Aborigines

The Colonial Office adopted two measures to safeguard Aboriginal land rights: the appointment of a protector and the embodiment of land rights in the Letters Patent, which had to be issued before the commission could dispatch the first shipload of colonists. The commissioners responded to Glenelg's demands of 2 January by proposing to appoint a protector who would be informed of any planned sale of land and who would determine whether the lands 'thus surveyed or any portion of them' were actually in the 'occupation or enjoyment of the Natives'. If so, such land would not be declared open to public sale 'unless the natives shall surrender their right of occupation or enjoyment by a voluntary sale'. Should the blacks refuse to sell their land it would be the duty of the protector 'to secure to the Natives the full and undisturbed occupation or enjoyment of their lands and to afford them legal redress against depredators [and] trespassers'.[12]

The commitment seemed clear and unequivocal. It was accepted as such by the government. In acknowledging receipt of the provisions Grey referred to the plan 'for the sale of lands in South Australia of which the object is to protect the Rights of the Aborigines'.[13]

The Colonial Office accepted the commission's proposals. But there were still problems. Glenelg believed that the protector, or indeed several such officers, armed with the authority suggested by the commissioners and supported 'by all necessary ministerial agency in the exercise of such authority', would be 'adequate security for the protection of the rights of the Aborigines'. But the appointments were to be reserved for the Crown; the protectors must be 'exempt from all dependence whatever on the Land Commissioners'.

Land Rights Frustrated, 1834–38

Glenelg appreciated that the suggested provisions would run up against the South Australian Act. He was certain that parliament would pass appropriate legislation to amend it, but given the need to move quickly if the venture was to survive at all, he was willing to let the colonists depart on the understanding that they accept the planned changes. Without that moral commitment to Aboriginal land rights it was Glenelg's 'clear opinion, that the Settlement itself should be postponed, until all necessary alteration in the Statute [had] been effected'. All future purchasers of South Australian land, he suggested, should be warned in writing of the impending changes to the legislation.[14] In a further letter Glenelg intimated that he regarded the 'subject as of paramount importance' and sought the opinion of the Law Officers of the Crown as to what method could be adopted so that powers in question could be 'effectually conveyed' to the protector. The Law Officers determined that it was necessary to either change the Act in parliament or have legislation passed by the South Australian Legislative Council as soon as it was established.[15] The commission assumed that the new legislation would be passed in England and actually drew up amendments that would provide for compensation for Aboriginal land but would ensure that all such negotiations would remain in their hands.

The clause that provided that 'the Commission alone shall have a right to treat with the Natives for the purchase of lands reserved to them' was presented to the Colonial Office in a draft bill designed to amend several aspects of the 1834 legislation. The clause read:

And be it further enacted, That it shall be lawful for the said Commissioners to assign or allot any part of the lands of the said Province to the Aboriginal natives thereof free of any Price . . . and also to make such compensation to the said Aboriginal Natives as to the said Commissioners shall seem just in compensation for their Interests in any Lands now occupied by them in the said Province.[16]

Glenelg and Stephen were not opposed to the idea of compensation. Far from it. But they were determined that the government and not the commissioners would oversee the matter. The commissioners should not be allowed to judge what compensation they were 'to pay to the Natives for the Lands to be taken from them', nor should they be responsible for regulations 'affecting that class of persons'. Indeed, such powers should not be 'admitted by the Government to any other authority than that of the Governor in the first instance and to his Majesty in the last resort'.[17] With this in mind, the Colonial Office gave instructions a few weeks later to Governor Hindmarsh indicating that it was his duty to

take an early opportunity after the Legislative Council shall have been formed to propose to that Body an enactment for investing the Protector with the necessary powers to enable him to give effect to the objects contemplated in his appointment.[18]

Did the delegation of power to the governor to establish the Office of Protector indicate a lack of serious commitment in the Colonial Office? Clearly not. Glenelg's procedure conformed closely to accepted Imperial practice of allowing self-governing colonies a large degree of autonomy. The Imperial government enunciated broad principles, leaving the colonists to put them into practice. Often the colonists resisted the Imperial will for years on end. This technique had been employed to bring about the reform of slavery in the West Indies in the 1810s and 1820s and in the East Indies in the 1830s. Writing of a bill to register all slaves, which the Imperial government sought to have passed in the colonies, the Secretary of State, Lord Bathurst, wrote in 1816 that

> it was the intention of the government to recommend in the most earnest manner to the colonial legislatures the adoption of some measure or other calculated to answer the principles of the Bill. He did not deny the right of the British parliament to bind the colonies by such a law, but it would be very indiscreet to act upon that right unless in cases where the object could not be accomplished by any other method.[19]

A modern historian of slavery observed that the attitude taken by ministers to the reform of slavery in the 1820s was to leave the whole of the actual government with the local institutions, a practice that the Imperial authorities regarded as 'beneficial to the country's interests, essential for preserving the Empire, and vital for solving the slavery question'.[20]

The Letters Patent

The appointment of a Protector of Aborigines was one of two methods adopted to ensure that Aboriginal land rights were protected in the new colony. The other was to enshrine the principles in question in the Letters Patent. The relevant clause read:

> Provided always, that nothing in these our Letters Patent contained shall affect or be constrained to affect the rights of any

Aboriginal natives of the said Province to the actual occupation or employment in their persons or in the persons of their descendants of any lands now actually occupied or enjoyed by such Natives.[21]

It was a clear definition of native title as understood in other parts of the empire. The Aborigines had rights – property rights. They should continue to enjoy those rights of possession, which could and should be inherited by their descendants like any other form of property.

It was significant that the same clause, without any substantial change of wording, was used in the charter that established New Zealand as a separate colony in December 1840 and provided for Maori native title. We can assume that it was no accident that the same form of words was used; that it signalled the recognition of native title in both colonies. We know that the Colonial Office regarded the New Zealand version as a statement of fundamental principle. Lord John Russell, Secretary of State at the time, explained that in the charter the Imperial authorities had 'distinctly established the general principle that the territorial rights of the Natives, as owners of the soil, must be recognised and respected'.[22] It is reasonable to assume that if these general principles were established in 1840 and expressed in the clause cited above they would also have been in place four years earlier when incorporated in South Australia's Letters Patent.

THE COMMISSION FIGHTS BACK

The South Australian commissioners had no doubt that the new men at the Colonial Office were serious and that their project had been caught in cross-currents caused by a decisive shift in policy. John Brown, the Emigration Agent, wrote in his diary just two days after the decisive meeting at the Colonial Office between Torrens and Glenelg:

> there is talk that the reason for the delay at the CO [Colonial Office] is the wish to bind us to some plan for the protection of the natives in order to satisfy the Saints in the House of Commons. That measures should be devised and enforced for their protection & civilization as far as possible is not only just & humane but politic; but that a Legislature should authorize the sale of land & the formation of a Colony in a part expressly declared by them for the purpose & then as soon as people have embarked their money & spent their time on such an assurance, suddenly finds out that there are natives and native rights which they ought to have first enquired about is beginning at the wrong end and if just to the Aborigines is unjust to the Colonists.[23]

The demands of the Colonial Office for a commitment to Aboriginal land rights created a sense of crisis among the would-be colonists already frustrated by long-delayed departure. Torrens recalled years later that Glenelg's demand that the commissioners prove the absence 'of a previous proprietary right on the part of any native tribe' was a 'startling announcement' that 'amounted to a veto on the establishment of the colony'.[24] Brown noted that after receiving the letter in question Torrens was 'exceedingly depressed' and 'altogether . . . very nervous'.[25] Three weeks later Torrens said that the colony was 'pretty well ended'.[26]

John Hindmarsh met Torrens when he emerged from his meeting with Glenelg on 2 January and reported that Torrens 'said the only difficulty was that Lord G. insisted upon the rights of the Aborigines being properly taken care of but that he the Col. did not see how to get over the difficulty'. Hindmarsh himself remarked: 'I really began to fear that we have no chance of getting out till after our Bill is amended which all allow it must be'.[27] When in the middle of negotiations with Glenelg, Torrens wrote to a fellow commissioner, 'Should we not resign and thus throw off the responsibility from our own shoulders?'[28]

In his discussion with the Colonial Office, Torrens appeared to concede a great deal. In a letter of late December (received at the Colonial Office on 28 December and probably written on 26 December) he offered to 'give precise and positive instructions' to the colonists 'not to colonize any district which the Aborigines may be found occupying or enjoying or possessing any right of property in the Soil'. The commissioners, he asserted, would provide the most ample measure of justice

> to the Aboriginal inhabitants by giving positive orders to the Colonial Commissioner of Lands to protect the Natives in the unmolested exercise of their rights of property in Land, should such a right be anywhere found to exist.

But Torrens went beyond specific suggestions and made more general commitments to the principle of Aboriginal land rights. The commissioners, he wrote, believed that hitherto in the colonisation of Australia 'the case of native occupancy has never yet been provided for before hand, and they are not only willing but desirous that South Australia should in this respect be made an exception to the general rule'. He concluded his letter with a flourish, promising that the colonists would prove

Land Rights Frustrated, 1834–38

by practical demonstration that 'the Civilization and Religion of Europe may be planted in savage lands, without invading the rights of the Aborigines'.[29]

In the instructions sent from London to Adelaide, the commissioners appeared to put their commitment into practice. In October 1836 they dispatched the second letter of instructions to their chief colonial officer, the Land Commissioner. It included the following provisions:

> You will see that no lands in occupation or enjoyment be offered for sale until previously ceded by the Natives to yourself. You will furnish the protector of the Aborigines with evidence of the faithful fulfilment of the Bargains or treaties which you may effect with the Aborigines for the cession of lands, and you will take care that the Aborigines are not disturbed in the enjoyment of the lands over which they may possess proprietary rights.[30]

The commissioners' first report to parliament underlined the commitment. The location of the colonists would be conducted 'on the principle of securing to the natives their proprietary right to the soil'. The cession of territory was to be 'perfectly voluntary' and the Aborigines who ceded their land would be permanently supplied with subsistence and afforded moral and religious instruction. The commissioners informed parliament that they had it 'under consideration' to reserve 16 acres in every 80-acre block sold (i.e. almost 6.5 hectares in every 32-hectare block) for the use of the Aborigines so that ultimately 20 per cent of all settled land would be held on their behalf, providing both land and income for their support.[31]

But despite the fine sentiments and elaborate plans, it is

doubtful if the commissioners ever had any intention of respecting Aboriginal land rights. From the first they aimed to outwit the zealous reformers in the Colonial Office. On 16 December 1835 John Brown noted in his diary that a letter had been received from the Colonial Office. 'There is nothing in it of any consequence,' he wrote,

> but a statement that the Government expect the Comm. in fixing the boundaries of the Province to occupy such ground only as is unoccupied by the Native. What is to be the interpretation of the word 'occupy' is the question. The Act itself declares the ground to be waste and unoccupied & this question, if raised at all, ought to have been raised before it was passed. But it is not occupied according to any law regulating possession which is recognized by civilized people.[32]

Torrens saw the problem in much the same light. He was a witness before the House of Commons Select Committee on the Disposal of Lands in the British Colonies in June 1836 when the first settlers were still on the sea, and was asked by Sir George Grey how the colonists were going to deal with the Aborigines. He explained that Lord Glenelg had appointed a protector whose duty it would be

> to see that no land which the aborigines really have in possession or enjoyment *(I believe they have none)* shall be taken for settlement, until a voluntary transfer of it shall have been made by the aborigines themselves.[33]

Torrens never changed his view despite the great weight of evidence that accumulated about Aboriginal land use and tenure. The Aborigines were, he believed, 'unlocated'; property in land was 'utterly unknown to them' and the wandering tribes 'never held a single acre in permanent occupation'.[34]

Clearly all the pious talk of securing 'this just and benevolent object', the written commitment, meant nothing. The leading figures in the venture knew all along that they would claim, on arrival in South Australia, that Aboriginal property rights, even the right to occupation and enjoyment, did not exist. That is why they phrased their promises so carefully. Torrens told Glenelg the colonists would protect the Aborigines in the unmolested exercise of their right to property *'should such a right be anywhere found to exist'*. In their first report to parliament, the commissioners indicated that 'the locations of the colonists will be conducted on the principle of securing to the natives their proprietary right to the soil, *wherever such rights may be found to exist'*.

In the end it was all a charade. Brown had put his finger on the fundamental issue at the very beginning of negotiations with the Colonial Office, when he observed that the question was what would be the interpretation of the word 'occupy'. The commissioners faced real problems with Glenelg, Grey and Stephen but they had history on their side, an Act which declared the ground waste and unoccupied and, once the colonists had got away, thousands of kilometres of ocean to insulate them against official displeasure. At the Antipodes, public opinion was overwhelmingly opposed to humanitarian zeal on behalf of the Aborigines, and to Exeter Hall (the headquarters in London of missionary and humanitarian organisations) meddling with colonial affairs.

The hypocrisy and duplicity of Torrens and his confidants were highlighted in their attitude to the Office of Protector of Aborigines. Having drawn up proposals for that role in the new settlement and presented them to the Colonial Office, they secretly planned to render the protector impotent long before he was appointed. Brown noted in his diary on 1 February 1836:

> I should have recorded that about a fortnight ago the Comis., by way of protecting themselves against any encroachments of the Protector of the Aborigines, passed & sealed an Order of the Board declaring *all* the lands of the Colony open to Public sale.[35]

Once it became clear that there was to be a protector of Aborigines, the commissioners sought to secure an appointment sympathetic to their views. Brown wrote on 7 January:

> C. Torrens this morning suggested to me that should the Govt. determine to appoint a P. of A., the Commissioners were exceedingly anxious that the office should be in the hands of the one who . . . thoroughly understood the principles of the Colony.[36]

The commissioners saw danger in the figure of George Fife Angas, the colony's most substantial financial backer. The problem was that Angas was firmly committed to the principles of Aboriginal land rights and had indicated that he would like to have overall responsibility in the matter. He had been in contact with Buxton on the question and was recognised in humanitarian circles as a kindred spirit. He became an active member of the Aborigines Protection Society. In a speech, 'The welfare of the Aborigines of South Australia', given at a dinner for Captain John Hindmarsh on his appointment as governor, Angas declared that the colonists would treat with the Aborigines 'for the purchase of those lands which they claim as belonging to them'.[37]

The fundamental conflict between the plans of Angas and the intentions of the commissioners was apparent to contem-

Land Rights Frustrated, 1834–38

porary observers. The Methodist Missionary Society prepared a discussion paper on the South Australian question and whether settlement would inevitably 'lead to the natives being dispossessed of the lands'. The author noted that the Act declared the lands were 'to be sold as *waste land* by the commissioners, but Mr. Angas speaks of the Colonists purchasing them of the Natives'.[38]

Angas was a focal point of discussion about the appointment of a protector at the Colonial Office on 2 January 1836. Hindmarsh wrote to Angas immediately after the events informing him of what had happened, explaining that he had been in the waiting room while Torrens was in discussion with Glenelg. Torrens emerged and told Hindmarsh that he did not see how 'to get over' Glenelg's insistence that the colonists purchase the land from the Aborigines. Hindmarsh wrote:

> it . . . occurred to me that you had expressed Some wish with respect to this subject. I therefore entreated the Colonel to go back to Lord Glenelg & Beg that you might be apptd. a Commissioner to Superintend the Inter[es]ts of the Aborigines. The Col. was not gone five minutes when he came out in high glee & his expression was that Lord Glenelg approved of the measure entirely. I sat down instantly to write you the letter of which this envelope was one half & the Col. went off to the Salopean [an inn?] where I was to follow as soon as I had done my letter, I did so & found him walking [in?] the Coffee room with Mr. Wakefield – after a little conversation I made some allusion to the appointment that you were to have & the Col. said but I don't think Mr. Angas would like to reside in the Colony, I replied why you never said anything about residing in the colony only that Ld. G. approved the measure entirely. I left them immediately & got back just in time to get yr. letter out of the Bag, & tear off

half the sheet & to give you this long story – Now I suspect that what Torrens told me first was correct & that Wakefield might have had some hand in the 2nd version.[39]

Torrens sent Brown down to Norfolk a few days later to try to recruit Buxton's influence in securing an appointment approved by the commissioners. Glenelg apparently contacted the various mission organisations seeking a suitable candidate and spent some time in negotiations with George Augustus Robinson before appointing him to the job of Chief Protector of Port Phillip. Angas maintained his interest in Aboriginal affairs but had no direct influence on policy in South Australia in the early years of settlement.

In the Colony

In the infant colony three Provisional Protectors performed their duties with varying degrees of enthusiasm and competence during the initial three years of settlement. The division of authority between the governor, who was responsible to the Colonial Office, and the Land Commissioner, who was the creature of the Colonization Commission, added to the difficulties faced by the protectors, especially as Torrens and his colleagues had made their mind up in advance about Aboriginal tenure and land use. The venture was a private one. It was always financially fragile. Any nonsense about Aboriginal land rights could seriously hinder the land sales on which the health of the whole scheme depended.

The attitude of the commissioners was epitomised by the Colonial Secretary, Robert Gouger, who wrote home in 1837 explaining that no legal provision, by way of purchase of land on their behalf, or in any other mode, has been yet made; nor do I think that with proper care it is at all necessary. I can see no reason why they should not, in a comparatively short time be made to understand our notions, and to depend upon their own exertions for a livelihood . . . At any rate, until it and other means shall have been tried and found fruitless, the enervating effect of specific legal protection should not be tried.[40]

What, then, were the protectors to actually do? Eventually the colonial officials had to give them some instructions, while at the same time avoiding any statutory commitment. In the middle of 1837 Gouger gave verbal instructions to Protector Bromley to the effect that he might claim for the Aborigines lands 'in their actual or peculiar occupation'.[41] But little came of it and Bromley was dismissed for incompetence soon after the instructions were given.

Gouger sent for Bromley's successor, William Wyatt, on 3 August and after meeting the other senior officials, 'a conversation ensued respecting the rights possessed by the Aborigines to the soil'.[42] A week later, official instructions were finally issued to Wyatt. He was to protect the Aborigines 'in the undisturbed enjoyment of their proprietary rights to such lands as may be occupied by them in any especial manner'. In becoming acquainted with the habits and customs of the Aborigines, the protector was to find out if in any part of the country they were 'in the practice of making use of the land for cultivation' or if they had fixed residences on any particular spot or if they used any piece of land for 'funeral purposes'. If so, the protector was required to report the facts to the colonial government 'without loss of time, in order that means may be taken to prevent its being included in the survey of sale'.[43]

The following May, Wyatt wrote to the governor seeking his support to achieve the reservation of land for the local tribes 'which did not appear to have been made' in land sales held up till that time. The governor approved, suggesting that the protector wait on the Land Commissioner and 'make such suggestions as he may deem proper', adding that he would be happy to lend his aid 'in so absolutely necessary a duty as preserving the interests of the Aborigines'.[44] But the Land Commissioner had other ideas and was a law unto himself. Wyatt duly made an official application for an Aboriginal reserve at the next land sales but was told that as the South Australian Act 'admitted of no reservation of the kind', his request was nugatory. The commissioner promised a written reply but it never arrived. In respect of any wider commitment to Aboriginal property rights, Wyatt agreed that as it had 'hitherto appeared that the natives occupy no lands in the especial manner' contemplated in his instructions, he 'felt it of no avail to keep [his] attention directed to it'.[45]

As Brown had realised, the crucial thing was to define what possession was and do it in such a way that no claim to land could ever be made on behalf of the Aborigines. Any pittance allowed to them could then be considered as charity, the product of European benevolence.

Betrayal

The hopes that the new colony would see the dawn of a better era for Australian Aborigines were dashed. There was deep disappointment, even a sense of betrayal, in humanitarian circles. For all their talk, the South Australians were doing no better than the dwellers of the convict colonies to the east.

A committee of English Quakers noted that notwithstanding the expression of 'just and humane views', the Aborigines were being 'deprived of their lands and means of subsistence without treaty, payment or compensation'.[46] The Aborigines Protection Society contrasted the sentiments expressed in the official reports of the South Australian commissioners with the situation at hand. 'It will doubtless be asked,' the editor of the society's journal observed,

> how the worthy and honourable gentlemen whose names are attached to the [Commissioner's Report] can have allowed a system to be established so completely at variance with the sentiments they have therein recorded?[47]

The Aboriginal question was debated in the colony. The 'rights of the Aborigines in the soil' were the subject of intense discussion at a meeting of the Adelaide Aborigines Committee in June 1838. While reporting the proceedings, a correspondent named O.T.R. observed that the instructions to the commissioners had directed that any land 'in the occupation or enjoyment of the Natives was to be considered their property' and that a sale or cession was to be negotiated. This, the writer argued, seemed to recognise 'a moral, if not a legal right of the natives to the land we now occupy, for it seems certain that at different periods of the year the whole of the districts surveyed ... was occupied by the natives'. Indeed, the Aborigines themselves 'often asserted that the land belonged to the "black fella"'.[48]

The editor of the *South Australian Gazette* believed that the Aborigines had received 'but a miserable instalment of the debt of justice we still owe them'. The settlers had met them upon the 'footing of British subjects – their claims of property in the soil distinctly recognized by our Sovereign and the Parliament of England'.[49] In September 1838 an Adelaide Quaker, Robert Cock, made his feelings known in a letter to the protector. He wrote:

> Sir,
> Please receive herewith the sum of £3–16–6 being the interest at the rate of 10%, on one fifth of the purchase money of the town lands purchased by me, on the 27th March, 1837.
>
> This sum, in accordance with the pledge given by the Colonisation Commissioners for this province, and in accordance with the principles therein signified in their first annual report, wherein it was stated they were to receive one-fifth of the lands to constitute a permanent fund for the support and advancement of the natives; I beg leave to pay the above sum for that purpose, seeing that the Commissioners as yet have neither fulfilled their pledge in this respect to the public, or carried out the moral principle signified. Under these circumstances it is impossible to let the question rest; and until that be done, I feel it my duty to pay to the proper authorities for the use of the natives this yearly rent.
>
> I disclaim this to be either donation, grant or gift; but a just claim the natives of this district have on me as an occupier of those lands.[50]

LAND RIGHTS IN HISTORY AND LAW

The importance of the land rights question in the early history of South Australia has been almost completely overlooked. Not that the period has lacked historians. The negotiations between the government and the commissioners are among

Land Rights Frustrated, 1834–38

the most widely covered aspects of Australian colonial history. Douglas Pike, the author of *Paradise of Dissent: South Australia 1829–1857* and a leading authority on the subject, gravely misinterpreted the negotiations between Torrens and the Colonial Office that took place in December 1835 and January 1836, writing that Glenelg's concern was that there should be better religious and educational facilities for settlers and Aborigines alike. There is little appreciation anywhere in the historical literature of just how serious the Colonial Office officials were about protecting Aboriginal land rights, that Torrens made a profound moral commitment to them or that Glenelg was quite willing to delay the departure unless the issue, a matter 'of paramount importance', was satisfactorily resolved.

This 'forgetting' has influenced South Australian self-perception in a number of ways. By overlooking the commitment made by the first colonists to respect Aboriginal land rights, the later history of white–Aboriginal relations in South Australia can be presented in a much more favourable light than would otherwise be possible. Leave that out and the record looks good, probably better than Tasmania, New South Wales and Queensland. Those things which were done for local blacks can be thought to flow from the benevolence of the colonists rather than a very inadequate response to obligations owed to the original owners of the soil.

But the self-deception went even deeper. South Australia saw itself as a child of the era of liberal reform, infused with the spirit of the Reform Bill and religious emancipation. What was discreetly dropped from the legacy was the powerful commitment to racial equality that ran through both the antislavery and Aboriginal protection movements. It was for this very reason that reform circles in Britain felt betrayed by events in

South Australia. When it came to the Aborigines, the pious South Australians didn't want a new beginning; they didn't want to revive in the Antipodes the spirit that had just freed 800 000 slaves; they found inconvenient the deep moral concern for the coloured races. Above all else they wanted to become colonials, to become like the 'old' Australians and brush the Aborigines aside without trouble or expense or compensation. In virtually ignoring the Aborigines, Pike wrote a far more accurate tribute to the spirit of the South Australian pioneers than he may have realised.

The failure of South Australian historians to address the question of Aboriginal land rights has been a matter of more than academic interest. It has influenced the way the issue has been perceived in the nation as a whole and has spilled over into both law and politics. If the events of 1835–36 are overlooked, the interpretation of the whole history of white–Aboriginal relations is distorted. Disregard the clear Imperial commitment to land rights — and above all, Glenelg's insistence that land should be purchased — and all later developments are misunderstood.

The consequence of this became apparent in 1971 when Justice Blackburn was called upon to examine South Australian history in the Gove Land Rights Case in the Northern Territory Supreme Court. Counsel for the Aboriginal plaintiffs argued, correctly, that the Letters Patent of 1836 guaranteed respect for land rights. Blackburn disagreed, concluding that the relevant clause was 'not intended to be more than the affirmation of a principle of benevolence' inserted in the document in order 'to bestow upon it a suitably dignified status'.[51] It may be thought unfair to expect judges to be their own historians. Blackburn's interpretation seems to reflect the traditional view of South Australian history.

Land Rights Frustrated, 1834–38

The problem was that if Blackburn had accepted that the Letters Patent meant what they said, his case – that there had never been any recognition of native title in Australia – I believe would have been completely undermined. As the South Australian Act was passed prior to the drawing up of the Letters Patent, and had the status of statute law (the circumstances of its passage through parliament notwithstanding), the reference to Aboriginal rights could be brushed aside as a strange but unimportant anomaly that wasn't meant to be taken seriously.

There was a real difficulty in explaining the deep contradictions between the Act and the Letters Patent. After all, one referred to rights of occupancy on land that the other declared to be uninhabited. Glenelg, Grey and Stephen were sharply aware of the problem. They were much too astute to miss it. That, indeed, was the whole point. But they thought it was the Act that was wrong – indeed, that it was a 'remarkable exception' to the mainstream of British Imperial policy. As members of a new administration determined to carry through sweeping reforms of colonial practice, they were not willing to accept the Act as it stood. The example of Tasmania was constantly before their eyes. They stressed that if the difficulty couldn't be resolved by negotiation, the establishment of the colony would have to be postponed until the Act was amended to provide for Aboriginal land rights. They were confident parliament would support such a move.

Given the need for an early departure of the ships in order to arrive in the southern spring, Glenelg was willing to compromise. In doing so he extracted a written commitment from the commissioners to respect Aboriginal rights and purchase their land from them, such transactions to be supervised by an Imperial official. The commission itself drew up an amendment to the Act providing for compensation for Aboriginal land. Rather than accept it, the Colonial Office instructed the governor to enact measures to cloak the protector in powers appropriate to the end sought. It is clear that Glenelg, Grey and Stephen were determined to provide for the acceptance of native title in South Australia, that the spirit of the Letters Patent would triumph over the provisions of the Act. Can anyone seriously doubt that in South Australia in 1836, as in New Zealand in 1840, the Imperial government 'distinctly established the general principle that the territorial rights of the Natives, as owners of the soil, must be recognised and respected'?

Blackburn's suggestion that provisions allowing for Aboriginal land rights were inserted in the Letters Patent merely as 'an affirmation of a principle of benevolence' indicates a fundamental misunderstanding of Imperial policy at the time. It also belittles the commitment of Glenelg, Grey and Stephen to reform of colonial policy. The implication is that the Colonial Office was not serious about land rights. It is only necessary to recall the role the three men played in the struggle against slavery, their policy towards white expansion in South Africa, their willingness to confront the Jamaican parliament in 1838 over conditions in prisons[52] and their determination to defend Maori land rights to appreciate that when Glenelg told the would-be colonists that in South Australia they were to purchase land from the Aborigines he meant exactly what he said.

It proved difficult to implement that policy in the colony during the first three years of settlement, but when the dual system of administration was scrapped and the new governor arrived, the land rights question was taken up with renewed vigour and commitment.

Land Rights Recognised, 1838–48

The British Government recognised native title in Australia in the 1830s. The several claims to sovereignty (1788, 1824, 1829) had not extinguished all Indigenous rights to land stemming from prior occupation of the continent.

Not much came of that recognition in the first years of South Australian settlement. The Colonization Commissioners saw to that. But between 1838 and 1848 three provisions were made by way of Imperial law to give some substance to the commitment to Aboriginal land rights. They were the establishment of reserves, the recognition of rights of use and occupancy on crown land and the provision for compensation to provide for education and welfare.

BATMAN'S TREATY, 1835–39

In May 1835, while the South Australian Colonization Commission planned the expedition to the Antipodes and Lord Glenelg was settling in at the Colonial Office, a small party of Tasmanian settlers sailed across Bass Strait and landed on the shores of Port Phillip Bay. On 6 June the leader of the party, John Batman, met local Aboriginal clans, subsequently claiming that he had negotiated a treaty by which means he became the owner of 243 000 hectares of prime grazing land. When they were informed of the proceedings both the New South Wales and the Imperial governments refused to recognise the transaction.[1]

Australian judges and historians have seized on the rejection of Batman's treaty as conclusive proof of official endorsement of the doctrine of *terra nullius*. This was a pivotal argument of Justice Blackburn in the Gove Land Rights Case of 1971. The treaty, he argued, was never officially considered 'to be in the nature of the purchases from Indians which were customary in America'. The fact that Batman's actions were regarded as 'simply a trespass on Crown Land' was a 'cogent demonstration of the total absence from official policy of any idea that aboriginals had any proprietary interest in the land'.[2] Legal historian Alex Castles bolstered the judge's assessment of the situation; arguing that the Colonial Office's disavowal of the treaty ended 'once and for all, the possibility that Aboriginal rights would be recognized administratively, except where these were accorded by statute'.[3] Historians of European– Aboriginal contact have followed the same interpretive trail, Bain Attwood observing that when Batman and his associates were rebuffed the authorities 're-iterated the principle of *terra-nullius*'.[4]

At first sight the argument appears persuasive. Batman's treaty was, after all, the only well-known transaction that worked on the assumption that the clans in question had an interest in the land. If the Aborigines were prevented from selling their land then surely this meant they had nothing to sell. The counterattack on this interpretation must advance from two different directions – from an assessment of the law as it was understood at the time, and from a close scrutiny of the reasons for the actions of the Colonial Office.

The relevant legal principles are clear and can be quickly

outlined. The doctrine of native title was firmly entrenched in British colonial law by the early nineteenth century and had informed practice in North America since the seventeenth century. As discussed earlier, the Indigenous people were seen to have a form of property based on prior possession.[5] The Crown held sovereign rights over the land and could exercise its exclusive right to extinguish the native title.

American colonial experience was outlined by James Kent in his classic *Commentaries on American Law*. Colonial governments had everywhere 'asserted and enforced' the exclusive right to extinguish Indian title to land, and they 'held all individual purchases from the Indian, whether made with them individually or collectively as tribes, to be absolutely null and void'.[6] The royal proclamation of 1763 clearly forbade any private purchases of Indian land of the kind negotiated by Batman: 'And, We do further strictly forbid, on Pain of our Displeasure, all our loving subjects from making any Purchases or Settlements whatever'.[7] The Crown's exclusive right of pre-emption was further entrenched by decisions in the courts in the United States and New Zealand between 1823 and 1847[8] and by the Treaty of Waitangi in 1840.

Paradoxically, Blackburn provided an able summary of the relevant legal situation in a section of his judgement in the Gove Land Rights Case entitled 'Principles applied to the acquisition of colonial territory'. The principles in question determined that

> subjects of a sovereign have no power to acquire for themselves title to land from aboriginal natives; any such purported acquisition operates as an acquisition by the sovereign. This principle operates whether the actions of the subject amount to a conquest of the aboriginal natives, or the conclusion of a treaty

with them, or merely a private bargain. The principle was often shortly described as the sovereign's right of pre-emption. Its existence and age are undoubted.[9]

It is a powerful rebuttal of the judge's own interpretation of the Batman business and that of the bevy of historians who have travelled in his footsteps. The government's rejection of the treaty was strictly in accord with the law of the period. It did not turn on the question of whether the Aborigines had any form of native title. It wasn't a question of the ability of the Port Phillip clans to *sell their land* but rather the inability of Batman *to purchase it* when confronted with the Crown's exclusive right of pre-emption.

THE COLONIAL OFFICE RESPONDS

The relevant legal principles are, then, both clear and certain. The response of the Colonial and Imperial governments needs more detailed exploration. In particular, it will be necessary to examine the reaction of the Colonial Office to four dispatches received from Australia between July 1835 and January 1837: three from Governor Bourke in New South Wales and one from Tasmania's Governor Arthur.

The first report of the Batman venture reached the Colonial Office from Tasmania in December 1835. In commenting on the matter, Governor Arthur made two distinct references to the problem of ownership and tenure. He observed that both Batman and the explorers Hume and Hovell had met Aborigines in the same part of Port Phillip, but that they had different names for the territory in question. This apparent overlapping of Aboriginal tenure would, he believed, 'render the original ownership doubtful'. Then, in an afterthought, Arthur addressed the whole issue of Indigenous rights to land, wondering if it could be true

> in contemplation of law, that a migratory savage tribe, consisting of from, perhaps, thirty to forty individuals, roaming over an almost unlimited extent of territory, could acquire such a property in the soil as to be able to convey it so effectually as to confer to the purchasers any right of possession which would be recognized in our courts of law.[10]

The immediate response of the Colonial Office was to oppose the Batman venture on practical grounds because all attempts to initiate new settlements had been 'of late years discountenanced' as leading to the establishment of 'fresh Settlements and fresh expenses'. But when it came to underlying principles, James Stephen refused to endorse Arthur's view. He would, he explained, not enter

> at present into the question of the right possessed by the Chiefs who were the Contracting parties to the Territory of which they agreed to dispose, or of the justice and fairness of the terms of the arrangement.[11]

Stephen's attitude can be better appreciated if we consider other memos written at much the same time as his response to Arthur, which was drafted on 17 December 1835. Two days earlier, Stephen had been dealing with exactly the same issue when outlining his concern about the extension inland of the boundaries of South Australia. While deflecting Arthur's questions about legal principles in his memo about Tasmanian settlers at Port Phillip on the 17th, he had no such qualms when writing to the South Australian Colonization Commission on the 15th emphasising his disquiet because the new colony

> might extend very far into the interior of New Holland and might embrace in its range numerous Tribes of People whose Proprietary Title to the Soil we have not the slightest ground for disputing.[12]

The Colonial Office received the second dispatch about Batman from Governor Bourke in April 1836. Bourke enclosed a copy of a proclamation he had issued the previous August. In refusing sanction to the purchase of land, the governor had declared that

> every such treaty, bargain, or contract with the Aboriginal Natives . . . for possession, title or claim to any land . . . is void and of no effect against the Crown and that all such persons who shall be found in possession of such lands . . . without the license or authority of His Majesty's Government . . . will be considered as trespassers.[13]

When approving Bourke's proclamation, Glenelg advanced arguments that have often been adduced in discussion of the Imperial government's attitude to the question of Aboriginal rights. He explained that although many circumstances had made him 'anxious that the Aborigines should be placed under zealous and effective protection' and that their rights 'should be studiously defended', he believed no advantage would accrue to them 'by recognizing in them any right to alienate to private adventures the land of the Colony'.[14] When read in context, the meaning is clear. It is not, as has often been suggested, a repudiation of native title. Rather it confirms a

Land Rights Recognised, 1838–48

key element of that doctrine: the inability of Aborigines to alienate land to private settlers or of settlers to purchase it.

The matter was considered again by the Colonial Office just over a year later in June 1837, in response to another dispatch from Governor Bourke. By that time the senior officials had read the legal opinion of Burge, Pemberton and Follett, which had been sought by the Port Phillip Association and which has been discussed earlier.[15] The opinion embodied a classic statement of the principles of native title: the colonising powers had gained 'ultimate dominion in and sovereignty over the soil', but the Indigenous people retained 'the rights of occupancy'. The three legal experts argued that it was essential

> that the powers of alienating those parts of the territory should be restricted. To have allowed them [the indigenes] to sell their land to the subjects of a foreign state would be inconsistent with the rights of the state . . . To have allowed them to sell to her own subjects would have been inconsistent with their relation of subjects.
>
> The restriction imposed on their power of alienation consisted in the right of pre-emption of these lands by that state, and in not permitting its own subjects or foreigners to acquire a title by purchase from them without its consent. Therein consists the sovereignty of a dominion or right to the soil asserted, and exercised by European government against the Aborigines, even while it continued in their possession.[16]

The legal opinion was examined by Glenelg and Stephen in June 1837. In a memo of 22 June, Stephen indicated his own and Glenelg's wholehearted acceptance of it and the accompanying doctrine of native title. In fact, Stephen wrote that Glenelg *perfectly concurred* with the lawyers' view as to 'the extent of the rights of the crown and the invalidity of the title upon which the Port Phillip Association relied'.[17] This was an important and revealing comment. Clearly the rights of the Crown as against Batman rested not on the doctrine of *terra nullius* but on its right of exclusive pre-emption of the native title. This strengthened the hand of the Crown against settlers claiming rights of possession on the basis of discovery and occupation. The land remained in the possession of the Aborigines by right of prior occupation up until the time the Crown chose to exercise its exclusive right to extinguish the native title.

The importance of the opinion of Burge, Pemberton and Follett has never been fully appreciated. But its influence was immediately apparent. Stephen was reading the opinion on 22 June 1837, and on the following day he drafted a dispatch which went out under Glenelg's signature a month later.[18] It was meant to be an important statement of principle and has generally been interpreted in that light. Stephen outlined for Bourke 'the general principles to be observed in [his] conduct towards the Aborigines'. Along with a declaration of the rights of the Aborigines as British subjects, Stephen observed that the governor exercised the sovereignty that had been 'assumed over the whole of their Ancient Possessions'.[19] In words that echoed the legal opinion he had just been reading, Stephen buried the concept of *terra nullius*. Indeed, the prior possession of the Aborigines was considered to be so obvious as to be a 'legal maxim'.[20]

Judges and historians have misinterpreted the significance of the rejection of Batman's treaty. It did not affirm the principle of *terra nullius*; nor did any of the official correspondence relating to that rejection.

THE NEW ZEALAND LAND GRAB

The question of individual purchase of Indigenous land arose again in 1840 when a group of prominent New South Wales settlers claimed that they had purchased vast areas of the South Island of New Zealand from Maori chiefs visiting Sydney. The New South Wales government, which was still responsible for the nascent colony, legislated to forestall the entrepreneurs. The resulting New Zealand Land Claims Bill of 1840 included the clause:

> And whereas no such individual or individuals can acquire a legal title to, or permanent interest in, any such tracts or portions of land by virtue of any gift, purchase, or conveyance by or from the chiefs or other individuals of such aboriginal tribes.[21]

With this Bill, Gipps effected by legislation exactly what his predecessor had done five years earlier by means of a proclamation. However, no one has ever argued that this action was proof that New Zealand was a *terra nullius,* that because the Maoris couldn't sell their land to individual settlers they were without land rights.

In justifying the legislation, Gipps provided a detailed account of the doctrine of native title and made it clear that it applied equally to Australia and New Zealand and was, indeed, part of colonial common law. When challenged to prove that native title was enshrined in English law he turned to the opinion of Burge, Pemberton and Follett, who he said were 'three of the most eminent of living lawyers'. In order to strengthen his argument Gipps referred back to his predecessor's action in the Batman affair. He conceded that Bourke had acted on the grounds that the Tasmanian settlers were trespassing on crown land and had not fully enunciated the doctrine of native title. Gipps argued that his predecessor had been right to adopt his course of action, which was 'sufficient for the exigency of the case, and there was no necessity for him entering on the wider question'[22] of underlying legal principles.

Gipps's speech, with its strong affirmation of native title and the assertion that it applied to Australia and New Zealand alike, was favourably received when it reached the Colonial Office six months later. There was no suggestion that Gipps had done anything more than provide 'a very able exposition' of principles that were 'received as political axioms' in official circles in both Sydney and London.[23]

South Australia, 1838–40

Between 1838 and 1840 South Australia's second governor, George Gawler, and his Land Commissioner, Charles Sturt, made a serious attempt to find a way of giving recognition to Aboriginal land rights while encouraging settlement at the same time.

Gawler had both public and private reasons for doing so. He was a deeply religious man with links to the humanitarian and missionary organisations, and we can assume that he was fully briefed on the Aboriginal question in the Colonial Office before he departed for the colony. He believed that land rights had been 'confirmed to them' both by the Letters Patent and the commissioners' instructions to their local officers. The royal instructions, he wrote, commanded that the Aborigines would be protected 'in the free enjoyment of their property' while the commissioners' instructions directed that the Aborigines should not be disturbed 'in the enjoyment of lands over which they may possess proprietary rights, and of which they are not disposed to make a voluntary transfer'. The colony itself was 'publicly known' to be founded on principles of the 'strictest regard to the original rights of the aboriginal inhabitants'.[24]

Gawler tried to implement principles that Torrens and his colleagues had sought to subvert. Even more important were the differing opinions about Aboriginal society held by the two administrations. Gawler and Sturt adopted the view, wide-spread in humanitarian circles, that the Aborigines had rights that arose from the irreducible fact of long and undisturbed possession. This was an interpretation with a long legal pedigree. The local Aborigines had exercised 'from time immemorial . . . distinct, defined and absolute rights of proprietary and hereditary possession'. They had 'natural indefeasible rights . . . vested in them as their birthright', which had arisen in 'remote and unknown antiquity'.

But it was not just the antiquity of the Aboriginal interest which earned them respect. The form of land tenure was sufficiently developed to be compared with that known to Europeans. The Aborigines had 'well understood and distinctly defined proprietary rights over the whole of the available land'; their sense of property was 'equally positive and well defined' as was that of the settlers themselves.[25]

Not that this should stand in the path of settlement. That was what the British were there for. But the Aborigines had an interest in the land that had to be considered. Compensation was unavoidable. The only question was how much and what form it should take. Gawler had been with the army in Canada, where Indians had exchanged land for cash payments or annual grants of consumer goods. He decided that the most appropriate method to use in Australia was to reserve some land in every district that came up for sale for the exclusive use of the Aborigines. Though their land holding would be substantially reduced in the process, it would be worth much more hectare for hectare as a result of European settlement. The local clans would be given the absolute right of selection, before all settlers, 'of reasonable portions of the choicest land, for their special use and benefit'.

Cash payment for land would bring only illusory benefit, as the North American experience had shown. 'In the degree of knowledge which they have attained,' Gawler explained, 'it would, however, have been to their great disadvantage to have entered into general treaties with them for the cession of land', inasmuch as such lands would certainly have been obtained 'for the most insignificant, ill-defined, and unsubstantial terms'. In developing their rationale for the creation of reserves, Gawler and Sturt argued that

> the invasion of those ancient rights by surveys and land appropriations of any kind, is justifiable only on the ground that they should, at the same time, reserve for the natives an ample sufficiency for their present and future use and comfort, under the new state of things into which they are thrown – a state in which we hope they will be led to live in greater comfort on a small space than they enjoyed before it occurred on their extensive original possessions.[26]

If in creating reserves Gawler was not acting on Colonial Office instructions, he certainly gained its subsequent approval. He presented his case to the incumbent Secretary of State, Lord John Russell, in 1840, including in his dispatch the correspondence he had exchanged with disgruntled settlers who strongly opposed his policies. In explaining his course of action, Gawler indicated he appreciated that the Aborigines had 'very ancient and hereditary possession of the available lands of this part at least of the territory'. Their system of land tenure was 'well defined'. His decision to allow the Aborigines prior selection 'before all other claimants' was, he argued, 'fully borne out by the Royal Instructions & the Commissioners' Regulations as well as inseparable from the natural right of man'.

The dispatch was considered by Russell, Stephen and two other senior Colonial Office officials. Stephen noted that Gawler had explained what had 'actually been done for securing lands to the Aborigines' and had in the letter and enclosures 'fully explained the principles on which he was acting'. Russell approved both the principles espoused and the practice outlined, while observing that Gawler was far from generous towards the Aborigines, reserving only 32 hectares out of 2023 sold to the settlers. 'I approve of the arrangement as far as it extends,' he wrote, 'but adverting to the very small portions of land assigned to the Aborigines out of extensive districts, I am of opinion that a more liberal provision should have been made for their support.'[27]

IMPERIAL ACTION

Both Gawler's governorship and his policy of creating Aboriginal reserves came to an abrupt end. His successor, George Grey, sought approval for land grants to Aborigines but was told by Lord Edward Stanley, Secretary of State after a change of government in 1841, that his action was illegal under the terms of the South Australian Act. The contradiction between Act and Letters Patent had emerged again, to be resolved in favour of the Act and the land-hungry settlers.

But by then the problem had been taken up again in Britain by the House of Commons Select Committee on South Australia. The Aboriginal question was brought to the notice of committee members by George Fife Angas. Indeed, it was Angas who drew the attention of the committee to the fact that the Act of 1834 gave no recognition of any Aboriginal right to land and made it impossible to create reserves in their favour. Angas's evidence was important and is worth examining in some detail. He was questioned about the nature of Aboriginal tenure and the dispossession of the clans around Adelaide.

> 2420. [Mr. *Wood*.] Have they been dispossessed of the land on which they were living? – The lands on which they were living they have been dispossessed of.
>
> 2421. Have they been removed from the places where they were residing by authority? – By the authority of the settlers who have purchased the lands. The government has allowed them a location on what is termed 'The Park', near Adelaide.
>
> 2422. [Captain *A'Court*.] Were they not migratory tribes? – No, they had distinct limits; every family had a location.
>
> 2423. [Mr. *Wood*.] Had they such a fixed residence previously to the settlement of any Europeans in the country? – Yes, it was accurately defined; not only was the district of the tribe defined, but the districts of the families of the tribe were so also.
>
> 2424. Defined in relation to each other? – Defined in relation to each other.
>
> 2425. Then did they recognise the rights of property in land? – In that sense they did.
>
> 2426. They respected each other's portions of land? – Clearly so. Those who trespassed upon others were put to death if they could be taken hold of.

2427. Have they been dispossessed of those portions? – Certainly; in every instance where the whites have settled down, they have dispossessed the natives of the portion of land which they formerly occupied.

2428. Has land been sold under the authority of the commissioners which was actually in the occupation of the Aborigines? – Most unquestionably.

2429. Have the aborigines been dispossessed in consequence? – I believe that to be the fact.

2430. Have you that upon the authority of information transmitted to you from the colony? – Pastor Kavel mentions that, in that particular locality at the Gawler river, they will have to be sent away so soon as the settlers go to it, in order to prevent mischief, and that he wishes to have a certain portion of land set apart for their particular use.

2431. That is a prospective case. Are you aware of any instance in which such dispossession has actually taken place? – I am persuaded that the land now occupied by the settlers was formerly belonging to the natives, and that they have in consequence been obliged to remove.

2432. Do you know any case where they were in actual possession, and have been obliged to remove in consequence of the occupation of the land by the settlers? – Yes, there is the Adelaide tribe; they have been obliged to remove, their lands having been occupied by the whites; that of course destroyed their means of subsistence from the kangaroos; they are now located on a small spot where they receive rations from the government.

2433. Is their location remote from the place of their former residence? – No, but it is a very small portion of their former possessions, probably not one-fiftieth part of it.

2434. Does it constitute part of the land on which they were situated? – It does in their case.

> 2435. Their hunting grounds for kangaroos have been curtailed? Yes, the land on which they are now placed belongs to the government; it is called the Park, and by the regulations of the government at Adelaide, they are there by sufferance; they have no right to the soil according to the Act of Parliament.[28]

Angas advocated a system of reserves which might eventually total as much as 10 per cent of the colony. He referred to the amount of land 'in proportion to the population in England as a criterion' and when applying the same principle to South Australia concluded that 4 hectares of good land and 12 hectares of what he called scrub land should be assigned to each individual.

The Aborigines Protection Society took a keen interest in the proceedings of the select committee. On its behalf Angas presented each member with a copy of Motte's pamphlet, *Outline of a System of Legislation for Securing Protection to the Aboriginal Inhabitants of all Countries Colonized by Great Britain*. Society members who were in the commons kept a close watch on proceedings. In the 1841 annual report the editor of the association's Papers and Proceedings remarked that members had 'hoped to be able to state authentically' the recommendations of the select committee so far as the Aborigines were concerned. This, the report continued,

> they are *not* yet enabled to do; but they believe they can with confidence anticipate, as the result of the enquiry, a measure of justice to the natives unprecedented in our colonization . . . It is with pleasure anticipated that from [the Society's appeals] reserves of land will be made for the inalienable possession of the natives . . .[29]

As the Aborigines Protection Society predicted, the select committee recommended the creation of reserves in South Australia, that the Imperial government 'should be authorized to reserve, and set apart' within the colony for the use of the Aborigines 'any lands which it may be found necessary so to reserve and set apart for the occupation and subsistence of such Aboriginal Inhabitants'.[30]

The government accepted the select committee's report and in the following year embodied many of its recommendations in the Imperial Crown Land Sale Act, Section Three of which provided for the creation of Aboriginal reserves in all the Australian colonies and in New Zealand.[31] While the provision in the Act was very general, merely making the creation of reserves possible, Imperial officials subsequently made it clear that they expected colonial governments to act on the Aborigines' behalf. In 1848, the then Secretary of State at the Colonial Office, Earl Grey, told Governor Fitzroy of New South Wales that reserves 'should be established where they do not exist, particularly in districts recently brought within the range of occupation' and that those 'already set apart for this purpose should be turned to account with all speed'.[32]

Reserves in Perspective

Reserves were set aside for Aborigines all over Australia during the second half of the nineteenth century. South Australia had fifty-nine small reserves in 1860, covering over 3645 hectares. It was a clear indication that the policy formulated by Gawler and Sturt had borne fruit.

In themselves, reserves were the strongest indication that Aboriginal land rights had been tacitly accepted in Australia and that compensation was required from the settlers. Colonists frequently adopted the view that reserves were given to the Aborigines as manifestations of benevolence and goodwill and carried no implication of rights lost and obligations incurred. It was one of the more obvious ways in which Australian settlers attempted to rewrite the history of their relations with the Aborigines. In itself this was a relatively harmless activity, but it had a major impact on the legal and political status of Aboriginal communities and the security or otherwise of their hold on reserves granted in the nineteenth and early twentieth centuries. Misinterpret the reasons for the creation of reserves and the whole history of land rights is distorted, a fact which became clear in the judgement of Justice Blackburn in the Gove Land Rights Case of 1971.

The decision to create reserves, Blackburn argued, implied 'not that the sovereign recognizes rights in the natives', but that it has power 'to dispose for their benefit of any lands –irrespective of what the natives claim'. There was, he concluded, 'not the slightest suggestion that this encouragement of the aboriginals to abandon their normal manner of life represented any recognition that they were entitled to any particular land'. The express creation of native reserves 'strengthens this manifestation of intention [to extinguish native title]; it does not detract from it'.[33]

Blackburn may or may not have been right in law, but he seems to have fundamentally misunderstood the motives that led to the creation of reserves in many parts of the empire. I believe he also failed to appreciate the strong links in the international law of the eighteenth and nineteenth centuries between the recognition of native title and the creation of reserves.

The issue is an important one, and it is necessary to place

the policy of granting reserves, introduced by the Imperial legislation of 1842, in its proper context. The earliest reserves in North America were created in the middle of the seventeenth century. When Indians ceded territory they commonly reserved areas of land for their own exclusive use. In 1658 the Assembly of Virginia enacted

> that for future no lands should be patented until 50 acres had been first set apart to each warrior or head of a family belonging to any tribe of Indians in the neighhourhood.[34]

Reservations were aptly named. To reserve means literally to keep something back, to keep in one's possession, to retain as one's own, to exempt from something. There is an even more precise legal meaning. In law, 'reservation' means to retain for oneself some right or interest in property that is being conveyed to another. American experience of the creation of reserves was summed up by the Supreme Court in a case in 1899. When land was reserved, it was a matter of a 'right acknowledged' rather than a 'favour conferred'.[35]

International law strongly supported the view that reserves were to be seen as islands of native tenure remaining above the flood tide of settlement. In a much quoted passage (see Chapter 1) Vattel argued that the Indians could be 'confined within narrower limits'. But they weren't to be completely dispossessed, they weren't to want for land. They just had to make do on a much smaller piece of territory. The United States House of Representatives Committee on Indian Affairs discussed the justification for the creation of reserves in 1830:

> The rigor of the rule of their exclusion from these rights (the rights of soil and sovereignty) has been mitigated, in practice, in

conformity with the doctrines of those writers upon natural law, who, while they admit the superior rights of agriculturalists over the claims of savage tribes in the appropriation of wild lands, yet, upon the principle that the earth was intended to be a provision for all mankind, assign to them such portion as, when subdued by the arts of the husbandman, may be sufficient for their subsistence. To the operation of this rule of natural law may be traced all those small reservations to the Indian tribes within the limits of most of the old states.[36]

In his classic 1928 study, *The Acquisition and Government of Backward Territory in International Law*, the English jurist M. F. Lindley summed up the situation that had existed in many parts of the world where European settlers had competed with native people for land. The opinion, he explained,

was generally held that where tribes or communities were occupying an inordinately large extent of land merely for hunting, or even for pasturing flocks and herds, there was no just reason why some part of it should not be taken and put to more productive uses. But it came to be recognized that sufficient land ought to be left to the original occupants for their sustenance, and there arose the policy of reserving definite areas for their exclusive use.[37]

There is no doubt that this is the way that reserves were understood in both humanitarian circles and the Colonial Office in the middle of the nineteenth century. They were an acknowledgement of prior ownership, of the perpetuation of native title after settlement, of the need for compensation. Gawler explained his policy in a letter to Angas in 1840. The local tribes, he argued, had a system of tenure that was 'positive and well defined', and the 'lowest degree of respect that might be shown to it' was to give them 'a preliminary choice of land suitable for their future limited location'.[38] Eyre believed that the Aborigines should have land 'reserved for them out of their own possessions, and in their own respective districts'.[39] At Port Phillip, Joseph Orton argued in favour of government action aimed at 'securing to them sufficient portions of their own native land as hunting ground'.[40] Prominent Western District pioneers petitioned the government to reserve for the local groups 'suitable portions of land within the territorial limits of the respective tribes'.[41] Robinson wrote to the Government Resident at Port Phillip in 1839 arguing that the 'remnant tribes' should be 'permitted to select in their own districts small portions of land'.[42] Twenty years later a Select Committee of the Victorian Legislative Council advocated the formation of reserves 'for the various tribes, on their own hunting grounds'.[43]

The creation of reserves in Australia in the middle of the nineteenth century was the consequence of a clear recognition of native title. It was, in Gawler's opinion, the lowest level of respect that could be accorded to the ancient rights of the Aborigines. Such an interpretation should occasion no surprise, given developments in other countries at the time. Reserves of one sort or another were set aside for Indigenous people in comparable societies (New Zealand, Canada, United States, South Africa), where native title was respected whatever else may have happened to the natives at the hands of the settlers. In Canada a new policy of creating reserves was established in the years 1828–30 to replace the earlier practice of purchasing Indian land outright. Under the new regime Indians were to be collected 'in considerable numbers . . . to settle them in villages with due portion of land for their cultivation and support'.[44] In South Africa in 1835 Governor D'Urban planned to establish 'locations' for the Bantu in the captured Queen Adelaide Province. He had no intention of extinguishing native title altogether, seeking rather 'to restrict and define the Kaffir's right to remain in occupation of their old homes'.[45] Just six weeks before he approved Gawler's plans for reserves in South Australia, Lord John Russell instructed the Government Resident in New Zealand to make provision for permanent reserves for the Maoris. The surveyor-general was to report 'from time to time' what particular tract of land 'it would be desirable that the natives should permanently retain for their own use and occupation'.[46]

The unity of Imperial policy was underlined by the Land and Emigration Commissioners, who told James Stephen in 1840 that they were

> inclined to think as we before stated that moderate reserves of land should be made in all those countries, which like New Holland, have been arbitrarily occupied. By moderate reserves, we mean reserves of that extent which would enable them to live, not as hunters, in which case no good would be done, but as cultivators of the soil.[47]

Reserves in settled districts was one way in which the Imperial government gave substance to its commitment to native title in Australia. A second way was financial compensation. The need to provide an 'equivalent' was widely accepted, as was the obligation to pay for the education, conversion and 'civilization' of the displaced tribes.

The question was tackled in the *Imperial Crown Land Sale Act 1842*, which gave the Crown discretion to use the proceeds of

Land Rights Recognised, 1838–48

land sales. Two years earlier the Colonial Office had decided that 15 per cent of land revenue should be spent on the indigenes in all new colonies. In a dispatch of August 1840, Russell told Governor Gipps that in his opinion 15 per cent of the land fund should be used for the Aborigines. The Australian governors were informed in September 1842 that they were to use an amount 'not exceeding in the whole 15 per cent of the gross proceeds of land sales for the benefit, civilization and protection of the Aborigines'.[48] This was meant to be taken seriously. In 1848 Earl Grey proposed the setting up of schools for both children and adults all over the colonies. 'The expense attending any measures of that nature,' he wrote, 'should constitute the very first charge upon the Land Revenue, a principle which Parliament has recognized in the Australian Land Sales Act'.[49]

The changes in attitude that had taken place towards Aboriginal land rights between 1834 and the end of the decade in political and financial circles in Britain were well illustrated by events that accompanied the planning for a proposed, but abandoned, colony at Australind in the south-west of Western Australia in 1841.

The major figures behind the venture had been associated with the founding of South Australia and included E. G. Wakefield, the spiritual father of the colony. In contrast to the plans of 1833–35, which ignored the presence of the Aborigines, the new colony was to proceed with full recognition accorded to native title. Wakefield made contact with prominent Aborigines Protection Society member Thomas Hodgkin and told him that he intended to appoint a commissioner, to be selected by the society, who would travel to Western Australia and 'inquire into the state of the natives, and on the spot devise the details of a better system of treatment to be adopted towards them'. There was a clear appreciation of Colonial Office concern for

Indigenous rights, while Hodgkin understood that 'very influential individuals in some degree connected with the Western Australian enterprise, had insisted on justice to the natives being made an essential condition of their adhesion to it'.[50]

The directors of the company and a delegation from the society met and drew up a joint proposal to be put to the government, which included, as the first of three measures, provision for

> an arrangement with the natives for the extinction of their title to the crown lands of the colony, and the security to these natives of a portion of land adequate to supply the means of their peaceful existence.[51]

The joint company/society petition to the Colonial Office embodied plans to send an officer to make an inspection of local conditions. In his letter to Lord Russell, the society secretary sought not just 'sanction and support' for the venture but also a commitment that the government 'so far recognizes the principle of aboriginal claims as to insure the adoption of any really practical measures which may be devised'.[52]

Russell agreed with the proposals and presumably accepted the principles implicit in them. An officer was appointed and plans made to send him to the colony. But by then the company was in deep financial trouble. Investors withdrew their money and the company's bank collapsed. The company severely pruned expenditure and refused to pay for the expedition to Western Australia. The whole scheme was in jeopardy and only a few colonists actually set sail for the Antipodes.

But while settlement in the south-west of Western Australia faltered, it was spreading rapidly throughout the grasslands of the Murray–Darling basin, creating an enormous problem for the Colonial Office and its Australian representatives. Namely, how to manage the squatting rush and how to preserve the rights of Aboriginal clans to remain on their homelands.

SEVEN

Pastoral Leases

The Port Phillip Protectorate was the principal means chosen by the Imperial authorities to implement in Australia the recommendations of Buxton's select committee. His strong commitment to Indigenous land rights and desire to discover the 'most judicious modes of securing to them some portion of their own land'[1] were apparent in plans that were put in place in many parts of the empire in the late 1830s and early 1840s. His original idea was to appoint protectors to defend Aboriginal property 'that they may not be cheated out of their land'. In the select committee report, the outline of the duties of the protectors included the following recommendations:

> Especially they should claim for the maintenance of the Aborigines such lands as may be necessary for their support. So long as agriculture shall be distasteful to them, they should be provided with the means of pursuing the chase without molestation.[2]

PORT PHILLIP PROTECTORS

When it came to appointing protectors for Port Phillip and drawing up specific instructions, Glenelg turned to George Arthur, then on leave in London after completing a twelve-year term in Tasmania. Arthur believed that recognition of native title was vital in order to avoid the bloodshed experienced in Tasmania. He was also aware of the contemporary legal view that native title was entrenched in the common law, and had a copy of the legal opinion of Burge, Follett and Pemberton in his private papers. In the instructions he drew up for the protectors, Arthur made two references to Aboriginal property. The protector was to encourage the Aborigines to 'engage in the cultivation of *their grounds*', to watch over 'their rights and interests' and to protect them by his personal exertions and influence 'from any encroachment *on their property*'.[3]

Whatever else Arthur may have planned for Port Phillip Aborigines, he clearly assumed that they would have some land to call their own, that they wouldn't want for land. The reference to 'rights and interests' suggested an expectation of some form of compensation from the settlers. This was certainly the way that the chief protector, G. A. Robinson, interpreted his task, referring again and again to his belief that the Aborigines should be allowed 'a reasonable share in the Soil of their fatherland'.[4]

From his arrival in Port Phillip, Robinson was shocked by the way in which the Aborigines were being swept aside by the tide of pastoral settlement. He noted in his journal in May 1839 that he had just had a long conversation with the surveyor-general, who

> showed me a Map of the Country – marked off into allotments comprising an Extent of I think fully 30 miles square – and not a single reserve for the blacks . . . I said that if a similar map was Exhibited to the people of England they would at once see the way the natives are treated. Their land sold from them and no provision made for their maintenance and this by the Govt which

are bound to protect them – There is a complete system of expulsion and Extermination for first the Purchaser of their lands drive them on to other Purchased lands and then on ad infinitum.[5]

Robinson's solution was like Gawler's: to create reserves within the traditional boundaries of the Aborigines' own land. 'It would appear but an act of common justice,' he wrote in 1839, that the local clans 'should be permitted to select in their own districts small portions of land.'[6]

His alarm grew as he travelled extensively through the Port Phillip district and witnessed first-hand the linked processes of settlement and dispossession. It appeared in the early 1840s that resident Aborigines had no legal standing when confronted by incoming squatters with pastoral licences. He took alarm at a judgement in the Supreme Court in Melbourne in December 1841. A squatter named Bolden was indicted for shooting an Aboriginal, Tackiar, who was on his pastoral run. Mr Justice Willis declared that he wished it to be distinctly understood

> that if a party receives a licence from Government to occupy a run, and *any person white or black comes on my run* for the purpose of *stealing my property*, I have a right to drive them off by every lawful means in my power . . . The blacks have no right to trespass unless there is a special clause in the licence from the government.[7]

Robinson returned to the question of Aboriginal rights to land in his annual reports which were ultimately sent to the Colonial Office in London. In 1845 he observed that the 'future protection and support of the Aboriginal natives' required what he called 'fixed localities' because they had 'no right in the property of the soil and were liable to be driven away from their own lands'.[8] The following year Robinson wrote with even more urgency because the squatters were contemporaneously engaged in an ultimately successful campaign to force the Imperial government to provide them with greater security of tenure. He pointed out to the Colonial Office that in all the intense discussion about the rights of the pastoralists there had been no mention of the 'claim of the Aborigines to a reasonable share in the Soil of their fatherland'.[9] He incorporated in his report an extract from a letter that he had received from his assistant protector, E. S. Parker, who had written from his station in the Loddon district that

> unless suitable reserves are immediately formed for their benefit, every acre of their native soil will shortly be so leased out and occupied as to leave them, *in a legal view, no place for the sole of their feet*. If the occupation of Crown Lands is to be settled by the Crown granting a Lease for years, the natives will be deprived of all *legal* rights to hunt over their own native land and according to the Dicta of certain high legal Authorities, may be forcibly excluded by the Lessee, from the tract of Country so leased . . . I have great reason to fear the legal rights acquired under a lease would be fully acted upon and the unfortunate natives might be hunted from Station to Station, without a Spot they can call their own.[10]

Robinson's report and its call for the Aborigines to receive a reasonable share of their traditional land apparently evoked no response in Australia. But when it reached the Colonial Office it was a different story. The first official to read it commented that it would be 'most unjust that the Natives should be extruded in the manner described . . . from the soil of which till recently, they were the sole occupants'. Of more importance was the reaction of the Secretary of State, Earl Grey, who wrote that Governor Fitzroy must be instructed to take care that the Aborigines were not to be driven off all the land that was being divided into grazing stations. Land should be reserved sufficient to allow the natives being maintained upon it, and to make up the deficiency of game 'with a view to their preservation from being exterminated'.[11]

The Colonial Office responded in a dispatch sent to Sydney in February 1848 in which Grey considered both the question of reserves and the need to find innovative ways to preserve Aboriginal rights to continue to live on the vast areas of land leased for pastoral purposes. He explained that

> the very difficulty of thus locating the Aboriginal Tribes absolutely apart from the Settlers renders it more incumbent on Government to prevent them from being altogether excluded from the land under pastoral occupation. I think it essential that it should be generally understood that leases granted for this purpose give the grantees only an exclusive right of pasturage for their cattle, and of cultivating such land as they may require within the large limits thus assigned to them, but that leases are not intended to deprive the natives of their former right to hunt over these Districts, or to wander over them in search of subsistence, in the manner to which they have been heretofore accustomed, from the spontaneous produce of the soil except over land cultivated or fenced in for that purpose.[12]

Grey returned to the subject in further dispatches as officials in both Britain and Australia wrestled with the problem of providing for the mutual rights of squatters and Aborigines over the same land, particularly as some leases had already been issued in New South Wales. In October 1848 he minuted on a further dispatch from Governor Fitzroy that

> I apprehend that it may fairly be assumed that HM (Her Majesty, i.e. the Government) did not intend and had no power by these leases to exclude the natives from the use they had been accustomed to make of these unimproved lands . . .[13]

What Grey was advocating was a unique form of tenure – a lease which provided for the pastoralists' exclusive right to use the land for grazing and to enclose those small areas required for gardens and fodder crops. The Aborigines continued to have the right to use the same land for the pursuit of their traditional life. The Colonial Office had conceded that Australian squatters needed some security of tenure over large areas of grassland. The economic viability of both industry and colony demanded it. But the spread of settlement was not to be at the cost of the Aborigines whose rights were also to be protected.

It took some time to find the means by which Aboriginal rights to use the land could be inserted into New South Wales pastoral leases. In the end an Order in Council was signed by the Queen on 18 July 1849 which gave the Governor power to impose on lessees such 'conditions, clauses of forfeiture, exceptions, and reservations, as may be necessary for securing the peaceable and effectual occupation of the land . . . and for preventing the abuses and inconveniences thereto . . .'[14] Following the issue of the Order in Council a condition was inserted in pastoral leases issued in New South Wales and in Queensland after 1859 which reserved to the Aboriginal inhabitants of the colony such free access to the said Run or Parcel of Land, hereby demised or any part thereof as will enable them to procure the Animals, Birds, Fish and other foods on which they subsist.[15]

The process required to protect Aboriginal property rights had been tortuous but by 1850 the Colonial Office officials believed that they had given the Aborigines of New South Wales legal protection. When responding to reports about frontier conflict in the Gwydir district in February 1850, Earl Grey reminded Governor Fitzroy that 'the practice of driving the Natives from the cattle runs is illegal, and they have every right to the protection of the law from such aggressions'.[16] What is more, Grey thought the matter 'one of very great importance'.[17]

The same result was achieved with greater ease in Western Australia and South Australia. In October 1849 Governor Fitzgerald of Western Australia sent to the Colonial Office three alternative schemes for the regulation of pastoral occupation of hitherto unsettled land. None of them mentioned the Aborigines or referred to their property rights. When Earl Grey read the material prepared by his officials he immediately noticed the lack of attention to the Aboriginal question. He wrote back to his officials accepting what they had written,

> except as to one point which has I think been overlooked – If I am not mistaken a question arose in New South Wales as to the right of leaseholders to exclude the natives from their runs and it was found necessary to give some additional instruction upon this point – It is material that this should be attended to in the present case.[18]

As a result of Grey's intervention a new clause was added to the draft Order in Council which declared that nothing contained in any pastoral lease

> shall prevent Aboriginal natives of this colony from entering upon the lands comprised therein, and seeking their subsistence therefrom in their accustomed manner . . .[19]

South Australia developed its own form of protection for Aborigines living on land leased for pastoral purposes. The Colonial Office sent Governor Young a copy of Earl Grey's dispatch to Governor Fitzroy of February 1848 which enunciated the basic principles underpinning the development of a form of tenure which protected the rights of both pastoralist and Aborigine. The Governor published a declaration about the protection of the Aborigines, observing

> that it would be expedient to insert a clause reserving the right of the natives to dwell upon lands held under lease, and to follow their usual customs in searching for food. I would also point out that the practice of driving the Natives from the cattle runs is illegal, and that they have every right to the protection of the law from such aggressions.[20]

South Australian leases contained a far more detailed list of Aboriginal rights than those in New South Wales and Western Australia, allowing

> for and on account of the present Aboriginal Inhabitants of the Province and their descendants . . . full and free right of ingress, egress and regress into upon and over the said Waste Land of the Crown . . . and in and to the Springs and surface water thereon

and to make and erect such wurlies and other dwellings as the said Aboriginals have been heretofore accustomed to make and take and use for food birds and animals . . .[21]

The Government's seriousness of purpose was illustrated in the correspondence on the matter which passed between the colonial officials. The Commissioner of Crown Lands, Charles Bonney, wrote in June 1851:

> I think such reservations should be inserted in the leases as will give the Government complete control in the matter. I am of opinion that knowledge that the Government is in possession of this power and that the runs are liable to be resumed for the use of the natives, will be sufficient to ensure the forbearance of the white people, and to render them rather desirous of conciliating the natives in order that no necessity may arise for the exercise of these powers.[22]

Earl Grey could not have wished for a more effective implementation of his desire that pastoral leases would not deprive the Aborigines of their former right to take their living from the land.

The bureaucratic manoeuvring, the exchange of dispatches, the drafting of memos – they are not the stuff of exciting history. They have evoked little interest compared with the great drama of settlement and dispossession that was acted out across the vast stage of inland Australia. But the creation of the pastoral lease by the Colonial Office had profound implications that only became fully apparent with the High Court's judgement in the Wik case in 1996. It is necessary to sum up the argument to this point.

1. Colonial Office action was a clear and demonstrable recognition of native title: the right to use and occupy land held under traditional title.

2. The Imperial authorities believed that the Aborigines had rights. They said so a number of times, both in public and private. Grey explained in his dispatch that grants of pastoral leases were not intended to deprive the Aborigines 'of *their former right*' to hunt and gather. In an internal Colonial Office memo, Gordon Gairdner, the senior official in charge of Australian affairs, explained that the object of Grey's proposals was 'the reservation in leases of Pasturage Land of *the rights of the Natives*', and the 'conveyancing to the Natives [of] the *continuance of their rights*'.[23] The Colonial Office had not created these rights. It had recognised their existence. It intended to provide for their *continuance*. The rights did not derive from statute law; they were embodied in the common law and stemmed from the Aboriginal prior occupation of the continent.

3. On all but enclosed *and* cultivated land the Aborigines could, as of right, continue to make use of the land as they had done since time immemorial. They could come and go as they pleased, hunt, fish, gather, reside. They had what were known as usufructuary rights. Such rights were an 'interest' in the land, a form of property, which could be passed on by inheritance like any other form of property. The owner of such an interest would expect compensation if it was extinguished by the Crown.

4. Aboriginal customary rights were to continue on land leased to pastoralists. The conclusion is irresistible that

they also continued to exist on crown land all over the continent and that where there were no Europeans their rights were unimpaired.

The pastoral lease continued to be the major form of tenure applied to the vast rangelands of inland Australia throughout the nineteenth and twentieth centuries. But their origin in the Colonial Office in the 1840s was almost completely forgotten. The reservation in favour of Aboriginal usufructuary rights was preserved in leases issued in Western Australia, South Australia and the Northern Territory but was no longer included in Queensland leases from some time in the early twentieth century. If the source of the leases was forgotten, so too was the Colonial Office intent — to give pastoralists some security of tenure but prevent them from gaining freehold title by means of adverse possession or prescription and the preservation of native title.

Grey's clear understanding that it was illegal to force Aborigines off leased pastoral land had little effect on the course of land settlement. Things might have been very different if the colonial governments had decided to enforce the law in favour of the Aborigines. But they never did. And what may be more perplexing is that none of the humanitarian individuals who spoke out against the treatment of the Aborigines ever sought to use the law — or even knew about it. Occasionally officials in colonial administrations referred to the reservations in favour of resident clans but there was little follow-up. Few pastoralists took the reservations in their leases seriously — or even knew they were there. They allowed Aborigines to remain on their runs or drove them off as the spirit moved them, with absolutely no fear of legal consequences. If they required Aboriginal labour — and a great many did — they encouraged the 'local blacks' to stay on their land. In this way Earl Grey's vision of pastoralists and Aborigines sharing the same land came to function, particularly in northern Australia, but not in the way that he might have expected.

EIGHT

A Forgotten Legacy

By the end of 1848, when Earl Grey's dispatch reached Australia with suggestions for the creation of more reserves and Aboriginal schools and recognition of usufructuary rights on crown land, the humanitarian movement had long since passed its zenith. James Stephen had just left the Colonial Office after an association of more than thirty years. New racial theories were winning converts in both Europe and America, clearing the way for the emergence of Social Darwinism later in the century. The Australian colonies were shortly to write their constitutions in preparation for self-government in 1856.

The new colonial governments were to be far less interested in Aboriginal rights than the Colonial Office had been. The colonists themselves had always resented Imperial concern for Aborigines. The British were seen at best as misguided idealists, at worst as dangerous meddlers in what was a purely domestic matter. The settlers always thought that they knew how to handle the blacks! Racist assumptions about the Aborigines had taken deep root in Australian society from the early years of settlement. Many felt that the Aborigines were unworthy of any rights at all. Even more were convinced that they would die out, obviating the need for any special effort or particular policies. The Imperial endeavour to give recognition to Aboriginal land rights was hotly disputed. Colonial progress and individual wellbeing both appeared to be threatened by too close attention to embarassing questions about land tenure. 'Exeter Hall' enthusiasts were often despised. They did the unpardonable: they made the settlers feel guilty. James Stephen made what was perhaps the most telling assessment of colonial attitudes, especially

> the hatred with which the white man regards the black. That feeling results from fear – from the strong physical contrasts which intercept the sympathy which subsists between men of the same Race – from the proud sense of superiority – from the consciousness of having done them great wrongs and from the desire to escape this pain of self reproach by laying the blame on the injured party.[1]

The three Imperial initiatives – reserves, compensation and recognition of usufructuary rights – fared badly in the new political and intellectual climate. In New South Wales, the oldest and largest colony, a select committee of the Legislative Council considered Grey's proposal for more reserves in 1849. Commissioners of crown lands actually made suggestions for appropriate sites. The committee, however, strongly opposed the move, arguing that the creation of new reserves would 'prove prejudicial to those settlers who would be ousted from a portion of their runs', a development that would interfere with 'the good feeling' that the committee thought was springing up between 'the white and black populations of the colony'.[2]

Some reserves created before 1856 survived; others were established. However, they were rarely seen as a measure of compensation, as something owed to Aborigines and belonging to them as a right. It was much more comforting to believe that reserves were gifts of a benevolent society. No colonial government spent anything like 15 per cent of land revenue on Aboriginal welfare. During the five-year period 1845–49 the New South Wales government spent between 2 and 3 per cent on Aboriginal welfare. After separation from the parent colony in 1859, the new Queensland government provided blankets once a year and not much else, apart from a native police force, over 200 strong at times, which was used to crush black resistance. Wealthy Victoria earned about £44 000 a year from land sales and rental during the 1860s and spent about 1 per cent of it on the Aborigines. South Australia did much the same.

In 1860 a select committee on the Aborigines investigated what had happened to expenditure in South Australia. Dr Matthew Moorhouse, the protector during the 1840s, explained that in 1842 the government had committed 10 per cent of land revenue to the Aborigines following the directive from Downing Street. But with the boom in land sales following the discovery of copper, it was decided that too much was going to the Aborigines. He was told at the time that the 'natives were to have what was absolutely necessary and the 10% was not to be enforced'.[3] With self-government small sums were voted for Aboriginal welfare, while at the same time rental for Aboriginal reserves let out to settlers was paid into consolidated revenue, reducing even further the actual financial commitment.

A study of the debates and decisions about Aboriginal land rights in the first half of the nineteenth century makes it clear that although it was almost inevitable that the Aborigines would lose their sovereignty to one of the major powers, it was far from inevitable that they would be denied property rights to every inch of their territory. The radical dispossession was not the inescapable legacy of Australian history or of English law. We are the legatees of a past that was, to a considerable extent, chosen by our forebears — not the past in general but a particular past, not the law in general but a self-serving version of the law, deeply tainted by the racism of colonial society and corrupted in its way as the legal systems in the slave colonies of the West Indies. The particular problem of Aboriginal land rights may have had its origin in accident or oversight, but expediency ensured its perpetuation long after it was known that Australia was inhabited and that the native people were in possession of their ancient homelands.

When colonial policies were scrutinised in the era of reform — the Reform Bill, catholic emancipation and the abolition of slavery — it was accepted that there were serious political and legal problems associated with Australian settlement. The treatment of Aboriginal land was anomalous; it was out of step with British and United States policy in North America and with policy adopted in New Zealand after 1840. It was also out of harmony with the major tradition of international law as enunciated in American and New Zealand courts and in the legal opinion of Burge, Pemberton and Follett. When the Imperial officials turned their attention to the question of native title in Australia, they had every reason to believe that they were merely bringing the country into line with principles and practices accepted elsewhere. The colonists, for their part, based their expectations on what had already happened in Australia up to that time. For a crucial period of forty years Aboriginal land rights had been ignored. That was the colonial reality; that was the way things were done at the Antipodes.

The conflicting views were brought into sharp focus when Glenelg told Torrens that the South Australian colonists would have to prove that no prior title existed. Torrens immediately sent his staff out to collect every available book on Australia and every piece of legislation relating to the country in order to prove the unfairness of Colonial Office demands when judged by local practice.

Even by the 1830s it was difficult to change the direction of colonial policy. Attitudes, habits of mind and action, were already entrenched. Colonists were committed to defending their own way of doing things against outside interference. The most common argument used to support colonial behaviour was that the Aborigines themselves were to blame: they were too primitive, nomadic, savage, and therefore had to be treated differently to Indigenous people elsewhere in the world. What is more, talk of Aboriginal rights threatened those who held land and those who aspired to hold it in the future. In the 1830s many of the landed elite occupied large areas of land as squatters with a very insecure title. The promise of abundant 'empty' land was a major lure for immigrants and capital alike. The dominant pastoral industry depended not just on sales of wool, meat and tallow but on the demand for animals to stock new pastures on an ever-expanding frontier. Abstract rights of savages meant little when weighed against such considerations.

Imperial interest in Aboriginal rights was widely dismissed as an example of unnecessary meddling with colonial affairs and was therefore rejected root and branch. But a more interesting and subtle reaction was to accept what the Colonial Office was doing very selectively, supporting such purely humanitarian aspects as protection of life and tight-fisted charity while rejecting the central emphasis on legal equality and land rights. In English humanitarian circles, Aboriginal rights meant native title; in the colonies they meant blankets, rations and protection from the cruder forms of violence. For Buxton, in England, the protectors were to see the indigenes weren't cheated out of their land. In Australia the protectors' role was seen as controlling the Aboriginal 'nuisance' and limiting the spread of frontier violence.

It's not that the settlers didn't understand what the Imperial authorities wanted. They understood only too well. Aborigines could have 'protection', but they couldn't have land. Richard Windeyer warned the Sydney humanitarians at the inaugural meeting of the Aborigines Protection Society in 1838 that while he agreed the blacks should be 'protected', it could only be done if public opinion supported the cause and 'to do this effectually, it was necessary to carry the country gentlemen along with them, but this they could not expect' if colonial reformers followed their London mentors and talked carelessly about land rights. But if they would only concede European prior rights of possession they could solicit the support of 'nineteen twentieths of the country gentlemen'.[4]

The problem was seen even more clearly in the behaviour of Governor Gipps, who arrived in New South Wales at the very time that Imperial concern about native people reached its height. Soon after he settled into office he decided to issue a proclamation about the position of the Aborigines. Difficulties of drafting, the outbreak of frontier violence and pressure from the 'country gentlemen' delayed publication and ensured that when it eventually emerged it lacked any reference to Aboriginal rights. Gipps had foreseen the problem during the long process of drafting. While commenting on a passage written by one of his officers, he warned of the danger of referring to Aboriginal rights 'lest we be called upon to acknowledge their right to possession of the soil'.[5]

The colonists were able to rob the Imperial reforms of their central driving force: the concern for Aboriginal rights to land and for compensation from the colonial governments. They achieved two objectives at the same time. They disarmed the first land rights movement and were able to characterise it as being foolishly idealistic and impractical. The 'well-meaning' but 'ineffectual' attempts at protection were remembered; the demand for land rights was forgotten, and forgotten very quickly, even by those concerned with Aboriginal welfare. Land rights virtually disappeared from the political agenda, no doubt helped by the ubiquitous belief that the Aborigines were a dying race.

The 'forgetting' of the land rights issue can be seen in the case of South Australia. A select committee on the Aborigines in 1860 'found some difficulty in tracing the history of the early efforts of the Colonists to provide for the necessities and ameliorate the condition of the native'.[6] Six years later the author of a book on the colony recalled that 'it was a special instruction' of the Imperial government that the Aborigines 'should be properly cared for' and for that purpose 'a Chief Protector of Aborigines was appointed in Adelaide'.[7] Within a generation of settlement, the fact that the colony was founded on the assumption that Aboriginal land would be purchased had been conveniently forgotten. The 'country gentlemen' had won their battle. Aborigines could be 'cared for', but all reference to land rights had been discarded.

In 1848 the Western Australian Colonial Secretary explained how the colonists subverted the intentions of the Imperial government, how

> the wishes and intentions of the home government towards them have been frequently frustrated, evaded, misrepresented

and successfully counteracted, opposed, not only in the face of positive instructions, but encountered by a dead weight of indisposition towards them by a covert opposition, a persevering system of obstruction, a pulling back of the wheels of Government which has proved sufficient to hinder any efforts that have been made to upraise the Aborigines.[8]

COULD IT HAVE BEEN DIFFERENT?

The settlers pictured the Imperial reformers as impractical idealists who were out of touch with colonial realities. This has generally been the view taken by Australian historians, although it is a sobering thought to remember that the slave owners had a very similar interpretation of the contemporaneous crusade against slavery. Members of the Aborigines Protection Society, of the mission organisations and of the Colonial Office were very well-informed about Australia; their assessment of colonial conditions was sound, their foreboding about the future justified by events.

Critics of colonial practice in both Britain and Australia saw clearly that unless respect was paid to Aboriginal land rights, relations between black and white would continue to deteriorate. The Reverend John Beecham warned that existing methods of colonisation would lead to a system of painful and angry intercourse 'for years to come'.[9] After working in New South Wales as attorney-general in the 1820s, Saxe Bannister argued that the heart of the problem was the 'unjust seizure' of the land. It had

> so completely cut off another means of gradual improvement, that the land itself, through exasperated feelings for the loss, is become an obstacle rather than an incentive to their civilization.[10]

In Australia, Bishop Polding made a similar assessment of the situation, explaining to a select committee of the New South Wales Legislative Council in 1845 that the 'want of success' in civilising the Aborigines

> must be attributed to the bad feeling and want of confidence, naturally caused by the mode in which possession has been taken of their country – occupation by force, accompanied by murders, ill-treatment, ravishment of their women, in a word, to the conviction on their minds that the while man has come for his own advantage, without any regard to their rights – Feeling this burning injustice inflicted by the white man, it is not in the nature of things that the black man should believe the white man better than himself, or suppose the moral and religious laws, by which the white man proposes the black man to be governed, to be better than those of his own tribe.[11]

The fears of the reformers were borne out by events. The blood continued to flow; many thousands of Aborigines died in those districts still unsettled in the 1830s. The killing went on for another century. It was 100 years from Governor Arthur's declaration of martial law to the Coniston massacre in central Australia in 1928. Australians have thought of this conflict as regrettable but unavoidable. Here above all is where the humanitarian and missionary critics of colonial practice have to be addressed. They argued that colonisation that ignored Indigenous land rights was bound to be too costly, that the Tasmanian experience would be repeated over and over again. But a majority of the settlers chose the old ways, eschewed reform, denounced attempts to respect Aboriginal rights. They were willing to pay the cost of forced expropriation – in insecurity, property loss, suppressed guilt. They could bear all that because the real price was paid in the destruction and desolation of Aboriginal tribes all over the continent.

Could it have been different? Not completely. Australian geography alone made control of frontier contact almost impossible. But had the three measures proposed by the Imperial government in the 1840s – compensation, reserves, usufructuary rights on crown land – been fully implemented, the situation would have been much improved. Greatly increased spending on food and shelter, education and health would not have solved all the problems of fringe-dwelling communities, but it would have made inroads into them. If more reserves had been created and preserved for the Aborigines, even if held in trust, they would have entered the twentieth century with at least some stake in the country. There seems to be no compelling reason why Australian courts could not have followed those both in Canada and the United States in determining that the Aborigines had a legal interest in reserves whenever and however created.

If the Aboriginal right to use and occupy all land held under lease had been defended by colonial governments and courts, the nature of frontier contact may have been very different. Settlers would have been forced to negotiate with resident Aboriginal clans and not shoot them off the ground. The successful pioneer would have been, of necessity, linguist, diplomat and ethnographer. Negotiations may have replaced brute force in the process of settling the land. This might appear fanciful, but there were enough examples of individual pioneers who did successfully follow this course to show that it could have been much more commonly adopted.

Aborigines did not forget that the land had once been theirs. Their sense of injustice continued to burn. A missionary who worked with Victorian Aborigines for many years in the second half of the nineteenth century observed that they took everything that the Europeans gave them 'as their due'. 'We have got their country,' he explained, 'and they get what is given as rent. All this makes it difficult to deal with them, and I must say that most of my troubles have come from this source'.[12] James Dawson, who was a keen student of Western District tribes, told a Victorian royal commission in 1877 that it was

> a mistake to imagine that they are not fully aware of the position the occupancy of their country by the white man has placed them in, and of their strong claims upon him for proper maintenance and protection. They are very sensitive on this point, and assert that they are entitled to be well housed, well clothed, and well fed in consideration for the loss of their 'hunting grounds'.[13]

In 1872 the blacks living around the Braidwood goldfield in southern New South Wales approached the local police inspector asking him to intercede with the government on their behalf. The spokesman for the local people wanted to get some land that they could call their 'own in reality', where they could 'settle down and which the old people [could] call their home'. He explained that 'everyone objects to our hunting on his land, and we think the blacks are entitled to live in their own country'.[14] Several other communities attempted to gain access to land in other parts of Australia in the last few decades of the nineteenth century.

BLACK HISTORY – WHITE HISTORY

The Aborigines probably knew little of the first campaign fought by philanthropic people and religious enthusiasts for land rights, or of the various attempts by the Imperial government to recognise their 'proprietary in the soil' and provide some form of compensation for land taken by the settlers. But by the twentieth century Aboriginal communities had a vigorous tradition of oral history, which provided an alternative version of white–Aboriginal relations. It included many stories of death and deprivation, but also embodied two beliefs about the British government — or more correctly about Queen Victoria. They were that the Queen had given the Aborigines freehold title to their reserves in recognition of their prior ownership of the land and had provided for their welfare as a way of compensating them for the loss of it.

This view wasn't entirely correct. There were no title deeds signed by the Queen hidden away in the archives. But the black oral tradition was in fact closer to the truth than the version of events that gained ascendancy among the white community during the late nineteenth and early twentieth centuries. The settler version included the belief that all Aboriginal rights had disappeared in 1788; that the British government had never recognised any form of native title in Australia; that if anyone was to blame for that situation it was the Aborigines themselves. They were either too primitive to be accorded land rights or too feeble to fight for them. What conflict there was — and it was forgotten remarkably quickly — was more a matter of crime than warfare or insurgency. It resulted not from usurped land but from the savagery of the blacks and the viciousness of disreputable whites who lurked on the outer fringes of settlement. When the settlers provided reserves or welfare for the Aborigines it was due to benevolence, and embodied no suggestion of rights overridden or obligations owing. During the first half of the twentieth century, white Australians wrote the Aborigines — and therefore the land question – out of their history altogether. They were therefore ill-prepared for the re-emergence of the land rights crusade in the 1970s and 1980s.

NINE

Mabo and Wik Remake the Law of the Land

On Wednesday 3 June 1992, the High Court of Australia delivered its judgement in the case of *Mabo v. Queensland*. It represented a legal revolution, one that was closely related to many of the themes dealt with in this book. The case and the book were related in other ways as well.

The question of Aboriginal and Islander land rights was a recurring theme of long discussions I had with the principal plaintiff, Eddie Mabo, during the late 1970s. While he spoke compellingly of his life as a boy on Murray Island and of his family's traditional land, I told him a little about Australian law – or as much as I knew of it at the time. I still vividly remember the occasion when a colleague and I explained to Eddie that, regardless of his customary rights, the whole of Murray Island was considered to be crown land and that, as Queensland's solicitor-general was later to tell the High Court, he and his fellow islanders were technically trespassers who could at any moment be legitimately driven off the island. On hearing this for the first time, Eddie stared at us for a long while in silence, with a look combining horror and incredulity. How could anything so obvious as his property rights be disregarded by the white man's law?

In a later conversation, and drawing on my meagre

knowledge, I suggested that legally the Murray Islanders would have a much stronger case in the courts than the Aborigines because they used the land for gardening – at that time I thought, as did many others, that the Aborigines had lost their land because they did not use it 'properly' or 'mix their labour with the soil'. I also had a rudimentary knowledge of the American concept of native title, which I explained to him.

Eddie Mabo's awareness of his parlous legal situation was sharpened a short time later when he went to the Torres Straits to work as a research assistant on an oral history project we were both involved in. He got as far as Thursday Island. He was refused permission to land on any of the other islands in the Straits. A reputation as a radical was a heavy burden in Queensland at the time. For Eddie, the rejection was devastating. He could not go home. He was not only landless in the eyes of white man's law, he was an exile as well.

The issue of land rights continued to be a concern at James Cook University at the time, and in 1981 the students' union held a conference on the subject. For the first time Eddie and some of his friends could discuss their problem with experts in the field, and the decision to pursue the matter through the courts was made. As the case negotiated its tortuous course, I began to question the concept of *terra nullius*. The relevant research resulted in *The Law of the Land*, the second edition of which appeared just after the eleven-year saga of the Mabo case came to an end, and seven months after Eddie Mabo's tragic and premature death.

The High Court decisively rejected the concept of *terra nullius*, arguing that it was a totally inappropriate foundation for the Australian legal system. In doing so, the court answered many of the stringent criticisms of Australian jurisprudence advanced in *The Law of the Land,* and in the process confirmed the arguments around which the book was crafted. Justice Brennan remarked that the 'fiction by which the rights and interests of the indigenous people in the land were treated as non existent' was justified by a policy that 'has no place in the contemporary law of this country'. Neither domestic nor international law could sustain the traditions of the past. Brennan explained:

> A common law doctrine founded on unjust discrimination in the enjoyment of civil and political rights demands reconsideration. It is contrary both to international standards and to the fundamental values of our common law to entrench a discriminatory rule which, because of the supposed position on the scale of social organisation of the indigenous inhabitants of a settled colony, denies them a right to occupy their traditional lands.[1]

The easy acceptance of *terra nullius* in Australia resulted from the confusion of sovereignty and property, as was argued earlier in the book. Justice Brennan noted that it is

> only the fallacy of equating sovereignty and beneficial ownership of land that gives rise to the notion that native title is extinguished by the acquisition of sovereignty.[2]

The court determined that the Murray Islanders had a form of land ownership in 1879, governed by their own customs and rules. In the same way, the Australian Aborigines owned their land at the time of the earlier claims of sovereignty in 1788, 1824 and 1829. No elaborate proofs were necessary to establish this fact. Brennan argued that the ownership of land within a territory 'in the exclusive occupation of a people must be vested in that people: land is susceptible of ownership, and there are no other owners'.[3]

Justice Toohey was equally succinct. 'If occupation by an indigenous people is an established fact at the time of annexation,' he asked, 'why should more be required?'[4] The type of land use, the different economic organisation of the various Indigenous societies, did not alter the situation. The central desert nomads were as much the owners of their land as the gardeners of Murray Island. Toohey explained:

> While this case concerns the Meriam people, the legal issues fall to be determined according to fundamental principles of common law and colonial constitutional law applicable throughout Australia. The Meriam people are in culturally significant ways different from the Aboriginal people of Australia, who in turn differ from each other. But . . . no basic distinctions need be made, for the purpose of determining what interests exist in ancestral lands of indigenous peoples of Australia, between the Meriam people and those who occupied and occupy the Australian mainland. The relevant principles are the same.[5]

Once sovereignty was claimed over the various parts of Australia, the Indigenous people became British subjects protected by the law in the same way as the immigrant English. Immediately on acquisition, Toohey explained, 'Indigenous inhabitants became British subjects whose interests were to be protected in the case of a settled colony by the immediate operation of the common law'.[6]

Justices Deane and Gaudron pursued the argument further. While the Crown gained what was known as the radical title to all the lands in the colony, the common law protected the property rights of the Indigenous inhabitants. The strong presumption of the common law was that interests in property which existed under native law or custom were not obliterated by the act of State establishing a new British Colony but were preserved and protected by the domestic law of the Colony.[7]

The High Court had brought Australian jurisprudence into line with Australian history. Justices Deane and Gaudron considered the problem of British intentions towards the Aborigines at the establishment of the first settlement, which were dealt with in the first chapter of this book. They believed that the normal practices of British colonisation should be assumed in the absence of any instructions to the contrary. They gave credence to the suggestion that official policy was influenced by Banks's advice that Australia was largely uninhabited. It is unlikely, they believed,

> that there was any actual but unexpressed intent on the part of the Crown that the State establishing the Colony of New South Wales should reverse the assumption of the common law or extinguish native interests in land throughout the more than 1.4 million square miles of the colony.

At the same time, they appreciated that

> notwithstanding that the rights of use or occupancy under a common law native title recognised by the law of a settled British Colony were binding upon the Crown, the native inhabitants of such a Colony in the eighteenth century were in an essentially helpless position if that title was wrongfully terminated by the Crown or those acting on its behalf.[8]

The court had clearly absorbed the lessons about Australian history embodied in the new historiography of European–Aboriginal relations that had been written over the previous twenty years. Law and history now coincided in the view that the Aborigines were not dispossessed in one apocalyptic moment in 1788 but in a piecemeal fashion over a long period of time. Brennan observed that

> Aboriginal rights and interests were not stripped away by the operation of the common law on the first settlement by British colonists, but by the exercise of a sovereign authority over land exercised recurrently by Governments. To treat the dispossession of the Australian Aborigines as the working out of the Crown's acquisition of ownership of all land on first settlement is contrary to history. Aborigines were dispossessed of the land parcel by parcel, to make way for expanding colonial settlement.[9]

In the case of Murray Island, the original native title survived from 1879 to the present. Nothing the Queensland government did during the intervening 113 years – no legislation, no executive act – extinguished the Islanders' rights 'as against the whole world to possession, occupation, use and enjoyment'[10] of their land. Aboriginal communities who were still living on their traditional lands and had not received freehold title under land rights legislation must be assumed to be the possessors of native title under the common law. Justice Brennan explained that where traditional connection with the land had been 'substantially maintained, the traditional community title of that clan or group can be said to remain in existence'.[11]

Justice Toohey argued that it was not so much a matter of continuity of tradition as continuity of possession that mattered:

But modification of traditional society in itself does not mean traditional title no longer exists. Traditional title arises from the fact of occupation, not the occupation of a particular society or way of life. So long as occupation by a traditional society is established now and at the time of annexation, traditional rights exist.[12]

Toohey made the even more crucial point that when there was any question about the existence of native title it was up to the Crown to show that the Aboriginal interest had been extinguished. 'Previous interests in the land may be said to survive,' he argued, '*unless* it can be shown that the effect of annexation is to destroy them'. The onus rests with 'those claiming that traditional title does not exist'.[13]

The court's reasoning focused attention on the critical question of when and how Aboriginal and Islander land rights were extinguished, if indeed they ever were. The judges accepted that the Aboriginal interest was extinguished bit by bit over a long period of time. They had no doubt about the capacity of government to extinguish the Aboriginal interest. But the intention to do so had to be plain and clear. In adopting this view, they referred not only to North American cases dealing with native title but also to Australian and English property law. Thus, in a case before the High Court in 1904 Samuel Griffith noted that 'it is a general rule to be followed in the construction of Statutes' that they were 'not to be construed as interfering with vested interests unless the intention is manifest'.[14] Native title in Australia was not extinguished by the creation of reserves or by legislation, which did no more than 'provide in general terms for the alienation of the waste lands of the colony or Crown land'.[15] But the Aboriginal interest was lost when there had been 'an alienation of land by the Crown inimical to the continuance of traditional title'. Justice Brennan explained that

> Where the Crown has validly alienated land by granting an interest that is wholly or partially inconsistent with a continuing right to enjoy native title, native title is extinguished to the extent of the inconsistency. Thus native title has been extinguished by grants of estates of freehold or of leases but not necessarily by grants of lesser interest.[16]

PASTORAL LEASES AND THE WIK CASE

It was widely appreciated that in the Mabo judgement the High Court had carried through a legal revolution. This was a view shared by commentators both inside Australia and outside it, more particularly in the common law world. Both supporters of the court and its numerous detractors understood the significance of the decision to recognise native title and thereby overturn the doctrine of *terra nullius*. The clear implication was that jurists and officials had been wrong in the past. They had failed to see that the Aborigines and Islanders had a traditional form of land ownership which could both be recognised and protected by the common law.

Under the new dispensation, all Indigenous communities had either once been landowners or, in the case of the Murray Islanders, still were because at no point had governments extinguished their rights in a clear and plain manner. The necessary assumption was that those communities which still lived on their own country, and where the land was not owned by someone else, could assume that, like the Murray Islanders, they would eventually be seen to have native title to their traditional lands. But the overwhelming view – shared by supporters and opponents of the court – was that only vacant crown land was in question, with Justice Toohey observing that nothing in the judgement should be taken to suggest that the titles 'of those to whom land has been alienated by the Crown may now be disturbed'.[17] Until 1996 it was assumed that this principle would apply to pastoral leases.

THE WIK CASE

Pastoral leases are one of the most common forms of land tenure in Australia. As we have seen above, they have been a feature of the pastoral industry since the middle of the nineteenth century. At the time of the Wik judgement there were 170 000 pastoral leases occupying 42 per cent of the country. Many covered marginal country with low carrying capacity but others provided access to prime grazing land. Some families had been on the same country for several generations and, not unreasonably, thought the land in question belonged to them. They had reason to think they were immune from any native title claims.

In the Mabo judgement the High Court had determined that the Crown had always been able to extinguish native title and had done so when granting a legal interest in land inconsistent with it. Both a freehold title and a lease would have this effect. Chief Justice Brennan had concluded that the grant of two small leases on the Murray Islands had extinguished native title in the specific areas. This was unsurprising. It was settled law that a lease gave the lessee exclusive possession for the term of the lease. The principle was embodied in the Native Title Act of 1993 which sought to incorporate the Mabo judgement in legislation. The Act declared that the High Court had held that native title was extinguished by valid government acts that are inconsistent with the continued existence of native title rights and interests, such as the grant of freehold or leasehold estates.[18]

The Wik case began in June 1993 when the Wik and Thayorre people of western Cape York sought a declaration of their native title rights over their traditional land, two parcels of which had been embodied in pastoral leases. Their case was heard in the Federal Court in January 1996. The decision went against them, with Justice Drummond declaring that the grant of pastoral leases had necessarily extinguished any native title that might have existed prior to the granting of the leases. The argument to the contrary was made more difficult because in Queensland the reservation in favour of Aboriginal use and access had been removed from pastoral leases before the ones relevant to the case had been issued. In this sense Queensland leases were quite different from those in Western Australia, the Northern Territory and South Australia.

Given the apparent facts of the case and judgement by Justice Drummond, it was confidently expected that on appeal the High Court would find that native title had not survived. The weight of legal representation was heavily tipped away from the Wik and Thayorre plaintiffs with the Commonwealth, Queensland, Victoria, South Australia, Western Australia and Northern Territory governments represented as well as several mining corporations with interests in the region. Mining and farming spokesmen were so confident as to the outcome that they pressed the High Court to hurry with their decision and so provide security to their industries.

By a majority of four to three the court overturned the judgement of Justice Drummond, declaring that the creation of pastoral leases did not confer on the grantee rights wholly inconsistent with the concurrent and continuing exercise of any rights or interests which the Wik peoples could prove to exist. And even more critically the majority of the court held that the grant of a pastoral lease did not necessarily extinguish all incidents of Aboriginal title.

The surprise and alarm provoked by the Wik case was expressed in an editorial headed 'Wik decision disappointing' in the *Financial Review* on the morning after the news broke. Farmers and miners, the editor observed

> have every right to be alarmed at yesterday's long-awaited High Court decision in the Wik case. Contrary to the expectations of most legal commentators, and State and Commonwealth governments alike, the High Court found that native title may still exist over land upon which pastoral leases have been granted.[19]

The leaders of the National Farmers Federation declared that development in Australia's rural industry would grind to a halt. Miners claimed that investment in their industry would dry up. The Queensland and Western Australian governments demanded a special premiers' conference to 'help clean up the mess'.[20] In January 1997, the Prime Minister, John Howard, met with State and Territory leaders who demanded that native title be extinguished on pastoral leases. In a press conference following the meeting Mr Howard observed:

> I've got to say again that the Wik decision has fundamentally altered one of the key understandings of the Native Title Act and it was never envisaged. The former Prime Minister positively asserted in his second reading speech that it was the view of the Government and he so assured the pastoral industry and he so

assured the mining industry that the grant of a leasehold estate extinguished native title.[21]

The political storm whipped up by Wik continued to rage throughout 1997 involving politicians, both chambers of the federal parliament, state governments, Aboriginal organisations, industry groups and independent commentators. The long-term consequences of the judgement are even now not fully apparent.

Why did the Wik decision create so much turmoil? Two things stand out. A lot of land was involved and, unlike vacant crown land, it had economic value and there were many powerful groups with attendant legal interests which the High Court had apparently diminished. The judgement was also quite unexpected, flying in the face of assurances issued by political leaders and weighty opinions delivered by expensive lawyers. So why did the judgement turn out as it did? Or rather why did four of seven judges decide that pastoral leases did not necessarily extinguish native title?

Mabo had established that Aborigines and Islanders had a form of land tenure which could be recognised by the common law. It could be extinguished by the action of the Crown and had been, historically, over large areas of Australia's most productive land. But it had to be extinguished in a clear and plain manner. The critical issue on which all else turned was whether a pastoral lease could effect the extinguishment in the way that a traditional common law lease certainly would. The answer was found not in exploring the characteristics of normal leases but in looking at the specific history of pastoral leases which established to the satisfaction of the majority on the bench that they were not at all like leases known to British law, their name notwithstanding. History was the key to understanding the nature of the pastoral lease and the majority of judges gave some time to the subject. Justice Toohey observed that what was important about the history of relevant land legislation in New South Wales and Queensland was that it was essentially the story of the relationship between the Crown and those who wished to take up land for pastoral purposes. It reflected

> the desire of pastoralists for some form of security of title and the clear intention of the Crown that the pastoralists should not acquire the freehold of large areas of land, the future use of which could not be readily foreseen.[22]

The four judges who found for the Wik peoples – Justices Toohey, Gaudron, Gummow and Kirby – stressed the importance of understanding where pastoral leases had come from, and how they had emerged from the particular geographical and historical circumstances of Australia. They were the product of statute, not the common law as made and moulded by judicial decision. 'To approach the matter by reference to legislation,' Justice Toohey observed

> is not to turn one's back on centuries of history nor is it to impugn basic principles of property law. Rather, it is to recognise historical development, the changes in law over centuries and the need for property law to accommodate the very different situation in this country.[23]

Given the importance of understanding the origins of the pastoral lease, Justices Kirby, Toohey and Gaudron focused on the policies of the Imperial government in the 1840s. Both Toohey and Kirby quoted from Earl Grey's dispatch to

Governor Fitzroy of 11 February 1848, indicating that leases granted to the squatters gave the grantee only an exclusive right of pasturage and did not provide any authority to deprive the Aborigines of their traditional rights.[24] The Colonial Office's direct intervention of 1848–50 provided, Kirby believed, 'the common starting point for the evolution of Crown leasehold tenure', including pastoral leases in all the Australian states.[25] Justice Gaudron concurred, observing that pastoral leases were not the creations of the common law but derived from the provisions and instructions emanating from the Colonial Office.[26] The direct link could be easily traced in the wording of later colonial and state laws dealing with pastoral land even where, as in the case of Queensland, the reservation in favour of Aboriginal traditional rights had been excised. Significantly, leases granted under the Queensland Land Act of 1910 – and this applied to two of three leases in question – were for 'pastoral purposes only'.[27]

So the critical point was not the nature of native title but the characteristics of pastoral leases and whether they could be thought to have extinguished the pre-existing rights of the Aborigines. The four judges in the majority were quite clear that they didn't. Toohey provided the best summary of a number of closely related arguments:

> A pastoral lease under the relevant legislation granted to the lessee possession of the land for pastoral purposes. And the grant necessarily gave the lessee such possession as was required for occupation of the land for those purposes. As has been seen, each lease contained a number of reservations of rights of entry both specific and general. The lessee's right to possession must yield to those reservations. There is nothing in the statute which authorised the lease, or in the lease itself, which conferred

on the grantee rights to exclusive possession, in particular possession exclusive of all rights and interests of the indigenous inhabitants whose occupation derived from their traditional title. In so far as those rights and interests involved going on to or remaining on the land, it cannot be said that the lease conferred on the grantee rights to exclusive possession.[28]

For the historian a related and intriguing question is why didn't colonial politicians actually extinguish Aboriginal traditional rights on pastoral leaseholds? A number of answers suggest themselves. As we have already seen, the reservations relating to Aboriginal rights were rarely if ever enforced by police, magistrates or the courts. This was very much the case in the self-governing colonies of eastern Australia, although in Western Australia, where until 1890 the Colonial Office still determined policy, Aboriginal rights were taken much more seriously. But over the vast pastoral lands of eastern Australia the reservations were never used to inhibit or control the actions of the pastoralists. There would have been outrage if they had been implemented, followed, no doubt, by legislation formally extinguishing native title. The prevailing view that the Aborigines had no right to land meant that extinguishment was quite unnecessary for there was nothing there to legislate out of existence. The equally powerful belief that the Aborigines were dying out further strengthened the likelihood that nothing would need to be done about the matter. Few colonists in the later nineteenth or early twentieth centuries would have imagined that one hundred years later a superior court would revive Aboriginal statutory rights which had lain dormant almost from the time that they were accorded recognition by the Colonial Office.

In the beginning the British had not dealt with the question of Indigenous property rights because they thought the continent was largely uninhabited, that is, there weren't any Aborigines to consider. When the Imperial authorities granted 'Responsible Government' to the five colonies of eastern Australia the colonial politicians didn't concern themselves with Indigenous property rights because they were sure none existed.

The irony of it all impressed Justice Kirby who noted that no Queensland legislation

> expressly abolished Aboriginal native title. This is scarcely surprising, having regard to the then understanding of the law, that such title had not survived annexation of Australia to the Crown. Nor did the legislation expressly provide for the curtailment or limitation of Aboriginal rights, or any manner of dealing with the land from which could be inferred the purpose of abolishing Aboriginal native title. Again, this is unsurprising, in the light of the understanding of Aboriginal legal rights at the time, the provisions in limited legislation about particular aspects of Aboriginal policy and the then prevailing policy of ignoring Aboriginals, leaving them as far as possible untouched by Australian law . . .[29]

The uproar which followed the Wik judgement did nothing to slow the momentum of native title claims or the pursuit of certainty, definition and justice through the Native Title Tribunal and the courts – the supreme courts of the states, the Federal Court and ultimately the High Court itself – all of which had to deal with the consequences which inevitably followed the overthrow of *terra nullius*.

TEN

The Aftermath of Mabo

In North America, many hundreds of native title cases have come before the courts since the 1820s when the Supreme Court first defined the concept. It is not surprising, then, that Australian courts have considered numerous native title cases since 1992 relating to matters not directly relevant to the Mabo judgement itself or only treated at the time in a general way. For his part, Eddie Mabo was intensely interested in claiming his traditional rights to the waters surrounding the Murray and Darnley islands and the related question of fishing and hunting among the offshore reefs and rocky outcrops. They were not pursued in his own case, but were taken up by other individuals and communities later in the 1990s.

In October 1999 the High Court delivered its judgement in the case of *Yanner v. Eaton* which related to the traditional right to hunt and the extent to which it was controlled by state (in this case, Queensland's) fauna protection legislation. How the case reached the High Court can be quickly outlined. Murandoo Yanner, a Ganggalida man from Queensland's Gulf Country, went hunting late in 1994 with members of his Gunnamulla clan. On two separate occasions the party took juvenile crocodiles from Cliffdale Creek, ate some of the meat and took both meat and skins home to put them in their freezers. Yanner's house was raided by Queensland police officers and he was charged before the Mount Isa Magistrates Court with having taken the crocodiles while not holding a licence or permit issued under the authority of the Fauna Conservation Act.

Perhaps to the surprise of many people the magistrate dismissed the charge. He concluded that Yanner's clan had been hunting crocodiles from before the time that the common law was introduced in Queensland and that the taking of juveniles had totemic significance. The Fauna Act did not prohibit or restrict native title holders from

> gaining access to the land or waters for the purpose of satisfying their personal, domestic or non-commercial communal needs and in exercise or enjoyment of their native title rights and interests.[1]

The Queensland government took the case to the state's Court of Appeal and won. The matter was remitted back to the Magistrates Court. Before this took place Yanner was given special leave to appeal to the High Court, where he won by a five to two majority.

During the proceedings many critical questions relating to the nature of native title were discussed. The Queensland and Commonwealth governments argued that the Fauna Act gave the Crown full, beneficial and absolute ownership of all wild fauna and had therefore extinguished any pre-existing native title rights. The majority of judges took the view, common in similar cases in Canada and New Zealand, that legislation which regulated fishing and hunting could not be construed as extinguishing native title rights as recognised by the Native Title Act which passed through the Federal Parliament in

1993. Queensland's Fauna Act did not prohibit Yanner from 'hunting or fishing for the crocodiles he took for satisfying personal, domestic or non-commercial communal needs'.[2] Unless native title had been explicitly extinguished, it had survived.

There was a similar result when the question of sea rights came before the High Court in the case of *The Commonwealth v. Yarmirr* in October 2001. It concerned the waters surrounding a group of small islands – of which Croker is the largest – lying off the coast of north-west Arnhem Land, roughly 200 kilometres from Darwin. The local estate groups or Yurwurrumu had received title to their land under the 1976 Northern Territory Land Rights Act. They now wanted their native title recognised over adjacent waters, much of it coming within the three nautical mile limit, asserting exclusive rights of ownership, occupancy, possession and use of the area in question.

Like other 'saltwater people' the Croker Islanders regarded the adjacent seas as much their property as the land. The leading academic authority on the subject, Nonie Sharp, explained that the 'rich and diverse sea traditions and beliefs' of the saltwater people of tropical Australia share a number of common themes. Property in the sea is inherited from ancestors. The tenures are clan-owned, extending across the foreshore to home reefs and lagoons. Mary Yarmirr, the first respondent in the Croker Island case, told the court that her clan's sea territory extended 'as far as my eyes can see'.[3] Spiritual inheritances from the sea itself link living saltwater peoples with the Creator Spirit Beings, sea deities and culture heroes whose sea journeys mark out sea territories and who remain ongoing presences. The saltwater people have comprehensive knowledge of the maritime territory – of tides and currents, reefs and channels, fish and shellfish and mammals.

In their submission to the Federal Court, anthropologists retained by the Croker Islanders listed the rights and interests which were claimed. They included the right of senior members of the Yurwurrumu to:

- be recognised as the traditional owners of the estate, including the seabed, the water and all life within it
- transmit all the inherited rights, interests and duties to subsequent generations, and to exclude or restrict others from entering any area of the estate
- control the use of and access to the subsistence and other resources, including the ritual resources, of the estate by all people including younger members of the Yurwurrumu and to engage in the trade and exchange of estate resources
- close off areas of the estate on the death of members and to decide when they shall be reopened to use
- speak for and make decisions about the significant places in the estate
- receive, possess and safeguard the cultural and religious knowledge associated with the estate and . . . to pass it on to the younger generation
- speak for and make decisions about the estate's resources, and the use of those resources, and the right and duties to safeguard them.[4]

The Croker Islanders lodged a native title claim in November 1994 and it was heard in the Federal Court in 1997. Justice Olney accepted that native title existed over all the areas of the sea and the seabed as claimed and in doing so rejected the contention of the Commonwealth that because the common law only applies as far as low water mark there could be no native title beyond that point. But the title was limited in a number of important ways. Use of the traditional areas was restricted to personal, domestic or non-commercial fishing for subsistence or cultural purposes, and to protecting places of cultural and spiritual knowledge.

But most significantly the court rejected any claim to exclusive possession or occupation of the sea because such power of exclusion would fly in the face of the right recognised universally in international law of so-called 'innocent passage' and of ancient common law rights to navigate and to fish. It was a result which satisfied neither side of the argument. The Commonwealth and Northern Territory governments asked the full Federal Court to strike down native title – the Croker Islanders to strengthen it. But the case emerged from the court in much the same way that it had entered it. A final appeal to the High Court brought little change. The bench split in three ways. Justices Callinan and McHugh found for the Commonwealth and would have struck down native title. Justice Kirby believed that native title rights should be considerably strengthened while still co-existing with rights to fish and right of passage. 'The result I favour in this case,' he wrote, 'is scarcely a surprising one':

> Indeed it appears a reasonable and just one. In the remote and sparsely inhabited north of Australia is a group of Aboriginal Australians living according to their own traditions. Within that group, as the primary judge [Justice Olney] accepted they observe their traditional laws and customs as their forebears have done for untold centuries before Australia's modern legal system arrived. They have 'a sea country' and claim to possess it exclusively for the group. They rely on, and extract, resources from the sea and accord particular areas spiritual respect. The

sea is essential to their survival as a group. In earlier times, they could not fight off the 'white man' with his superior arms; but now the 'white man's' laws have changed to give them, under certain conditions, the superior arms of legal protection. They yield their rights in their 'sea country' to rights to navigation, in and through the area, allowed under international and Australian law, and to licensed fishing, allowed under statute. But, otherwise, they assert a present right under their own laws and customs, now protected by the 'white man's' law, to insist on effective consultation and a power of veto over other fishing, tourism, resource exploration and like activities within their sea country because it is theirs and is now protected by Australian law. If that right is upheld, it will have obvious economic consequences for them to determine – just as the rights of other Australians, in their title holdings, afford them entitlements that they may exercise and exploit or withhold as they decide. The situation of this group of indigenous Australians appears to be precisely that for which Mabo was decided and the Act enacted. The opinion to the contrary is unduly narrow.[5]

But Kirby's eloquent appeal won no converts on the bench. The majority judgement of justices Gleeson, Gaudron, Gummow and Hayne upheld the Federal Court findings that there was a fundamental inconsistency between the asserted native title rights and interests and the common law public rights of fishing and navigation. 'These two sets of rights,' they declared, 'cannot stand together'.[6]

A central question in all discussion of native title is that of extinguishment. In Mabo the High Court determined that Aborigines and Islanders were in possession of the continent when at various times the British claimed sovereignty over the land mass. The incoming common law gave protection to native title but over a long period of time it was gradually extinguished in favour of the incoming settlers. How and when extinguishment happened is an important question for Indigenous people, jurists and historians alike. It has been considered in a number of cases that have reached the High Court, notably *Fejo and Mills v. The Northern Territory*, *Western Australia v. Ward*, and *The Yorta Yorta Aboriginal Community v. Victoria*.

The Yorta Yorta case was initiated in February 1994 when the community lodged an application with the Native Title Tribunal. It was accepted and in September a mediation process was initiated, beginning with a conference in the Shepparton Town Hall followed by meetings in other towns in the region. Wayne Atkinson, a leading member of the Yorta Yorta community, recalled the opening of the Shepparton meeting:

> The Yorta Yorta presentations went to the heart of what it is to be Yorta Yorta. We raised the big issues about land care and management and spoke of the degrading treatment of the waterways, and the loss of plant and animal life. Some of the elders spoke of the land, and of the ancient forests looking tired and in need of rest. In hindsight, it felt as though the tide of history was at least turning in our favour. It felt as though we were on the edge of a new start.[7]

But the mediation process broke down and in May 1995 the claim was referred to the Federal Court.

The Yorta Yorta claim related to scattered areas of crown land within the traditional ancestral territory straddling the Murray River, including the Barmah and Moira state forests and land around the Goulburn and Ovens rivers. The case attracted intense interest. It was the first one to relate to native title within an area of close settlement. Many individuals and interest groups ranged up against the Yorta Yorta claim. In all, 470 opponents came forward including cattlemen, water users, timber millers, recreational fishermen, beekeepers, municipal councils and state governments. The case was also the first one to be mounted by a community that had been dispossessed of much of its land by the middle of the nineteenth century.

For seven years *The Yorta Yorta Aboriginal Community v. Victoria* made its way through three hearings – before a single judge in the Federal Court, the full Federal Court and finally the High Court which handed down its decision in December 2002. In all, eleven judges considered the question. Only one of the three judges in the full Federal Court and two of seven in the High Court were willing to accept that the community had made a valid native title claim. Though criticised in detail by his colleagues, the original trial judge, Justice Olney, put his stamp on the case from the beginning.

He argued that the claimant group had failed what he termed the 'test of occupation', a state of affairs which had existed for over a century for

> notwithstanding the genuine efforts of members of the claimant group to revive the lost culture of their ancestors, native title rights and interests once lost are not capable of revival. Traditional native title having expired, the Crown's radical title expanded to a full beneficial title.

The point was driven home in numerous related passages, all of which doomed the Yorta Yorta quest for native title. Olney declared that the evidence did not support a finding

> that the descendants of the original inhabitants of the claimed land have occupied the land in the relevant sense since 1788 nor

that they have continued to observe and acknowledge, throughout that period, the traditional laws and customs in relation to land of their forebears. The facts in this case led inevitably to the conclusions that before the end of the nineteenth century the ancestors through whom the claimants claim title had ceased to occupy their traditional lands in accordance with their traditional laws and customs. The tide of history has indeed washed away any real acknowledgement of their traditional laws and any real observance of their traditional customs. The foundation of the claim to native title in relation to land previously occupied by those ancestors having disappeared, the native title rights and interests previously enjoyed are not capable of revival.[8]

Olney's judgement faced some criticism as it was considered in the higher courts. It was thought that he applied conditions which made it almost impossible to prove cultural continuity; that he privileged European written accounts over Aboriginal oral testimony; and that he did not focus sufficiently on current laws and customs as required by the Native Title Act which, Justice Kirby pointed out, related to the question of whether the Yorta Yorta people 'now acknowledge and observe traditional laws and customs by which they have a connection with the land and waters claimed by them'.[9] But, if anything, the fact that the original judgement was upheld despite accompanying criticism emphasised how emphatic the defeat of the Yorta Yorta was and how significant it was in relation to any future native title claims to emerge from areas of early European settlement. As if to emphasise the critical point, Justice Olney referred four times to the impact of 'the tides of history' washing away any hope that many communities had that they could achieve recognition of their land rights by following a path through the courts blazed by Eddie

Mabo and his legal team. Those groups who had felt the impact of settlement most severely and for the longest period of time were the very ones who could expect least from the native title process. That was the inescapable conclusion following the High Court's rejection of the Yorta Yorta claim by a five to two majority in December 2002.

The Larrakia people of the Darwin area suffered a similar defeat in the High Court in September 1998 in *Fejo v. The Northern Territory*. They had sought to establish their native title over land within the Darwin metropolitan area and to prevent its subdivision by the territory government. The land in dispute had been granted in fee simple by the South Australian government in 1882 but had been compulsorily acquired by the Commonwealth in 1927. It was not used as planned and in 1980 it once again became vacant crown land. In December 1997 the Larrakia people sought a declaration from the Federal Court recognising their native title.

There were, then, only two substantial issues to be considered by the High Court when the case was presented. The first was whether a grant of freehold extinguishes native title so that no form of native title can co-exist with freehold title. The second was whether extinguishment was permanent and absolute or if it was possible for native title to revive or be re-recognised when the land returned to the Crown. The court's answer was both simple and emphatic. Six judges provided a joint judgement. Justice Kirby wrote one of his own. But all were of one mind. Native title was completely extinguished by the grant of a freehold estate. No co-existing or concurrent rights could survive, not because of the actual use of the land in question but because of the legal rights conferred by the respective titles. The grant of freehold extinguished native title permanently, regardless of the land being held by the Crown in the future. Native title cannot revive after the grant of a freehold title even if the Indigenous society in question and Indigenous law survives.[10]

Most interest attached to the individual judgement of Justice Kirby, the most liberal member of the bench. However, if anything, his arguments were more emphatic than those of his colleagues. He argued that there were two basic considerations in the court's decision. The first was that a court should not destroy or contradict an important and settled principle of the legal system. The second, that in every society rights in land which afford an enforceable entitlement to exclusive possession were basic to social peace and order 'as well as to economic investment and prosperity'. There was a fundamental inconsistency between fee simple and native title. Kirby explained that the

> inconsistency lies not in the facts or in the way the land is actually used. It lies in a comparison between the inherently fragile native title right, susceptible to extinguishment or defeasance, and the legal rights which fee simple confers.[11]

These principles were not affected by the actual use of the land – by the facts on the ground. Unused, unoccupied land held under freehold title could wipe out native title even while traditional owners continued to live there and an absentee title holder didn't. 'Doubtless,' Kirby observed, 'the bundle of interests we now call native title would continue, for a time at least, within the world of Aboriginal custom'. He conceded that such Aboriginal interests might 'still do so'. But all to no avail. In his peroration he declared

> Legal history, authority and principle therefore combine. But they are also supported by considerations of legal policy . . . Native title is extinguished by a grant in fee simple. This statement of law must be taken as settled. It does not admit of qualification.[12]

Rather than bringing the debate to an end, Kirby's determination to see the whole matter as settled raises more questions than it answers. What, for instance, are the unexplained 'considerations of legal policy'? Are we to assume this is a roundabout way of referring to politics? Was the High Court reacting to the uproar that followed the Wik judgement still at its height when the Fejo case was being considered – to the two-pronged attack on the court's so-called 'judicial activism' and the widely expressed, sedulously fanned fears about suburban backyards?

It was as though the need to allay land owners' insecurities led to a policy of isolating native title from any outside source of jurisprudential support – either from the common law or from native title traditions in comparable countries. The critical question at hand was whether a freehold title could be encumbered by an unextinguished native title. The political sensitivity of the question in the late 1990s scarcely needs emphasising. But the common law has innumerable devices directly relevant to the matter. Titles can be, and are, encumbered with easements, rights of way, profits and a whole range of unwritten customary rights which do not derive from legislation. English property law allows for many situations where competing or complementary rights can co-exist. The fact that native title had its origins outside the common law does not seem to provide a convincing case for how it should be protected once it comes within it. This was surely true of a

The Aftermath of Mabo

vast array of customary law and of land titles in the Celtic fringe of the United Kingdom that were quite different from fee simple – titles in Ireland, the Isle of Man, and the Shetland and Orkney islands, for instance. Kirby argues as though the extraordinary flexibility of British property law lost its character when it was brought to Australia. The very flexibility that was the product of the slow expansion of English power throughout the British Isles failed to operate when the same process of colonisation took place at the Antipodes. It is pertinent that the pastoral leases were created by Colonial Office officials steeped in British legal traditions.

Having insisted that British property law had no relevance to an understanding of the characteristics of native title, the High Court then turned its attention to the jurisprudential traditions of other settler societies. Here too any external buttress to native title was to be taken away. Kirby explained that care must be exercised in the use of judicial authorities of other former colonies and territories of the Crown 'because of the peculiarities which exist in each of them arising out of historical and constitutional developments, the organisation of the indigenous people concerned and applicable geographical or social considerations'.[13] Kirby's colleagues cut more quickly to the chase, declaring that

> No guidance in these issues can be gleaned from comparative law. The position of indigenous peoples in Australia is distinguished from those in other common law jurisdictions.[14]

What are we to make of this declaration of jurisprudential autarchy? If Australian conditions are so distinctive that native title law in other settler societies has no relevance, surely the same must be true of international human rights law?

And for anyone who has read the Mabo judgement, the pronouncement appears even stranger. The whole point of that judgement was that the bench reached beyond Australian law to consider cases from the United States, Canada and New Zealand and colonial cases which reached the Privy Council. There could have been no judgement without this broadening out of Australian jurisprudence and the opening of it to native title traditions of the other settler societies. Do the remarks in the Fejo case suggest that this process is now at an end? That, having emerged from its provincial shell, Australian law is to retreat into isolation because other jurisdictions provide Indigenous people with rights, and protection of those rights, which would be politically embarrassing?

The difficulties inherent in the court's position can be seen most clearly in relation to the question of the extinguishment of native title. Justice Kirby observed that the concept of extinguishment of Indigenous land rights as a result 'of the advancing claims to legal title of the settlers' originated in the decision *Johnson v. McIntosh*.[15] But what went unremarked was that American law demanded a far more rigorous test before extinguishment could be allowed and that it was quite possible for freehold title to be burdened by an unextinguished Indigenous interest. The principles involved were most clearly enunciated by Justice Douglas in the 1941 Supreme Court case *United States v. Santa Fe Railway Co*. The case arose from circumstances familiar in Australia. In 1866 a railway company was granted land occupied by the Walapai Indians, who held native title to the area. But because there was no extinguishment of the Indian interest, it remained as an 'encumbrance' on the fee simple, despite a change of ownership, and was still an encumbrance in 1941.[16] The principle at stake has been reaffirmed in later cases. In *Edwardson v. Morton* the courts declared that Indian use and occupancy rights can be extinguished only by the United States acting through Congress, and until they are extinguished they remain as an encumbrance on the fee simple regardless of who holds it.[17]

Native title in North America seems to be a tougher form of tenure than the one the High Court has bestowed on Australia and can survive a grant of fee simple in a way not accorded the feeble Antipodean strain. Or perhaps fee simple is more voracious in Australia than anywhere else in the world. Justice Kirby enthusiastically proclaimed the feebleness of native title in Australia. 'So fragile is native title,' he declared, and so susceptible is it to extinguishment that the grant of a freehold title 'blows away the native title forever'.[18]

That is a most convenient doctrine for a settler society to implant in its jurisprudence. If you can no longer sustain *terra nullius* in the face of world opinion, an 'inherently fragile' native title is the next thing.[19] Having given birth to native title, the High Court decided to bind its feet before it could develop any jurisprudential strength and mobility. The conquest and dispossession had to be confirmed, put beyond question. Nothing must be permitted to 'cast doubt upon the validity of fee simple throughout Australia'.[20]

But the existence of a fragile title which can be blown away forever by the Crown has implications that have never been examined by the courts – and understandably so. A fragile title inescapably implies a far from fragile, all-powerful sovereign – a Leviathan – who has powers to deal with the subjects' property which would have warmed the heart of King John. In dealing with Indigenous subjects the Australian judiciary has accorded the Crown powers that have not been exercised in Britain for centuries. One of the fundamental aspects of the common law was the long-developed capacity it provided to strictly limit the power of the Crown to diminish the property interest of the subject. Centuries of tradition have been cast aside in order to define a form of tenure which the Crown can blow away forever. It should come as no surprise then that the High Court has advocated the use of blinkers to prevent litigants from looking beyond Australia, declaring that no guidance could be gleaned from comparative law when the matter of tenures comes up for review. It would not be entirely perverse to look back nostalgically to the days when appeals could be taken to the Privy Council which, by its very nature, has to consider comparative law.

The difficulty began with Mabo. This has been cogently argued by Kent McNeil, one of the world's leading scholars in the field and whose book *Common Law Native Title* was widely consulted while the Mabo case was proceeding through the courts. His 1996 article, 'Racial Discrimination and Unilateral Extinguishment of Native Title',[21] is a powerful *tour de force*. His argument is straightforward and considers the way in which the High Court dealt with the extinguishment of native title in the Mabo judgement.

McNeil begins with the axiomatic principle that the Crown can extinguish the title of the subject provided it has been effected by legislation and has been done in a clear and plain way. Where he takes issue with the court is in relation to the assumption that native title can be extinguished by the grant of a competing interest in land. Grounding his case in British legal precedent, he establishes that the Crown cannot extinguish the real property rights of its subjects by granting their lands to others, unless it has unambiguous statutory authority to do so. In fact this 'fundamental limitation on the Crown's power'[22] is the central theme of the paper. The Australian judges have argued that because native title is not a creature of the common law it is more susceptible to extinguishment than a title that is. McNeil argues and establishes that the protection of the common law 'clearly extends to all pre-existing rights regardless of their source'.[23] Consequently Justice Brennan's assertion that native title can be extinguished by inconsistent crown grant because the title does not originate from a crown grant 'is simply wrong'.[24] At common law, McNeil demonstrated

> the Crown does not have the power to extinguish any rights of its subjects, whatever their source, by grant . . . for hundreds of years the common law has provided the same protection to land titles which are not derived from grants as it has to titles that are.[25]

Because the High Court determined that native title could be extinguished in a way in which no other tenure was susceptible, McNeil concluded that the Mabo decision was highly discriminatory. His challenge is important and needs to be read at length:

> We have seen that the majority in *Mabo No. 2* decided that native title could be extinguished by unilateral executive action without any legal obligation to pay compensation. We have examined the explanations given for that decision, and found them to be wanting. Moreover, we have seen that the decision violates funamental common law principles and conflicts with case law of high authority. Clear and plain statutory authority apart, the Crown simply does not have the power to extinguish legal rights to land, except for defence purposes in time of war, in which case compensation must be paid. Were the law otherwise private

rights would be exposed to arbitrary executive action. The Crown would be able to commit what would amount to acts of state against its own subjects, and the rule of law would cease to be effective to protect property rights.

While these fundamental principles, which have been well established in the common law since at least the seventeenth century, are clearly part of Australian law, the majority in *Mabo No. 2* chose not to apply them to Aborigines and Torres Strait Islanders. In doing so, the Court treated the indigenous people differently from other Australians. Where indigenous land rights are concerned, the Court created an exception to the rule that, statutory authority and wartime conditions apart, the Crown cannot derogate from existing rights by inconsistent grant or appropriation. This is clearly discriminatory.[26]

Another striking and discriminatory feature of the Mabo judgement was the decision that the extinguishment of native title did not create any obligation to pay compensation. Once again this flies in the face of long-settled principles of the common law and 'violates fundamental constitutional protections of the rights of subjects going back to Magna Carta'.[27] The principal of compensation had been affirmed in African cases brought before the Privy Council in much more recent times. In the 1957 case of *Adeyinka Oyekan v. Musendiku Adele* Lord Denning considered what he called the 'guarding principles' of British colonial law, remarking that

> in inquiring . . . what rights are recognised, there is one guiding principle. It is this: The courts will assume that the British Crown intends that the rights of property of the inhabitants are to be fully respected. Whilst, therefore, the British Crown, as Sovereign, can make laws enabling it compulsorily to acquire

land for public purposes, it will see that property compensation is awarded to every one of the inhabitants who has by native law an interest in it: and the courts will declare the inhabitants entitled to compensation according to their interests, even if those interests are of a kind unknown to English law.[28]

The High Court's decision to effectively pre-empt any attempt to seek compensation for historic injustice and the failure of government to provide alternative means to the same end can be contrasted to the situation in Canada, the United States and New Zealand.

In each country it was decided that contemporary standards demanded that all previous dealings with the Indigenous people should be open to scrutiny and, where necessary, compensation should be paid. Each set up a form of judicial tribunal to hear cases and assess the behaviour of the past by the standards of today – the Americans in the 1940s, the Canadians in the 1970s, and the New Zealanders in the 1980s.

This process was undertaken despite the fact that in all three countries treaties had been negotiated and land had normally been purchased by the state. Indians and Maoris have been able to bring cases forward to prove that treaties and agreements in the past were unfair, or not fulfilled, or obtained by trickery or duress. New Zealand inquiries go back to 1840, American to 1790 and Canadian to the middle of the eighteenth century. Despite the inherent difficulties of the situation, the arguments in these countries have been about legal or quasi-legal documents, negotiated at a particular point in time with specific conditions, which can be reassessed and renegotiated. In North America hundreds of cases are involved. During its thirty-two-year life from 1946 to 1978, the United States Indian Claims Commission heard over 500 cases.

Many of them related to treaties signed in the nineteenth century, but by no means all of them. The Congress first faced the problem of Indians who had not signed treaties in the 1930s. In 1935 a number of Special Jurisdiction Acts were passed, which allowed Indian tribes to proceed in the Court of Claims against the United States in order to seek compensation for the loss of native title. The court was given power

> to hear, examine, adjudicate and enter judgement on all claims which the Indians may have against the United States for lands taken from them by the United States without compensation, or from the failure or refusal of the United States to protect the interest of the Indians in their lands or other property.[29]

In 1946 Congress established the Indian Claims Commission to hear claims for compensation or restitution in cases where treaties were unfair or had been violated and, more significantly for the Australian case, where the Indians had only moral claims on the state — 'claims based upon fair and honourable dealings that are not recognised by any existing rule of law or equity'.[30]

The phrase 'fair and honourable' dealing in the Indian Claims Commission Act played an important role in a variety of court cases that are of great relevance to the situation of the Aborigines in the Australian legal system. The vexed question of forced removal from traditional lands came before the courts in the 1967 case of *Lipan Apache Tribe v. The United States*. The Apaches claimed that they had been driven from their lands in 1858–59 by United States forces acting in concert with Texan settlers. The Court of Claims concluded that if the facts of the matter could be established, the Indians would have a legitimate claim for compensation.[31]

Similar standards were applied in other cases where Indian tribes had lost their land in the absence of a treaty and without compensation. In 1946 the Oregon Alcea Band of Tillamooks took the United States to court, claiming compensation for the loss of their land in the 1850s. The Supreme Court concluded that

> taking original Indian title without compensation and without consent does not satisfy the 'high standards and fair dealing' required of the United States in controlling Indians Affairs. The Indians have more than a moral claim for compensation.[32]

Developments have followed a similar course in Canada. Since the early 1970s, Indian communities have been able to take claims to a Special Claims Branch of the Department of Indian Affairs when they have a grievance relating to the treaties signed with colonial and federal governments. In 1991 a specific claims commission was established to speed up the process of research and negotiation. But of more interest to Australians is the comprehensive claims process, which since 1973 has dealt with Indian and Inuit communities in the Yukon, North West Territories and northern Quebec, where treaties were never negotiated.

This process was set in motion by the Supreme Court's judgement in the Calder case in 1973. It had strong similarities with the Mabo case. Six of the seven judges concluded that native title had existed in British Columbia, despite the absence of treaties in the province. Three of the six believed that native title persisted, while three argued that it had been extinguished at some point after European settlement by assorted legislative and executive actions of the colonial government. Prior to this judgement it had been widely believed that Indian rights only existed if they had been recognised by treaty. The Calder decision clearly suggested that unextinguished native title existed, not just in British Columbia, but right across the north of the country as well.

The Canadian federal government responded to the decision six months after it was handed down. The intention was to enter into a series of agreements that, after negotiation, would see the Indians and Inuit agree to a 'release of the general and undefined native title' in return for freehold title to a proportion of the land in question, compensation, hunting and fishing rights. In a policy statement, the Minister for Indian Affairs declared:

> The Government is now ready to negotiate with authorised representatives of these native peoples on the basis that where their traditional interests in the lands can be established, an agreed form of compensation or benefit will be provided to native peoples in return for their interest.[33]

Since then the process of modern treaty-making has dealt with Indian, Inuit and Metis communities in British Columbia, Quebec and right across the north. Settlements have dealt with much more than land and have included compensation, hunting and fishing rights, resource development, environmental protection, service delivery and self-government.

New Zealand's Waitangi Tribunal was established in 1975 to determine whether or not the Crown had complied with its obligations under the Treaty of Waitangi of 1840. For the first ten years the tribunal was restricted to the investigation of contemporary claims, but in 1985 the relevant Act was amended to allow for retrospective grievances to be examined, extending the brief to include all actions and policies of the Crown since 1840. Understandably the tribunal has been overwhelmed with hundreds of claims. The attendant frustration has affected the standing of the tribunal but among many things it has commissioned large-scale historical research of a kind that in Australia has been reserved for military history. Several large settlements have been reached which should be much better known in Australia. The Tainui tribe of the Waikato district sought redress for thousands of hectares of land confiscated after the New Zealand Wars of the 1860s. The settlement of 1995 included a cash payment of NZ$70 million and the return of 19000 hectares of land worth approximately NZ$100 million. As part of the settlement the Crown issued a formal apology for historic wrongdoing which read in part:

1. The Crown acknowledges that its representatives and advisers acted unjustly and in breach of the Treaty of Waitangi in its dealings with the Kiingitanoa and Waikato in sending its forces across the Mangataawhiri in July 1863 and in unfairly labelling Waikato as rebels.

2. The Crown expresses its profound regret and apologises unreservedly for the loss of lives because of the hostilities arising from its invasion, and at the devastation of property and social life which resulted.

3. The Crown acknowledges that the subsequent confiscations of land and resources under the New Zealand *Settlements Act 1863* . . . were wrongful, have caused the Waikato to the present time to suffer feelings in relation to their lost land akin to those of orphans, and have had a crippling impact on the welfare, economy and development of the Waikato.[34]

Conclusion

As I write it is almost eleven years since the High Court handed down its decision in the Mabo case. I often wonder what Eddie Mabo would have thought of the judgement and the subsequent developments. Many years ago, before the case began, I used to jokingly tell him that he would one day become famous. I'm sure neither of us imagined that his name would become known not just in Australia but overseas, and that his case would be regarded as a symbol of the global struggle for Indigenous peoples' rights. Some aspects of his fame would have delighted him: in particular, I think of the T-shirts that were worn by Murray Islanders for years after the case concluded. They bore a picture of Eddie along with the slogan: 'Captain Cook Stole Our Land – Eddie Mabo Got it Back'.

He would also have been pleased that following his lead, the native title process has made more progress in the Torres Strait than anywhere else in the country. In 1999 and 2000 there were seven consensual determinations of native title on Moa, Saibai, Dauan, Mabuiag and Coconut islands, and the York Islands. He would have strongly supported Murandoo Yanner's right to carry out traditional hunting practices and would have celebrated his win in the High Court. The Croker Island decision would have angered him with its limited recognition of sea rights, and he would have been deeply frustrated that so little progress has been made towards the creation of an autonomous self-governing region in the Torres Strait on the model of Norfolk Island.

Having devoted the last ten years of his life to the long campaign through the courts – back and forth between the Queensland Supreme Court and the High Court – Eddie would not have been entirely surprised that everything has taken so long; that so little has been achieved despite the huge investment in time and money. No doubt the eleventh anniversary will lead to many critical assessments of the native title process, the lack of progress, and the hundreds of outstanding claims.

What will have been achieved by then? A handful of cases where native title has been affirmed in the courts; some agreements outside them; a few land-use agreements and negotiated contracts between native title holders and resource companies. Their significance should not be underestimated. But it is so much less than many people hoped for and expected in those heady days in June 1992.

Native title itself, whether achieved under the aegis of the federal Native Title Act of 1993 or the earlier Northern Territory legislation of 1986, has not necessarily improved conditions in land-holding communities. In some places they may have deteriorated. The Canadian way of proceedings seems now to have been preferable, where land tenure was settled alongside all those other questions which determine the viability of usually remote communities – service delivery, local government, funding, resource development.

Having lived most of his adult life in north Queensland, Eddie would not have been surprised by the vehemence of opposition to native title. The Queensland government legislated to extinguish all property rights of Torres Strait Islanders in 1986 and would have succeeded if the High Court hadn't stepped in and struck down the Coastal Lands Declaratory Act by a slim majority. And the determined opposition of governments continued. They have fought – often in league with one another – almost every attempt to broaden the meaning of native title. In the process they have extended the time needed for settlement and greatly increased the cost of litigation. And, for the last eleven years, federal and state ministers, leaders of commerce and industry, and prominent conservative intellectuals have railed against the Mabo and Wik decisions and the judges who made them. The reaction to the Wik decision in 1996 was symptomatic. From the start a vociferous campaign was launched by the federal government, by the Prime Minister and his deputy and powerful industry bodies to extinguish or curtail the very limited rights which had unexpectedly survived the brutal process of colonisation.

The Mabo judgement was so much more important than its immediate objective – deciding who owned a small group of islands in the farthest corner of the country. It presented Australia with the opportunity to come to terms with a great historic injustice. And that opportunity was taken up by many people. The prime minister at the time, Paul Keating, some of the state premiers and parliaments, the churches and thousands of individuals expressed their regret, demonstrated their commitment to reconciliation and signed sorry books.

But there has been no officially funded campaign to fully account for past injustice; none of the research programs that were part of the work of the Indian Claims Commission in the United States and of the Waitangi Tribunal in New Zealand. The decision by the courts to dismiss any hope of seeking compensation for lost land closed off one avenue that might have led to a rigorous assessment of the past. The two royal commissions into deaths in custody and taking of children had a major impact on the community and indicated that there was a hunger for large-scale investigative research.

Eleven years ago the Aborigines and Islanders that I knew were both burdened with and vivified by a profound sense of historic injustice. Despite Mabo and Wik, Yanner and Croker Island, despite the Land Rights Act and the Land Fund, despite a decade-long process of reconciliation, I suspect that sense of injustice remains. A great opportunity created by the Mabo judgement has been squandered. The response has too often been grudging and legalistic. It is symptomatic that Australian courts have quite consciously rejected the idea that the Crown had a duty of care — a fiduciary relationship — towards the Indigenous people. That has been accepted in the United States since the nineteenth century and has more recently been incorporated in the law in Canada and New Zealand. It is not that the Australian judiciary is unaware of this. They have decided not to walk in that direction. But the idea that the process of colonisation itself and the concomitant extinguishment of Aboriginal title created lasting obligations is not a new one in Australia. It was forcefully put by Earl Grey, the Secretary of State for the Colonies, who in 1850 declared that in 'assuming their Territory the Settlers in Australia have incurred a moral obligation of the most sacred kind . . .'[1] It is a message that many people still don't want to hear.

ABBREVIATIONS

ACC	Australian Council of Churches
AIAS	Australian Institute of Aboriginal Studies
APS	Aborigines Protection Society
APS*P&P*	Aborigines Protection Society *Papers & Proceedings*
BPP	*British Parliamentary Papers*
CO	Colonial Office
CLR	*Commonwealth Law Reports*
DLR	*Dominion Law Reports*
FLR	*Federal Law Reports*
HCA	High Court of Australia
HPD	*Hansard's Parliamentary Debates*
HRA	*Historical Records of Australia*
HRNSW	*Historical Records of New South Wales*
JRAHS	*Journal of the Royal Australian Historical Society*
NSWLC	New South Wales Legislative Council
SAA	South Australian Archives
SAAP	*South Australian Parliamentary Papers*
WLR	*Weekly Law Reports*

NOTES

Wherever possible, original sources have been used. Publishers are given only for works published after 1900.

Introduction
1. Quoted in V. Windeyer, 'A birthright and inheritance', *Tasmanian University Law Review*, 1 Nov. 1962, vol. 1, no. 5, p. 635.
2. J. Bouvier, *A Law Dictionary*, 11th edn, Philadelphia, 1866, p. 258.
3. J. Selden, *Of the Dominion or Ownership of the Sea*, London, 1652, p. 21.
4. *South Australian Gazette*, 23 July 1840.
5. *Cooper v. Stuart*, 1889.
6. *FLR*, 17, 1971, p. 270.
7. *Australian Law Journal*, 29, 1985, p. 346.
8. ibid.
9. See H. Reynolds, *Frontier*, Allen & Unwin, Sydney, 1987, Ch. 7.

Chapter 1: Who Was in Possession?
1. W. Tench, *Sydney's First Four Years*, Angus & Robertson, Sydney, 1961, p. 41.
2. *Millirpum v. Nabalco*, FLR, 17, 1971, p. 245.
3. *Williams v. Attorney-General*, NSW, *Commonwealth Law Review*, 16, 1913, p. 439.
4. K. Roberts-Wray, *Commonwealth and Colonial Law*, Stevens, London, 1966, p. 631. See also G. Bennett, 'Aboriginal title in the common law', *Buffalo Law Review*, 27, 1978, pp. 617–35; T. J. Lawrence, *The Principles of International Law*, 4th edn, Macmillan, London, 1910, pp. 156–7.
5. See for instance Hugh Morgan's letter in the *Age*, 29 Mar. 1986.
6. H. Grotius, *The Rights of War and Peace*, London, 1738, vol. 2, p. 550.
7. J. Story, *Commentaries on the Constitution of the United States*, 5th edn, Boston, 1891, p. 6.
8. *Worcester v. Georgia*, 1832, quoted in M. F. Lindley, *The Acquisition and Government of Backward Territory in International Law*, Longmans, London, 1926, p. 29.

9. ibid., pp. 26–7.
10. H. Grotius, *The Freedom of the Seas*, Oxford University Press, New York, 1916, p. 11.
11. J. G. Heineccius, *A Methodical System of Universal Law*, London, 1743, vol. 1, p. 182. See also R. Phillimore, *Commentaries upon International Law*, London, 1854, vol. 1, p. 289; W. E. Hall, *A Treatise on International Law*, 8th edn, Clarendon Press, Oxford, 1924, p. 125; H. Taylor, *A Treatise on International Public Law*, Callaghan, Chicago, 1901, p. 128.
12. Hall, op. cit., p. 129. See also T. A. Walker, *The Science of International Law*, London, 1893, pp. 160–1; T. A. Walker, *A Manual of Public International Law*, Cambridge, 1895, pp. 29–39; F. Wharton, *A Digest of the International Law of the United States*, Washington, 1886, vol. 3, p. 839; T. D. Woolsey, *Introduction of the Study of International Law*, Boston, 1860, p. 119; Roberts-Wray, loc. cit.
13. See Roberts-Wray, loc. cit.; Lawrence, loc. cit.; A. Polson, *Principles of the Law of Nations*, London, 1848, p. 28.
14. Lawrence, op. cit., pp. 151, 160. See also G. H. Hackworth, *Digest of International Law*, Govt Printing Office, Washington, 1940, vol. 1, p. 402; A. S. Keller et al., *Creation of Rights of Sovereignty through Symbolic Acts, 1400–1800*, Columbia University Press, New York, 1938, p. 4.
15. Quoted by J. Goebel in *The Struggle for the Falkland Islands*, Yale University Press, New Haven, 1927, p. 115.
16. J. Kent, *Commentaries on American Law*, 11th edn, Boston, 1867, vol. 3, p. 485.
17. J. Westlake, *International Law*, Cambridge University Press, Cambridge, 1904, pp. 105–7.
18. Lawrence, op. cit., p. 151.
19. Heineccius, op. cit., vol. 1, p. 176.
20. E. de Vattel, *The Law of Nations*, vol. 3, Washington, 1916, p. 84.
21. G. F. von Martens, *The Law of Nations*, 4th edn, London, 1829, p. 67.
22. H. J. S. Maine, *Ancient Law*, London, 1861, p. 246. See also T. E. Holland, *Lectures on International Law*, Sweet & Maxwell, London, 1933, p. 113; Phillimore, op. cit., vol. 1, pp. 264, 267; C. Van Bynkershoek, *A Treatise on the Law of War*, Philadelphia, 1810, pp. 107, 211.

23. F. K. von Savigny, *Treatise on Possession*, 6th edn, London, 1848.
24. ibid., pp. 10, 143, 149–51. See also J. Kelleher, *Possession in the Civil Law*, Calcutta, 1888; J. M. Lightwood, *A Treatise on Possession of Land*, London, 1894.
25. T. Twiss, *The Oregon Question Examined*, New York, 1846, p. 113.
26. C. Wolff, *Jus Gentium*, Clarendon Press, Oxford, 1934, pp. 157–60.
27. Heineccius, op. cit., vol. 1, p. 179.
28. Vattel, op. cit., 1760 edn, pp. 89–91.
29. ibid., pp. vii–ix.
30. ibid., p. 152.
31. ibid., pp. 38, 91, 152.
32. Lightwood, op. cit., p. 111.
33. L. A. Warkoenig, *Analysis of Savigny's Treatise on the Law of Possession*, Edinburgh, 1839, p. 4.
34. Vattel, op. cit., 1834 edn, p. 35.
35. H. W. Challis, *The Law of Real Property*, 1888, quoted in G. C. Cheshire, *The Modern Law of Real Property*, 10th edn, Butterworths, London, 1967, p. 121.
36. M. Hale, *The History of the Common Law*, 5th edn, London, 1794, vol. 2, pp. 7, 9.
37. *Tyson v. Smith*, 1838.
38. *Falmouth v. George*, 1828.
39. F. Pollock, *The Land Laws*, London, 1898, p. 1.
40. *Jones v. Williams*, 1837, *All England Law Reports*, 1835–42, p. 424.
41. *Harper v. Charlesworth*, 1825, *All England Law Reports*, 1824–34, p. 68.
42. *Lord Advocate v. Young*, *Appeals Cases*, 12, 1887, p. 556.
43. Pollock, op. cit., p. 31.
44. *Harper v. Charlesworth*, loc. cit.
45. Lightwood, op. cit., p. 12. See also *Lord Advocate v. Lord Blantyne*, *Appeals Cases*, 4, 1879.
46. *Jones v. Williams*, op. cit., p. 425.
47. Grotius, *The Freedom of the Seas*, op. cit., pp. 11–13.
48. Selden, op. cit., p. 17. See also J. W. Textor, *Synopsis of the Law of Nations*, Carnegie Institute, Washington DC, 1916.
49. Selden, op. cit., pp. 17–18.
50. See for instance R. L. Meek, *Social Science and the Ignoble Savage*, Cambridge University Press, Cambridge, 1976.
51. H. Home, *Sketches of the History of Man*, 2nd edn, Edinburgh, 1778, vol. 1, pp. 116–17.

52. H. Home, *Historical Law-tracts*, 2nd edn, Edinburgh, 1761, pp. 94–5.
53. W. Falconer, *Remarks on the Influence of Climate . . .*, London, 1781, p. 272. See also A. Ferguson, *An Essay on the History of Civil Society*, 4th edn, London, 1783, pp. 135–6.
54. J. Millar, *The Origin of the Distinction of Ranks*, 3rd edn, London, 1781, pp. 188, 189.
55. J. Locke, *Two Treatises of Government*, 4th edn, London, 1713, p. 15.
56. W. Blackstone, *Commentaries on the Laws of England*, 18th edn, London, 1823, vol. 2, pp. 3, 5, 8, 261.
57. ibid., p. 258.
58. ibid., p. 3.
59. Savigny, op. cit., p. 5.
60. W. Blackstone, *A Discourse on the Study of the Law*, Oxford, 1783, p. 68.
61. Grotius, *The Freedom of the Seas*, op. cit., p. 27.
62. Bennett, op. cit., pp. 618–19.

Chapter 2: By What Tenure?

1. J. Banks, *The Endeavour Journal*, Angus & Robertson, Sydney, 1962, vol. 2, pp. 122–3.
2. *Copious Remarks on the Discovery of New South Wales*, London, 1787, p. 51; *The History of New Holland*, London, 1787, pp. 230, 232.
3. *HRA*, 4, 1, p. 330.
4. 4 & 5 Will, IV C.95.
5. See *Appeals Cases*, 14, 1889, p. 291; *FLR*, 17, 1971, p. 243; *Australian Law Journal*, 53, 1975; *Wilson v. Terry*, 1849, in J. G. Legge, *A Selection of Supreme Court Cases*, Sydney, 1896, p. 508.
6. Blackstone, op. cit., *Commentaries*, vol. 1, p. 104.
7. G. Lester, Aboriginal Land Rights, D. Juris. thesis, Osgoode Law School, 1981, p. 198.
8. *Appeals Cases*, 14, 1889, p. 291. (Emphasis mine.)
9. Blackstone, *Commentaries*, op. cit., vol. 2, p. 7.
10. Quoted in Reynolds, op. cit., p. 179.
11. F. de Victoria, *De Indis*, Carnegie Institute, Washington DC, 1917, p. 125.
12. Grotius, *The Rights of War and Peace*, loc. cit.
13. Grotius, *The Freedom of the Seas*, op. cit., pp. 13, 19.
14. E. W. Landor, *The Bushman*, London, 1847, pp. 187–8.
15. *Sydney Morning Herald*, 22 July 1846.

16. Vattel, op. cit., 1758 edn, p. 309.
17. *US v. Percheman*, 1833. See also H. Wheaton, *Elements of International Law*, Clarendon Press, Oxford, 1936, p. 346.
18. Wolff, op. cit., p. 157.
19. Twiss, op. cit., p. 124.
20. *Appeals Cases*, 6, 1881, p. 773.
21. Y. Blum, *Historic Titles in International Law*, Nijhoff, The Hague, 1965, pp. 99–100.
22. E. Campbell, 'Prerogative rule in New South Wales, 1788–1823', *JRAHS*, 50, 1964, pp. 161–90.
23. H. Broom, *Constitutional Law*, London, 1885, vol. 1, p. 225.
24. ibid., p. 231.
25. C. Viner, *A General Abridgement of Law and Equity* (1791), quoted by Lester in Aboriginal Land Rights, op. cit., p. 273.
26. R. J. King, 'Terra Australia: Terra Nullius aut Terra Aboriginium', *JRAHS*, 72, 2, Oct. 1986, p. 82.
27. *HRA*, loc. cit.
28. Glenelg to Torrens, 15 Dec. 1835, CO 13/3.
29. Blackstone, *Commentaries*, op. cit., vol. 2, p. 56.
30. *FLR* 17, 1971.
31. Blackstone, *Commentaries*, op. cit., vol. 3, p. 79.
32. Roberts-Wray, op. cit., p. 626.
33. See *White v. McLean*, 1890.
34. Quoted in B. Slattery, *Ancestral Lands: Alien Laws*, University of Saskatchewan, Saskatoon, 1983, p. 291.
35. F. P. Prucha, *American Indian Policy in Formative Years*, University of Nebraska, Lincoln, 1970, p. 140.
36. *Mitchell v. US*, 1835. The other cases were *Fletcher v. Peck*, 1810; *Johnson v. McIntosh*, 1823; *Worcester v. Georgia*, 1832; *Cherokee Nation v. Georgia*, 1834.
37. Papers Relative to Affairs of New Zealand, *BPP*, 1847, pp. 64–7.
38. Correspondence Respecting the Colonization of New Zealand, *BPP*, 1841, p. 68.
39. ibid., pp. 63–4.
40. *Hamlet of Baker Lake v. Minister of Indian Affairs*, DLR, 107, 1980, p. 513.
41. *DLR*, 34, 1973, p. 203.
42. *R. v. Secretary of State*, All England Law Reports, 1985, pp. 124–5.
43. *All England Law Reports*, 1957, p. 788.

44. Roberts-Wray, op. cit., p. 636.
45. J. Cook, *The Voyage of the* Resolution *and* Discovery, ed. J.C. Beaglehole, Cambridge University Press, Cambridge, 1967, p. ccxxiii.
46. J.C. Beaglehole (ed.), *The Journals of Captain Cook on His Voyages of Discovery*, 2 vols, Cambridge University Press, Cambridge, 1955–74, vol. 1, p. 514.
47. Committee on Transportation, *House of Commons Journals*, 40, 1785, p. 1164.
48. Twiss, op. cit., pp. 85, 90. See also J. Simsarian, 'The acquisition of legal title to *terra nullius*', *Political Science Quarterly*, 53, 1938, p. 121.
49. Quoted in King, op. cit., p. 77.
50. Selden, op. cit., p. 22.

Chapter 3: Reconnaissance and Reassessment

1. Tench, op. cit., p. 35.
2. *HRNSW*, 2, p. 664.
3. J. Hunter, *An Historical Journal*, London, 1793, p. 52.
4. Tench, op. cit., p. 52.
5. *HRNSW*, vol. 1, part 2, pp. 287, 324.
6. *An Authentic and Interesting Narrative of the Late Expedition to Botany Bay*, Aberdeen, 1789, p. 30.
7. Tench, op. cit., pp. 51–2.
8. *HRNSW*, vol. 1, part 2, pp. 289–90.
9. ibid., pp. 302, 321.
10. Tench, op. cit., p. 220.
11. *HRNSW*, vol. 5, p. 771.
12. Phillip to Sydney, 13 Feb. 1790, *HRA*, 1, 1, p. 160; King, op. cit., p. 275.
13. Hunter, op. cit., p. 62.
14. Tench, op. cit., pp. 225–6; Mrs Macarthur to her friends, *HRNSW*, 2, p. 504.
15. *HRNSW*, 2, p. 718.
16. Tench, op. cit., p. 226. See also the experience of Barrallier in *HRNSW*, 5, p. 771.
17. D. Collins, *An Account of the English Colony in New South Wales*, Reed, Sydney, 1975, vol. 1, p. 497.
18. ibid., p. 122.
19. See Reynolds, op. cit., p. 136.

20. *HRNSW*, 5, p. 513.
21. E. J. Eyre, *Journals of Expeditions of Discovery*, London, 1845, vol. 1, p. 351.
22. APS, *Report of the Sub-committee on Australia*, London, 1838, pp. 17, 18.
23. F. Tuckfield Journal, La Trobe Library, MSS 655, p. 174.
24. G. Grey, *Journals of Two Expeditions of Discovery*, London, 1841, vol. 2, p. 263.
25. Eyre, op. cit., vol. 2, p. 247.
26. ibid, pp. 246–7.
27. *HRNSW*, 5, p. 514.
28. *Perth Gazette*, 3 Aug. 1839.
29. Grey, op. cit., vol. 1, pp. 228, 231.
30. J. Grant, *The Narrative of a Voyage of Discovery*, London, 1803, p. 127.
31. T. L. Mitchell, *Journal of an Expedition into the Interior of Tropical Australia*, London, 1848, p. 412.
32. L. Leichhardt, *Journal of an Overland Expedition in Australia*, London, 1847, pp. 354–5.
33. Mitchell, op. cit., p. 413.
34. Grey, op. cit., vol. 2, p. 12.
35. Walker to Watson, 5 Nov. 1821, Bonwick Transcripts, Box 52.
36. S. Nind, 'Description of the natives of King George's Sound', *Journal of the Royal Geographical Society*, 1, 1831, p. 44.
37. Walker to Watson, 5 Dec. 1821, Bonwick Transcripts, Box 52.
38. Quoted in Reynolds, op. cit., p. 140.
39. P. de Strzelecki, *Physical Description of New South Wales and Van Diemen's Land*, London, 1845, p. 340.
40. Walker to Watson, loc. cit.
41. Quoted in *Westminster Review*, Jan. 1830, p. 183.
42. Letter from a Gentleman, Oct. 1826, Methodist Missionary Society, In Correspondence, 1812–26.
43. Report from the Select Committee on Aborigines, *BPP*, 7, no. 538, 1836, p. 183.
44. Quoted in Reynolds, loc. cit.
45. Orton to Methodist Mission Society, Methodist Missionary Society Papers, 18 July 1839.
46. Arthur to Goderich, 7 Jan. 1832, CO 280/33, p. 164.
47. *BPP*, 7, no. 538, 1836, p. 680.
48. C. G. Teichelmann, *Aborigines of South Australia*, Adelaide, 1841, p. 6.

49. Eyre, op. cit., vol. 2, p. 297.
50. Gawler to Angas, 10 July 1840, Angas Papers, South Australian Public Library.
51. J. Henderson, *Observations on the Colonies of New South Wales and Van Diemen's Land*, Calcutta, 1832, p. 149.
52. W. H. Breton, *Excursions in New South Wales, Western Australia and Van Diemen's Land*, London, 1833, p. 188.
53. Grey, op. cit., vol. 2, p. 252.
54. See Reynolds, loc. cit.
55. J. Backhouse, *Extracts from the Letters of James Backhouse*, London, 1838, pp. 40, 57.
56. Breton, op. cit., pp. 188–9.
57. Grey, op. cit., vol. 2, p. 236.
58. Strzelecki, loc. cit.
59. Henderson, op. cit., p. 151.
60. C. Sturt, *Two Expeditions into the Interior of Southern Australia*, London, 1833, vol. 2, pp. 126, 212.
61. *South Australian Gazette*, 28 Apr. 1838.
62. G. F. Moore, *A Descriptive Vocabulary*, London, 1842, p. 3.
63. CO 13/16.
64. *South Australia in 1842*, London, 1843, p. 22.
65. CO 13/16.
66. *The Colonist*, 19 Oct. 1838.
67. Letterbook of Joseph Orton, Mitchell Library, MSS. A1719, 28 Jan. 1842.
68. CO 13/16.
69. *HRA*, 4, 1, p. 414.
70. *Nireaha Tamaki v. Baker*, *Appeals Cases*, 1901, p. 577.
71. G. Arden, *Latest Information with Regard to Australia Felix*, Melbourne, 1840, p. 91.
72. Walker to Watson, 29 Nov. 1821, Bonwick Transcripts, Box 51.
73. *BPP*, 19, no. 259, 1831, p. 83.
74. Arthur to Glenelg, 22 July 1837, CO 280/84.
75. CO 18/31.
76. CO 201/272.
77. CO 201/286.
78. *HRA*, 1, 19, pp. 48–9.
79. *BPP*, 34, no. 627, 1844, p. 25.
80. CO 202/56.

81. CO 201/286; 18/34.
82. CO 13/6.
83. *South Australian Gazette*, 25 July 1840.
84. J. Orton Journal, 28 Jan. 1842.
85. G. A. Robinson Papers, vol. 2, Journal, 21 Dec. 1833.
86. APS*P&P*, Nov.–Dec. 1839, p. 137.
87. *The Colonist*, 12 Dec. 1838.
88. ibid., 27 Oct. 1838.
89. *Sydney Gazette*, 19 Aug. 1824.
90. *Sydney Herald*, 5 Dec. 1838.
91. *The Colonist*, loc. cit.
92. APS, *Seventh and Eighth Annual Reports*, London, 1844, p. 67.
93. ibid.
94. *Morning Chronicle*, 15 June 1844.
95. G. A. Robinson Papers, vol. 61, Mitchell Library.
96. APS, *Seventh and Eighth Annual Reports*, op. cit., p. 66.
97. *BPP*, 7, no. 538, 1836, p. 19.
98. Select Committee on the Aborigines, NSWLC, 1845, pp. 7–10.
99. J. Bischoff, *Sketch of the History of Van Diemen's Land*, London, 1832, p. 192.
100. *BPP*, 19, no. 259, 1831, p. 55.
101. Eyre, op. cit., vol. 1, p. 167.
102. Darling to Arthur, Arthur Papers, vol. 28.
103. Tasmanian Colonial Secretary, CSO/1/316, Tasmanian State Archives.
104. APS*P&P*, 1839, p. 140.
105. *BPP*, 34, no. 627, 1844, p. 282.
106. *Sydney Morning Herald*, 7 Oct. 1843.
107. Parker to Robinson, 20 June 1839, Port Phillip Papers, Mitchell Library.
108. E. S. Parker Journal, July–Aug. 1843, Port Phillip Papers, Mitchell Library.
109. W. Thomas Journal, 1841–42, Thomas Papers, Mitchell Library.
110. Tuckfield, op. cit., p. 176.
111. N. Plomley (ed.), *Friendly Mission*, Tasmanian Historical Research Association, Hobart, 1966, p. 88.
112. Arthur Papers, vol. 28, Mitchell Library.
113. G. A. Robinson, Letterbook, 1841–45, Robinson Papers, Mitchell Library.

Chapter 4: The First Land Rights Movement

1. J. Stephen, *Essays in Ecclesiastical Biography*, 4th edn, London, 1860, pp. 550–1.
2. G. Stephen, *Anti-slavery Recollections*, London, 1854, p. 231.
3. C. Buxton (ed.), *Memoirs of Sir Thomas Fowell Buxton*, London, 1848, p. 106.
4. ibid., p. 363.
5. R. H. Mottram, *Buxton the Liberator*, Hutchinson, London [1946], p. 108.
6. C. Buxton, op. cit., p. 360.
7. ibid., p. 361.
8. CO 323/218.
9. *BPP*, 7, no. 425, 1837, p. 5.
10. *HPD*, 29, 1835, p. 549.
11. ibid.
12. *BPP*, 7, no. 538, 1836, p. 516; 7, no. 425, 1837, p. 5.
13. *The Colonist*, 10 Oct. 1838.
14. CO 323/225.
15. ibid.
16. S. Motte, *Outline of a System of Legislation*, London, 1840, p. 15.
17. APS, *Fourth Annual Report*, London, 1841, p. 6.
18. C. Buxton, op. cit., p. 359.
19. APS, *First Annual Report*, London, 1838, p. 7.
20. *The Colonist*, 27 Oct. 1838.
21. APS, *Fourth Annual Report*, op. cit., p. 109.
22. Orton to Methodist Missionary Society, op. cit.
23. Motte, op. cit., p. 30.
24. C. J. Napier, *Colonization, Particularly in South Australia*, London, 1835, p. 94.
25. T. F. Buxton, reported in *The Colonist*, 17 Oct. 1838.
26. Ibid.
27. *HPD*, 24, 1835, p. 549.
28. Arthur to Goderich, 6 Apr. 1833, *BPP*, 44, no. 617, 1834, p. 165.
29. *HPD*, loc. cit.
30. Napier, loc. cit.
31. Arthur to Goderich, 7 Jan. 1832, *BPP*, 44, no. 617, 1834, p. 163.
32. The Aboriginal death rate has been recently challenged by Keith Windschuttle. See his book *The Fabrication of Aboriginal History*,

Macleay Press, Sydney, 2002. The most authoritative work is by N. J. B. Plomley. He estimated that during the period of the Black War, the Tasmanian Aboriginal population declined from 1500 to 350. See his book *The Aboriginal/Settler Clash in Van Diemen's Land, 1803–1831*, Queen Victoria Museum, Launceston, 1992, pp. 10–11.

33. APS, *Fifth Annual Report*, London, 1842, p. 120.
34. ibid., p. 24.
35. APS, *Fourth Annual Report*, op. cit., p. 120.
36. R. Anstey, *The Atlantic Slave Trade and British Abolition*, Macmillan, London, 1975, p. 194.
37. J. Stephen, op. cit., p. 544.
38. C. Buxton, op. cit., p. 360.
39. Backhouse, *Letters*, op. cit., p. 50.
41. *The Colonist*, 27 Oct. 1838.
41. APS, *Third Annual Report*, London, 1840, p. 68.
42. Quoted in Reynolds, op. cit., p. 85.
43. ibid.
44. *The Colonist*, 17 & 20 Oct. 1838.
45. Sermon as transcribed in W. Thomas Diary, 1839, Thomas Papers, Mitchell Library.
46. Quoted in Reynolds, op. cit., p. 142.
47. APS, *Address*, no. 1, p. 6.
48. Napier, op. cit., p. 96.
49. *HPD*, 29, 1835, p. 549.
50. APS, *Address*, loc. cit.
51. *BPP*, 7, no. 425, 1837, p. 5.
52. Arthur to Glenelg, 22 July 1837, CO 280/84.
53. Ibid.
54. *BPP*, 7, no. 538, 1836, p. 680.
55. *BPP*, 7, no. 425, 1837, p. 515.
56. Ibid., p. 510.
57. Ibid., p. 10.
58. Backhouse, *Letters*, loc. cit.
59. F. C. Irwin, *The State and Position of Western Australia*, London, 1835, p. 28.
60. *BPP*, 7, no. 425, 1837, p. 121.
61. P. Johnston, *Memoirs*, p. 59.
62. J. Stephen, op. cit., p. 16.

63. C. E. Stephen, (ed.), *Sir James Stephen: Letters*, Gloucester, 1906, p. 45.
64. C. Buxton, op. cit., pp. 366–7.
65. *BPP*, 39, no. 279, 1836, pp. 366–7.
66. C. Buxton, op. cit., p. 358; *The Colonist*, 17 Oct. 1838.
67. CO 323/225.
68. CO 280/55.
69. CO 396/1.
70. CO 13/4.
71. CO 202/36.
72. C. Buxton, op. cit., p. 368.
73. ibid., p. 364.
74. South Australian Colonization Commission Letterbook, 6 Jan. 1836, CO 386/137.
75. The only mention of Glenelg's instructions comes in an excellent but almost unknown article by R. Gibbs, 'Relations between the Aboriginal inhabitants and the first South Australian colonists', *Proceedings of the Royal Geographical Society of Australasia, South Australian Branch*, 61, 1959–60, pp. 61–78.

Chapter 5: Land Rights Frustrated, 1834–38

1. *HPD*, 3, 25, 1834, pp. 429, 700–12, 911, 1047.
2. Napier, op. cit., p. 213.
3. *Westminster Review*, July 1835, p. 239.
4. *BPP*, 7, no. 425, 1837, p. 515.
5. ibid., p. 4.
6. ibid.
7. Torrens to Grey, ? Dec. 1835, CO 13/3.
8. CO 396/1.
9. CO 13/3.
10. ibid.
11. ibid.
12. CO 13/5.
13. ibid.
14. CO 13/4
15. CO 13/4; 13/5.
16. CO 13/8; 396.
17. CO 13/4.
18. CO 13/4; 396/2.

19. D. J. Murray, *The West Indies and the Development of Colonial Government, 1801–1834*, Clarendon Press, Oxford, 1965, p. 97.
20. I. Gross, 'The abolition of Negro slavery and British parliamentary politics, 1832–3', *Historical Journal*, 23, 1980, p. 64.
21. CO 13/3.
22. *BPP*, 17, no. 311, 1841, p. 51.
23. Diary of John Brown, 4 Jan. 1836, South Australian Public Library.
24. R. Torrens, *Statement of the Origin and Progress of the Colony of South Australia*, London, 1849, p. 70.
25. Brown Diary, op. cit., 17 Dec. 1835.
26. ibid., 12 Jan. 1836.
27. Hindmarsh to Angas, 2 Jan. 1836, Angas Papers, South Australian Public Library.
28. Torrens to Shaw Le Fevre, n.d., Le Fevre Papers, South Australian Public Library.
29. CO 13/3.
30. Colonization Committee Letters to their Officers, 1836–40, SAA.
31. *BPP*, 36, 491, 1836, pp. 8–9.
32. Brown Diary, op. cit., 16 Dec. 1835.
33. *BPP*, 11, no. 512, 1836, p. 322.
34. Torrens, op. cit., p. 69.
35. Brown Diary, op. cit., 1 Feb. 1836.
36. ibid., 7 Jan. 1836.
37. C. Mann, *Report of the Speeches Delivered at a Dinner Given to Capt. John Hindmarsh*, London, 1835, p. 16.
38. Methodist Missionary Society Papers, M.126.
39. Hindmarsh to Angas, loc. cit.
40. R. Gouger, *South Australia in 1837*, London, 1838, p. 58.
41. South Australia Executive Council, 18 July 1837, CO 15/1.
42. *South Australian Gazette*, 18 May 1839.
43. ibid., 12 Aug. 1837; 12 May 1839.
44. Wyatt to Strangways, 15 May 1838; SAA, 24 Jan. 1838.
45. *South Australian Gazette*, 18 May 1839.
46. *Tracts Relative to the Aborigines*, London, 1843, p. 7.
47. APSP&P, 5, 1839, p. 139.
48. *South Australian*, 16 June 1838.
49. *South Australian Gazette*, 12 May 1839.
50. Reprinted in APSP&P, 5, 1839, p. 137.

51. *FLR* 17, 1971.
52. See R. L. Schuyler, *Parliament and the British Empire*, Columbia University Press, New York, 1929, p. 183.

Chapter 6: Land Rights Recognised, 1838–48

1. For an account of the Batman treaty see A. H. Campbell, *John Batman and the Aborigines*, Kibble Books, Malmsbury, Vic., [1987].
2. *FLR* 17, 1971, p. 257.
3. A. C. Castles, *An Australian Legal History*, Law Book Co., Sydney, 1982, p. 519.
4. B. Attwood, 'Writing the Aboriginal past', *Overland*, 114, May 1989, p. 131.
5. See Chapter 2.
6. Kent, op. cit., vol. 3, p. 379.
7. Slattery, loc. cit.
8. See Chapter 2.
9. *FLR* 17, 1971, p. 200.
10. CO 280/58.
11. ibid.
12. CO 13/3.
13. CO 201/247.
14. ibid.
15. See Chapter 2.
16. CO 201/255.
17. ibid.
18. CO 201/260.
19. *HRA*, 1, 19, p. 48.
20. ibid.
21. Correspondence Relative to New Zealand, 1835–42, *BPP*, 17, no. 311, 1841, p. 68.
22. ibid., pp. 68–9.
23. ibid., pp. 63, 78.
24. *South Australian Register*, 23 July 1840.
25. ibid.; Gawler to Angas, 10 July 1840, Angas Papers, South Australian Public Library.
26. *South Australian Register*, 23 July 1840.
27. CO 13/6.
28. *BPP*, 4, no. 119, 1841, p. 394.
29. APS, *Fourth Annual Report*, op. cit., p. 29.

30. *BPP*, 4, no. 119, 1841, Resolution XXI.
31. 5 & 6 VIC. C.36; *HRA*, 1, 22, p. 280.
32. *HRA*, 1, 26, p. 227.
33. *FLR*, 17, 1971, p. 253.
34. F. Cohen, 'Original Indian title', *Minnesota Law Review*, 28, 1947, p. 35; A. H. Snow, *The Question of Aborigines*, Govt Printing Office, Washington DC, 1919, p. 76.
35. *Jones v. Meehan*, US Law Reports, 175, 1899, pp. 11–12.
36. Snow, loc. cit.
37. M. F. Lindley, op. cit., p. 34.
38. Gawler to Angas, loc. cit.
39. Eyre, op. cit., vol. 2, p. 296.
40. Orton to Methodist Missionary Society, op. cit., 13 May 1839.
41. *BPP*, 34, no. 627, 1844, p. 52.
42. Robinson, Letterbook, op. cit., 1839–42.
43. Report to Select Committee, Victorian Legislative Council *Votes & Proceedings*, 1858–59, D8, p. v.
44. R. J. Surtees, 'The development of an Indian reserve policy in Canada', *Ontario Historical Society Journal*, 61, June 1969, p. 92.
45. W. M. Macmillan, *Bantu, Boer and Briton*, Faber, London, 1929, p. 125.
46. *BPP*, 311, no. 17, 1841, p. 52.
47. *HRA*, 1, 20, p. 740.
48. CO 202/44; *HRA*, 1, 20, p. 776; *HRA*, 1, 22, pp. 281–6; CO 13/27.
49. CO 202/54.
50. APS, *Correspondence Concerning the Natives of Western Australia*, London, 1841, pp. 1–12. See also CO 397/5; 397/6.
51. ibid.
52. ibid.

Chapter 7: Pastoral Leases

1. C. Buxton, op. cit., pp. 360–4.
2. *BPP*, 7, no. 425, 1837, p. 83.
3. CO 201/274.
4. G. A. Robinson, Annual Report of Chief Protector of Aborigines, 1846, CO 201/382.
5. Journals 1839–49, Robinson Papers, 14.
6. Robinson Letterbook, op. cit., 1839–42, Robinson Papers, 25.

7. Reported in the *Port Phillip Gazette*, 4 Dec. 1841.
8. Annual Report for 1845, enclosure no. 12 in dispatch Gibbs to Stanley, 1 April 1846, CO 201/366.
9. Annual Report for 1846, enclosure in dispatch Fitzroy to Grey, 17 May 1847, CO 201/382.
10. ibid.
11. The comments are on dispatch Fitzroy to Grey, 17 May 1847, CO 201/382.
12. Grey to Fitzroy, 11 Feb. 1848, CO 201/382.
13. Note of Grey on dispatch Fitzroy to Grey, 11 Oct. 1848, CO 201/400.
14. *New South Wales Government Gazette*, 26 April 1850, pp. 685–6.
15. Report of the Select Committee of the New South Wales Legislative Council on Crown Lands, *NSWV&P*, vol. 11, p. 1137.
16. Grey to Fitzroy, 10 Feb. 1850, CO 208/58.
17. CO 201/400.
18. Fitzgerald to Grey, 24 July 1849, CO 18/51. Draft of dispatch, Grey to Fitzgerald, 23 May 1850, CO 397/9.
19. The *Western Australia Government Gazette*, 17 Dec. 1850, pp. 1–4.
20. *South Australian Government Gazette*, 30 Jan. 1851.
21. Quoted in *Millirpum v. Nabalco*, *FLR*, 17, 1971, p. 260.
22. South Australian State Records, GR6 24/6/1851, 24 June 1851, cited by R. Foster, 'The Origin of the Protection of Aboriginal Rights in South Australian Pastoral Leases', Native Title Research Unit, Issues paper no. 24, IAISIS, Canberra, Aug. 1998, p. 6.
23. Gairdner memo on Fitzroy to Grey, 11 Oct. 1848, CO 201/400.

Chapter 8: A Forgotten Legacy

1. C.O. 201/309.
2. Select Committee on the Aborigines and the Protectorate, NSWLC *Votes & Proceedings*, 1849, vol. 2, p. 1.
3. Select Committee on the Aborigines, *SAPP*, vol. 3, 1860, pp. 4, 5, 96.
4. *The Colonist*, 27 Oct. 1838.
5. S.G. Foster, 'Aboriginal rights and official morality', *Push from the Bush*, 11 Nov. 1981, p. 75.
6. *SAPP*, 3, no. 165, 1860, p. 5.
7. A. Forster, *South Australia*, London, 1866, p. 420.

8. Western Australia Colonial Secretary, CSO 1848/173/36, Battye Library.
9. *BPP*, 1836, p. 515.
10. S. Bannister, *Humane Policy*, London, 1830, p. 51.
11. NSWLC *Votes & Proceedings*, 1845, p. 9.
12. B. Attwood, 'Blacks and Lohans', PhD thesis, La Trobe University, 1985, p. 205.
13. Royal Commission on the Aborigines, *Victorian Parliamentary Papers*, 3, 1877–78, no. 76, p. 550.
14. M. Brennan, *Australian Reminiscences*, William Brooks, Sydney, 1907, p. 213.

Chapter 9: Mabo and Wik Remake the Law of the Land

1. *Mabo and Others v. The State of Queensland*, High Court of Australia, pp. 29, 30.
2. ibid., p. 39.
3. ibid., p. 40.
4. ibid., p. 187.
5. ibid., p. 176.
6. ibid., p. 179.
7. ibid., p. 71.
8. ibid., pp. 83, 84.
9. ibid., p. 58.
10. ibid., p. 1.
11. ibid., p. 48.
12. ibid., p. 191.
13. ibid., p. 180.
14. *Clissold v. Perry*, 1901, 1 CLR, p. 373.
15. *Mabo v. Qld*, op. cit., p. 195.
16. ibid., p. 59.
17. *Mabo and Others v. The State of Queensland* (no. 2), 1992, 175, *CLR*, p. 196.
18. Quoted by E. Wilheim, 'Queensland pastoral leases and native title', *Aboriginal Law Bulletin*, vol. 3, no. 89, Feb. 1997, p. 20.
19. *Financial Review*, 24 Dec. 1996.
20. ibid.
21. Press conference transcript, 22 Jan. 1997.
22. *The Wik Peoples v. The State of Queensland*, High Court of Australia, FC 96/044, p. 57.

23. ibid., p. 58.
24. ibid., pp. 67, 199.
25. ibid., p. 200.
26. ibid., p. 104.
27. ibid., p. 61.
28. ibid., p. 70.
29. ibid., p. 202.

Chapter 10: The Aftermath of Mabo

1. *Yanner v. Eaton*, [1999], *HCA* 53, p. 4.
2. ibid., p. 11.
3. N. Sharp, 'Following in the seamarks? The salt water people of tropical Australia', *Indigenous Law Bulletin*, April 2000, p. 4.
4. *The Commonwealth v. Yarmirr*, [2001], *HCA* 56, pp. 37–8.
5. ibid., pp. 320–21.
6. ibid., p. 44.
7. W. Atkinson, 'Mediating the mindset of opposition: The Yorta Yorta case', *Indigenous Law Bulletin*, vol. 5, no. 15, Feb.–March 2002, p. 8.
8. *Australian Indigenous Law Reporter*, vol. 4, no. 1, March 1999, p. 112.
9. *The Yorta Yorta Aboriginal Community v. Victoria* [2002], *HCA* 58, p. 10.
10. *Fejo v. The Northern Territory*, op. cit., p. 37.
11. ibid., p. 54.
12. ibid., p. 55.
13. ibid., p. 53.
14. ibid., p. 37.
15. ibid., p. 56.
16. *US v. Santa Fe*, 314 U.S. 1941, pp. 339–59.
17. *Edwardson v. Morton*, 369 Fed. Supp. 1973, p. 1359.
18. *Fejo v. The Northern Territory*, op. cit., p. 57.
19. ibid., p. 56.
20. ibid., p. 55.
21. *Australian Indigenous Law Bulletin*, vol. 1, no. 2, 1996, pp. 181–221.
22. ibid., p. 188.
23. ibid., p. 193.
24. ibid., p. 196.
25. ibid.
26. ibid., p. 216.
27. ibid., p. 202.
28. 1957, 1, *WLR*, (PC), p. 880.

29. *US v. Alcea Band of Tillamooks*, 329, US 40, 1946.
30. United States Indian Claims Commission, *Final Report*, 1978, Washington, p. 7.
31. *Lipan Apache Tribe v. US*, 180 Ct. Cl. 487, 1967.
32. *US v. Alcea Bank of Tillamooks*, loc. cit.
33. Statement of Jean Chretien quoted in *R. v. Sparrow*, 70 DLR (4th), 385, 1990, p. 405.
34. T. Bennion, 'New Zealand: Indigenous land claims and settlements' in B. Keon-Cohen, ed., *Native Title in the New Millennium*, AIATSIS, Canberra, 2001, p. 271.

Conclusion
1. Grey to Fitzroy, 10 Feb. 1850, CO 202/58.

BIBLIOGRAPHY

OFFICIAL PRINTED SOURCES

BRITAIN
House of Commons, Sessional Papers

1831, 19, No. 259: Van Diemen's Land. Return to an Address . . . for Copies of all Correspondence between Lieutenant-Governor Arthur and His Majesty's Secretary of State for the Colonies, on the Subject of the Military Operations lately carried on against the Aboriginal Inhabitants of Van Diemen's Land.

1831, 19, No. 261: New South Wales. Return to an Address . . . dated 19 July 1831 for Copies of Instructions given by His Majesty's Secretary of State for the Colonies, for Promoting the Moral and Religious Instruction of the Aboriginal Inhabitants of New Holland or Van Diemen's Land.

1834, 44, No. 617: Aboriginal Tribes (North America, New South Wales, Van Diemen's Land and British Guinea).

1836, 7, No. 538: Report from the Select Committee on Aborigines (British Settlements).

1836, 11, No. 512: Select Committee on the Disposal of Lands in the British Colonies.

1836, 39, No. 279: Caffre War and the Death of Hintze.

1836, 39, No. 426: First Annual Report of the South Australian Colonization Commissioners.

1837, 7, No. 425: Report from the Select Committee on Aborigines (British Settlements).

1837–38, 29, No. 97: Second Annual Report of the South Australian Colonization Commissioners.

1839, 17, No. 225: Third Annual Report of the South Australian Colonization Commissioners.

1839, 34, No. 526: Australian Aborigines . . . Copies or Extracts of Dispatches Relative to the Massacre of Aborigines of Australia . . .

1841, 4, Nos 119 & 394: Select Committee on South Australia.

1841, 17, No. 129: Correspondence Relating to the Settlement of South Australia.

1841, 17, No. 311: Correspondence Respecting the Colonization of New Zealand.

1843, 33, No. 141: Port Essington: Copies or Extracts of Any Correspondence Relative to the Establishment of a Settlement . . .

1843, 32, No. 505: Papers Relative to the Affairs of South Australia, (especially pp. 267–340).

1844, 34, No. 627: Aborigines (Australian Colonies) . . . Return to an address . . . for Copies or Extracts from the Dispatches of the Governors of the Australian Colonies, with the Reports of the Protectors of Aborigines . . . to illustrate the Condition of the Aboriginal Population of said Colonies . . .

1897, 61, No. 8350: Western Australia: Correspondence Relating to the Abolition of the Aborigines Protection Board.

New South Wales
Legislative council, Votes and Proceedings

1838: Report from the Committee on the Aborigines Question.

1839, 2: Report from the Committee on Police and Gaols.

1841: Report from the Committee on Immigration with . . . Replies to a Circular Letter on the Aborigines.

1843: New South Wales (Aborigines). Return to an address by Dr Thomson . . . comprising details of Government Expenditure on Aborigines, 1837–43, and a large collection of correspondence relating to the protectorate and the missions.

1844, 1: New South Wales (Aborigines). Return to an address by Sir Thomas Mitchell . . . for numbers of whites and Aborigines killed in conflicts since the settlement of the Port Phillip District.

1845: Report from the Select Committee on the Condition of the Aborigines.

1849, 2: Select Committee on the Aborigines and the Protectorate.

South Australia
Parliamentary Papers

1860, 3, No. 165: Select Committee on the Aborigines.

Victoria
Legislative Council, Votes and Proceedings

1858–59, D8: Select Committee on the Aborigines.

Bibliography

DOCUMENTARY COLLECTIONS

Historical Records of Australia, Series One, 1–25, Series Three, 1–6, Series Four, 1.
Historical Records of New South Wales, 1–7.

OFFICIAL MANUSCRIPT SOURCES

Australian Joint Copying Project: Colonial Office Records, Files nos:
 CO 13/3, 13/4, 13/5, 13/9, 13/11, 13/22
 CO 201/274, 201/309, 201/382, 201/383, 201/400
 CO 202/36, 202/42, 202/44, 202/54, 202/58
 CO 280/55, 323/225, 386, 396/1, 396/2, 397/5, 397/6.

ARCHIVES OFFICE OF NEW SOUTH WALES

Colonial Secretary's Correspondence: In Letters (special bundles):
 Aborigines, 4/7153
 Aborigines 1833–35, 4/2219.1
 Aborigines 1836, 4/2302.1
 Aborigines 1837–39, 4/2433.1
 Aborigines 1849, 4/1141
 Aborigines 1849, 4/2831.1
 Aborigines 1852, 4/713.2
 Aborigines and the Native Police 1835–44, 4/1135.1
 Aboriginal Outrages, 2/8020.4
 Port Phillip Papers, 1839, 4/2471
 Port Phillip Papers, 1840, Part 1, 4/2510
 Port Phillip Papers, 1840, Part 2, 4/2511
 Port Phillip Papers, 1841, Part 1, 4/2547
 Port Phillip Papers, 1842, Part 1, 4/2588B
 Port Phillip Papers, 1842, Part 2, 4/2589B
 Port Phillip Papers, 1846, 4/2745-2
 Letters Received from and about Wide Bay, 1850–57, 4/7173
 Raffles Bay, 4/2060.2
 Reports on the Border Police, 1843–46, 4/7203
 Letters from Moreton Bay, 1843, 4/2618.1

Bathurst 1815–23, 4/1798
Bathurst 1824, 4/1800
Bathurst 1826, 4/1801
Bathurst 1824–26, 4/1799
Supreme Court Records
Papers Relating to the Aborigines, 1796–1839, 1161.

MITCHELL LIBRARY

Aborigines MSS A/611.
Letters from Government Officials, MSS A/664.
Queensland Native Police: Answers to Questionnaire, 1856, MSS A467.
Letterbook, Commissioner of Crown Land, Darling Downs 1843–48, MSS A1764-2.

TASMANIAN STATE ARCHIVES

Papers Relating to the Aborigines, 7578.
Reports on the Murders and Other Outrages Committed by the Aborigines, CSO/1/316.
Records Relating to the Aboriginals, CSO/1/317.
Reports of Mr G. A. Robinson Whilst in Pursuit of the Natives, CSO/1/318.
Papers of the Aborigines Committee, CSO/1/319.
Reports of the Roving Parties, CSO/1/320.
Suggestions Relative to the Capture of the Natives, CSO/1/323.
Papers Relating to the Black Line, CSO/1/324.

BATTYE LIBRARY, PERTH

Swan River Papers, 9, 10.
Colonial Secretary: In Letters, Volumes concerned with the Aborigines:
 53, April, May 1837
 54, June, July 1837
 56, October 1837
 89, 1840
 95, 1841
 108, 1842
 173, 1848
 2315/1888.

STATE LIBRARY OF SOUTH AUSTRALIA

Governors Dispatches GRG/2/6/1.

Letterbook of the Government Resident, Port Lincoln 3/379.

Colonization Commissioners, Letters to Resident Commissioner, GRG 48/5.

Dispatches to the Colonization Commissioners, 1838–41, GRG 48/4.

Colonization Commissioners, Letters to their Officers, 1836–40, GRG 48/1.

Colonial Secretary: In Letters, 1837–41, GRG/24/1; 1842–45, GRG/24/6.

Colonial Secretary's Letterbooks, GRG/24/4/3; GRG/24/4.

Protector of Aborigines Letterbook 1840–57, GRG/52/7.

VICTORIAN PUBLIC RECORDS OFFICE

Records of the Port Phillip Aboriginal Protectorate, especially the boxes: Westernport, North-Western District, Mainly In-Letters, Mt Rouse.

QUEENSLAND STATE ARCHIVES

New South Wales Colonial Secretary, Letters Received Relating to Moreton Bay and Queensland, 1822–60.

Microfilm copies of material from State Archives of NSW, Reels A2/1–A2/48, including the special bundles and A2/48, which contains Commissioner of Crown Lands re Aborigines in the District, 1854 Government Resident, Moreton Bay re complaints about the Native Police 1857; correspondence concerning the police firing on the Aborigines; Native Police: Moreton Bay 1857, Reels A2/47.

Native Police Papers QSA/NMP 48/100, 48/111, 48/120.

Government Resident, Moreton Bay, QSA/RES/2 and 3, 48/101, 48/102.

Letterbook of Commissioner for Crown Lands, Wide Bay and Burnett, 24/9/53–30/12/54, QSA/CCL/35/889 and 1/1/55–13/12/57, QSA/CCL/30/11.

Letterbook of W. H. WISEMAN, 5/2/55–30/5/60, QSA/CCL/7/61.

Colonial Secretary: In Letters, 1860–90, the QSA/Col/A files and the Special Bundles Relating to the Aborigines, QSA/Col/139–QSA/Col/144.

OTHER MANUSCRIPT SOURCES

MITCHELL LIBRARY

Papers of Sir GEORGE ARTHUR, especially vol. 19, Letters received 1827–28, MSS A/2179, vol. 20, 1829–30, MSS A2180 and vol. 28, Aborigines 1825–37, MSS A2188, Tasmanian Aborigines, MSS A612.

J. BACKHOUSE, G. Walker, Report of a Visit to the Penal Settlement, Moreton Bay, MSS B706.

J. BACKHOUSE, G. Walker, Reports, MSS B707.

Rev. W. BEDFORD, Papers 1823–43, MSS A76.

H. W. BEST Diary, 20/9/62–15/4/63 MSS B515/1.

ARTHUR BLOXHAM Diary, May–July 1863, MSS B515/1.

BONWICK Transcripts, Series 1, Boxes 49–53.

J. E. CALDER, Papers, MSS A597.

E. J. EYRE, Autobiographical Narrative of Residence and Exploration in Australia, 1832–39, MSS A1806.

W. GARDNER, Productions and Resources of the Northern Districts of NSW, 2 vols, 1842–54, MSS A176/1, A176/2.

Diary of JOHN GILBERT, 18/9/44–22/6/45, MSS A2587.

A. C. GRANT, Early Station Life in Queensland, MSS A858.

JESSE GREGSON Memoirs, MSS 1382.

J. GUNTHER, Correspondence and Notes on New South Wales Aborigines, MSS A1450.

—— Journal 1836–65, MSS B504.

—— Lecture on the Aborigines, MSS B505.

HASSALL Correspondence, MSS A1677.

J. D. LANG, Papers, 20, MSS 2240.

A. LE SOUEF, Personal Recollections of Early Victoria, MSS A2762.

D. MATTHEWS, Papers, MSS A3384.

R. B. MITCHELL, Reminiscences 1855–66, MSS B575.

ANDREW MURRAY, Journal of an Expedition 1859–1860, MSS 736.

Reminiscences of Mr JAMES NESBIT, MSS A1533.

J. ORTON, Letterbook, MSS A1719.

J. RAVEN, Reminiscences of a Western Queensland Pioneer, MSS A2692.

Papers of G.A. ROBINSON, MSS A7021–A7093, especially:
    Port Phillip Protectorate, 1839–40, MSS A7035
    Port Phillip Protectorate: Correspondence 54–57a and other papers, 1839–49, MSS A7075–7078-2

Port Phillip Protectorate, Official Reports, 59–61, 1841–49, MSS A7078–MSS A7082.
R. SADLIER, Papers, MSS A1631.
T. H. SCOTT, Letterbooks, MSS A850.
J. F. STEVENS, Histories of Pioneers, MSS 1120.
TELFER, Reminiscences, MSS A2376.
WILLIAM THOMAS Papers, especially his journal for 1844–47, uncatalogued MSS 214/2 and 3.
L. E. THRELKELD, Papers, MSS A382.
R. WINDEYER, On the Rights of the Aborigines of Australia, MSS 1400.

TASMANIAN STATE ARCHIVES
Van Diemen's Land Company Papers, Letters and Dispatches, 1828–46, VDC 5/1–7.

BATTYE LIBRARY, PERTH
L. C. BURGESS: Pioneers of Nor'-West Australia, PR 40.
L. F. CLARKE, West Australian Natives: My Experiences with Them, PR 2766.
Mr WILLIAM COFFIN, Oral History Tape, PR 9893.
Extracts from the Diary of Lieut. G. F. DASHWOOD in Perth, September 1832, PR 956/FC.
CONSTANCE NORRIS, Memories of Champion Bay or Old Geraldton, Q994.12/GER.
Journals of TREVARTHON C. SCHOLL, 1865–66 QB/SHO.
N. K. SLIGO, Reminiscences of Early Westralian Goldfields, Q 994.1/SLI.
Report on the Rev. JOHN SMITHERS re the Swan River Aborigines, 1840, PR 1785a.
Reminiscences of Mr F. H. TOWNSEND, PR 3497.
Diary of Dr S. W. VIVEASH, QB/VIV.
F. F. B. WITTENOOM, Some Notes on his Life QB/WIT.

STATE LIBRARY OF SOUTH AUSTRALIA
Papers of G. F. ANGAS, A461, PR6 174.
JOHN BROWN papers, M36–37.
J. B. BULL Reminiscences 1835–94, SAA 950.
Resolution of the Bush Club, 9/5/1839, A546/B8.
Letters Written by JOHN MUDGE . . . whilst a trooper at Pt. Lincoln and Mt. Wedge, 1857–60, SAA 1518.

SIMPSON NEWLAND, The Ramingaries (Encounter Bay) Tribe of Aborigines, A571/A4.

SHAW–LE FEVRE papers, PR6/226.

Papers of GEORGE TAPLIN, SAA 186/1/1–6. Journal, Letters Received, Lecture on Narrinyeri Tribe, History of Port Mackay.

Extracts from the Diary of MARY THOMAS, SAA 1058M.

La Trobe Library, Melbourne

Diary of NEIL BLACK, typescript, September 1839–May 1840, Box 99/1.

Journal of PATRICK COADY BUCKLEY, 1844–53, 6109, Box 214/7.

Papers of JAMES DREDGE: Notebook, 421959; Letterbook, 421961.

FOSTER FYANS, Reminiscences, 1810–42, 6940.

W. H. HOVELL, Remarks on a Voyage to Western Port, 7/11/26–25/3/27 CY, 8, 1/32 c.

H. MEYRICK, Letters to his family in England, 1840–47, 7959.

W. THOMAS, Brief Remarks on the Aborigines of Victoria, 1839, 7838Lt.

Journal of FRANCIS TUCKFIELD, 655.

Oxley Library, Brisbane

HARRY ANNING, Thirty Years Ago, OM172/123.

ARCHER Family Papers, including Durundur Diary, 1843–44, Some Letters Mainly from Australia, 1835–55.

Diary of Captain G. GRIFFIN at Whiteside, 1/1/47–16/5/49, OM72-42.

ROBERT HAMILTON, Diary at Mt Auburn Station, 18/11/61–3/9/62, OM68/28/Q2.

Reminiscences of Mrs ADELAIDE MORRISON OM69/8/f1.

Letter of T. W. WELLS to H. C. A. HARRISON, 24/10/61, OM66/2/f2.

Australian National Library

Church Missionary Society Records, FM4 1453–1523:
   JAMES GUNTHER, Letters 1837–42, Journals, 1837–40
   JOHN HANDT, Letters 1830–43, Journals 1832–41, Report 1835
   WILLIAM PORTER, Letters 1838–41, Journal 1838
   WILLIAM WATSON, Letters 1832–42, Journal 1832–37, Reports 1832–40.

HAGENAUER Letterbooks, MSS 3343.

MATHEW HALE Papers, FM4/1063.

London Missionary Society, FM 338–445:

Australian Letters 1798–1855
Australian Journals 1800–1842, including W. SHELLEY, R. HASSALL, L. E. THRELKELD.
Methodist Missionary Society Records, FM4 1398–1421:
Correspondence – In: Australia, 1812–26, 1827–36, 1837–42.
Microfilm of Australian Joint Copying Project.

RHODES HOUSE, OXFORD
Papers of the Anti-Slavery Society, MSS British Empire S22.
Letterbook of J. P. PHILLIPS, 1850–54, MSS Australia S1.

BOOKS, ARTICLES, THESES

Aboriginal Land Rights Commissioner, *Second Report*, AGPS, Canberra, 1974.
Aborigines Protection Society, *Correspondence Concerning . . . the Natives of Western Australia*, London, 1841.
―― *First Annual Report*, London, 1838.
―― *Second Annual Report*, London, 1839.
―― *Third Annual Report*, London, 1840.
―― *Fourth Annual Report*, London, 1841.
―― *Fifth Annual Report*, London, 1842.
―― *Seventh and Eighth Annual Reports*, London, 1844.
―― *Report of the Sub-committee on Australia*, London, 1838.
C. K. ALLEN, *Law in the Making*, 6th edn, Clarendon Press, Oxford, 1958.
S. AMOS, *Lectures on International Law*, London, 1874.
R. ANSTEY, *The Atlantic Slave Trade and British Abolition, 1760–1810*, Macmillan, London, 1975.
R. T. ANSTEY, 'Capitalism and slavery', *Economic History Review*, 21 Aug. 1968, pp. 307–20.
G. ARDEN, *Latest Information with Regard to Australia Felix*, Melbourne, 1840.
W. ATKINSON, 'Mediating the mindset of opposition: the Yorta Yorta case', *Indigenous Law Bulletin*, vol. 5, no. 15, Feb–March. 2002, p. 8.
B. ATTWOOD, 'Black and Lohans', PhD thesis, La Trobe University, 1985.
―― 'Writing the Aboriginal past', *Overland*, 114, May 1989, pp. 6–8.
Australian Council of Churches, *Aboriginal Land Rights*, ACC, Sydney, 1982.

Australian Indigenous Law Bulletin, vol. 1, no. 2, 1996, pp. 181–221.

Australian Indigenous Law Reporter, vol. 4, no. 1, Mar. 1999, p. 112.

Australian Mining Industry Council, *Aboriginal Land Rights*, AMIC, Dickson, ACT, 1985.

An Authentic and Interesting Narrative of the Late Expedition to Botany Bay, Aberdeen, 1789.

J. BAALMAN, 'The neglected profit à prendre', *Australian Law Journal*, vol. 22, Nov. 1948, pp. 302–5.

J. BACKHOUSE, *Extracts from the Letters of James Backhouse*, 3rd edn, London, 1838.

K. BAKER (ed.), *The Land Rights Debate: Selected Documents*, Institute of Public Affairs, Melbourne, 1985.

J. BANKS, *The Endeavour Journal, 1768–1771*, 2 vols, ed. J.C. Beaglehole, Angus & Robertson, Sydney, 1962.

S. BANNISTER, *Humane Policy: or, Justice to the Aborigines*, London, 1830.

R. H. BARTLETT, 'Aboriginal land claims at common law', *West Australian Law Review*, 15, 1983, pp. 293–346.

P. J. BAYNE, *A Makarrata: The Legal Options*, Aboriginal Treaty Committee, Canberra, 1981.

—— 'Symbolism', *Aboriginal Law Bulletin*, 5 Aug. 1982, pp. 5–6.

J. C. BEAGLEHOLE (ed.), *The Journals of Captain Cook on His Voyages of Discovery*, 2 vols, Cambridge University Press, Cambridge, 1955–1974.

G. BENNETT, 'Aboriginal title in the common law', *Buffalo Law Review*, 27, 1978, pp. 617–35.

J. E. BENNETT, *Historical and Descriptive Account of South Australia*, London, 1843.

T. BENNION, 'New Zealand: Indigenous Land Claims and Settlements' in B. Keon-Cohen (ed.) *Native Title in the New Millenium*, AIATSIS, Canberra, 2001.

H. BERMAN, 'The concept of aboriginal rights in the early legal history of the United States', *Buffalo Law Review*, 27, 1978, pp. 637–67.

J. BISCHOFF, *Sketch of the History of Van Diemen's Land*, London, 1832.

W. BLACKSTONE, *Commentaries on the Laws of England*, 2 vols, 18th edn, London, 1823.

—— *A Discourse on the Study of the Law*, Oxford, 1783.

Y. BLUM, *Historical Titles in International Law*, Nijhoff, The Hague, 1965.

C. BOLT & S. DRESCHER (eds), *Anti-Slavery, Religion and Reform*, Dawson, Folkestone, England, 1980.

J. BOUVIER, *A Law Dictionary*, 2 vols, 11th edn, Philadelphia, 1866.

G. BOWYER, *Commentaries on Universal Public Law*, London, 1854.

M. BRENNAN, *Australian Reminiscences*, William Brooks, Sydney, 1907.

W. H. BRETON, *Excursions in New South Wales, Western Australia and Van Diemen's Land*, London, 1833.

B. BRIDGES, 'Aborigines and the land question in New South Wales', *JRAHS*, 56, 2, June 1970, pp. 92–110.

J. L. BRIERLY, *The Law of Nations*, Clarendon Press, Oxford, 1928.

H. BROOM, *Constitutional Law*, 2 vols, 2nd edn, London, 1885.

C. BUXTON (ed.), *Memoirs of Sir Thomas Fowell Buxton*, London, 1848.

C. VAN BYNKERSHOEK, *A Treatise on the Law of War*, Philadelphia, 1810.

A. H. CAMPBELL, *John Batman and the Aborigines*, Kibble Books, Malmsbury, Vic., [1987].

E. CAMPBELL, 'Prerogative rule in New South Wales, 1788–1823' *JRAHS*, vol. 50, 1964, pp. 161–90.

D. CARNE, *Land Rights: A Christian Perspective*, Alternative Publishing Co-op., Chippendale, NSW, 1980.

T. H. CARSON, *Prescription and Custom*, Sweet & Maxwell, London, 1907.

A. C. CASTLES, *An Australian Legal History*, Law Book Co., Sydney, 1982.

—— 'The reception and status of English law in Australia', *Adelaide Law Review*, vol. 2, 1963, pp. 1–31.

Catholic Commission for Justice and Peace, *Aboriginal Land Rights*, CCJP, Sydney, 1985.

M. CHARLESWORTH, *The Aboriginal Land Rights Movement*, Deakin University, Waurn Ponds, Vic., 1983.

G. C. CHESHIRE, *The Modern Law of Real Property*, 10th edn, Butterworths, London, 1967.

C. CLARK, *A Summary of Colonial Law*, London, 1834.

P. COBBETT, *Leading Cases and Opinions on International Law*, 2nd edn, London, 1892.

F. COHEN, 'Original Indian title', *Minnesota Law Review*, 28, 1947, pp. 28ff.

—— 'The Spanish origin of Indian rights in the law of the United States', *Georgetown Law Journal*, 31, Nov. 1942, pp. 1–21.

D. COLLINS, *An Account of the English Colony in New South Wales*, 2 vols, ed. B. H. Fletcher, Reed, Sydney, 1975.

J. COOK, *The Voyage of the Resolution and Discovery 1776–1780*, ed. J. C. Beaglehole, Cambridge University Press, Cambridge, 1967.

Copious Remarks on the Discovery of New South Wales, London, 1787.

R. COUPLAND, *The British Anti-Slavery Movement*, 2nd edn, F. Cass, London, 1964.

R. CRANSTON, 'The Aborigines and the law', *University of Queensland Law Journal*, 8, 1973, pp. 62–78.

M. CRATON, 'Proto-peasant revolts: the late slave rebellions in the British West Indies', *Past and Present*, 85, Nov. 1979, pp. 99–125.

—— *Sinews of Empire*, Temple Smith, London, 1974.

—— *Testing the Chains*, Cornell University Press, Ithaca, 1982.

M. CRATON, J. WALVIN & D. WRIGHT, *Slavery, Abolition and Emancipation*, Longman, London, 1976.

E. S. CREASY, *First Platform of International Law*, London, 1876.

P. CUMMING & N. MICKENBERG, *Native Rights in Canada*, 2nd edn, Indian–Eskimo Association of Canada, Toronto, [1972].

J. DALRYMPLE, *An Essay Towards a General History of Feudal Property*, London, 1759.

D. B. DAVIS, *The Problem of Slavery in the Age of Revolution, 1770–1823*, Cornell University Press, Ithaca, 1975.

C. W. DE KIEWIET, *A History of South Africa*, Oxford University Press, London, 1941.

M. J. DETMOLD, *The Australian Commonwealth*, Law Book Co., Sydney, 1985.

J. DUNBAR, *Essays on the History of Mankind*, London, 1780.

E. ELSE-MITCHELL, 'Territorial conquest – Phillip and afterwards', *Victorian Historical Journal*, 43, Aug. 1975, pp. 429–46.

D. ELTIS & J. WALVIN (eds), *The Abolition of the Atlantic Slave Trade*, University of Wisconsin Press, Madison, 1981.

E. EVATT, 'The acquisition of territory in Australia and New Zealand', *Grotian Society Papers*, 1968, pp. 16–45.

H. V. EVATT, 'The legal foundation of New South Wales', *Australian Law Journal*, vol. 11, Feb. 1938, pp. 409–24.

E. J. EYRE, *Journals of Expeditions of Discovery*, 2 vols, London, 1845.

F. H. N., 'The case of Tanistry', *North Ireland Legal Quarterly*, vol. 9, May 1952, pp. 215–21.

W. FALCONER, *Remarks on the Influence of Climate . . .*, London, 1781.

A. FERGUSON, *An Essay on the History of Civil Society*, 3rd edn, London, 1781.

A. FORSTER, *South Australia*, London, 1866.

S. G. FOSTER, 'Aboriginal rights and official morality', *Push From the Bush*, 11 Nov. 1981, pp. 68–85.

E. J. B. FOXCROFT, *Australian Native Policy*, Melbourne University Press, Melbourne, 1941.

R. GIBBS, 'Relations between the Aboriginal inhabitants and the first South Australian colonists', *Proceedings of the Royal Geographical Society of Australasia, South Australian Branch*, 61, 1959–60, pp. 61–78.

J. GOEBEL, *The Struggle for the Falkland Islands*, Yale University Press, New Haven, 1927.

R. GOUGER, *South Australia in 1837*, London, 1838.

J. GRANT, *The Narrative of a Voyage of Discovery*, London, 1803.

G. GREY, *Journals of Two Expeditions of Discovery*, 2 vols, London, 1841.

I. GROSS, 'The abolition of Negro slavery and British parliamentary politics, 1832–3', *Historical Journal*, 23, 1980, pp. 63–85.

H. GROTIUS, *The Freedom of the Seas*, 1609, Oxford University Press, New York, 1916.

—— *The Rights of War and Peace*, 2 vols, London, 1738.

—— *De Jure Belli Ac Pacis: Libri Tres*, 2 vols, 1646, facsimile edn, Clarendon Press, Oxford, 1925.

G. H. HACKWORTH, *Digest of International Law*, vol. 1, US Govt Printing Office, Washington DC, 1940.

Sir MATTHEW HALE, *The History of the Common Law*, 2 vols, 5th edn, London, 1794.

W. E. HALL, *A Treatise on International Law*, 8th edn, Clarendon Press, Oxford, 1924.

H. W. HALLECK, *Halleck's International Law*, 2 vols, London, 1878.

S. HALLIFAX, *An Analysis of the Roman Civil Law Compared with that of England*, Cambridge, 1774.

A. HARRIS (An Emigrant Mechanic), *Settlers and Convicts*, Melbourne University Press, Melbourne, 1954.

S. HARRIS, *'It's Coming Yet . . .': An Aboriginal Treaty Within Australia Between Australians*, Aboriginal Treaty Committee, Canberra, 1979.

J. G. HEINECCIUS, *A Methodical System of Universal Law*, 2 vols, London, 1743.

J. HENDERSON, *Observations on the Colonies of New South Wales and Van Diemen's Land*, Calcutta, 1832.

F. VON DER HEYDTE, 'Discovery and visual effectiveness in international law,' *American Journal of International Law*, vol. 29, 1935.

The History of New Holland, London, 1787.

B. HOCKING, 'Aboriginal land rights: war and theft', *Australian Law News*, vol. 20, October 1985, pp. 22–5.

—— 'Does Aboriginal law now run in Australia?', *Federal Law Review*, 10, 1979, pp. 161–87.

—— Native Land Rights, Master of Law thesis, Monash University, 1970.

E. HODDER, *George Fife Angas*, London, 1891.

W. HOLDSWORTH, *An Historical Introduction to the Land Law*, Oxford University Press, 1927.

M. J. HOLLAND, *Life and Letters of Zachary Macaulay*, Edward Arnold, London, 1990.

T. E. HOLLAND, *The Elements of Jurisprudence*, Oxford, 1880.

—— *Lectures on International Law*, Sweet & Maxwell, London, 1933.

P. HOLLIS (ed.), *Pressure from Without in Early Victorian England*, Edward Arnold, London, 1974.

H. HOME, *Historical Law-tracts*, 2nd edn, Edinburgh, 1761.

—— *Sketches of the History of Man*, 2nd edn, Edinburgh, 1778.

J. HOOKEY, 'The Gove Land Rights Case', *Federal Law Review*, 5, 1972, pp. 85–114.

—— 'Milirrpum and the Maoris', *Otago Law Review*, 3, 1976, pp. 63–75.

J. HUNTER, *An Historical Journal*, London, 1793.

F. C. IRWIN, *The State and Position of Western Australia*, London, 1835.

P. JOHNSTON, *Extracts from Priscilla Johnston's Journal*, Carlisle, 1862.

J. KELLEHER, *Possession in the Civil Law, Abridged from the Treatise of von Savigny*, Calcutta, 1888.

A. S. KELLER, O. J. LISSITZYN & F. J. MANN, *Creation of Rights of Sovereignty through Symbolic Acts, 1400–1800*, Columbia University Press, New York, 1938.

D. G. KELLY, 'Indian title', *Columbia Law Review*, 75, 1975, pp. 655–86.

J. KENT, *Commentaries on American Law*, 4 vols, 11th edn, Boston, 1867.

R. J. KING, 'Terra Australia: Terra Nullius aut Terra Aboriginum', *JRAHS*, vol. 72, no. 2, Oct. 1986, pp. 75–91.

P. KNAPLUND, *James Stephen and the British Colonial System, 1813–1847*, University of Wisconsin Press, Madison, 1953.

E. W. LANDOR, *The Bushman*, London, 1847.

J. LATHAM, 'The migration of the common law: Australia', *Law Quarterly Review*, vol. 76, 1960, pp. 54–8.

T. J. LAWRENCE, *The Principles of International Law*, 4th edn, Macmillan, London, 1910.

S. D. LEDRUM, 'The "Coorong Massacre": natural law and the Aborigines at first settlement', *Adelaide Law Review*, vol. 6, Sept. 1977, pp. 26–43.

J. G. LEGGE (comp.), *A Selection of Supreme Court Cases*, 2 vols, Sydney, 1896.

L. LEICHHARDT, *Journal of an Overland Expedition in Australia*, London, 1847.

J. D. LESHY, 'Indigenous peoples, land claims and control of mutual development', *University of NSW Law Journal*, 8, 1985.

G. S. LESTER, Aboriginal Land Rights, 2 vols, D. Juris. thesis, Osgoode Law School, 1981.

—— 'Respect for Aboriginal occupation', *Australian Law Journal*, vol. 45, Dec. 1971, pp. 773–4.

G. LESTER & G. PARKER, 'Land rights: the Australian Aborigines have lost a legal battle, but . . .', *Alberta Law Review*, 11, 1973, pp. 189–237.

J. M. LIGHTWOOD, *A Treatise on Possession of Land*, London, 1894.

M. F. LINDLEY, *The Acquisition and Government of Backward Territory in International Law*, Longmans, London, 1926.

M. R. LITCHFIELD, 'Confiscations of Maori land', *Victorian University Law Review*, 15, 1985, pp. 335–62.

J. LOCKE, *Two Treatises of Government*, 4th edn, London, 1713.

J. LOGAN, *Elements of the Philosophy of History*, Edinburgh, 1781.

J. LORIMER, *The Institutes of the Law of Nations*, 2 vols, Edinburgh, 1883.

K. LYSYK, 'The Indian title question in Canada', *Canadian Bar Review*, 51, 1973, pp. 450–80.

J. MACDONNELL, 'Occupation and *res nullius*', *Journal of the Society of Comparative Legislation*, vol. 1, 1899, pp. 276–86.

P. G. McHUGH, 'Aboriginal title in New Zealand courts, *Canterbury Law Review*, 2, 1984, pp. 235–65.

R. C. MACLAURIN, *On the Nature and Evidence of Title to Realty*, C. J. Clay, London, 1901.

W. M. MACMILLAN, *Bantu, Boer and Briton*, Faber, London, 1929.

K. MADDOCK, *Your Land is Our Land*, Penguin, Ringwood, Vic., 1983.

H. S. MAINE, *Ancient Law*, London, 1861.

C. MANN, *Report of the Speeches Delivered at a Dinner Given to Capt. John Hindmarsh*, London, 1835.

H. T. MANNING, 'Who ran the British empire, 1830–1850?', *Journal of British Studies*, 5, 1965, pp. 88–121.

W. O. MANNING, *Commentaries on the Law of Nations*, 2nd edn, London, 1875.

J. MARSHALL, *The Constitutional Decisions of John Marshall*, 2 vols, ed. J. P. Cotton, Da Capo Press, New York, 1969.

G. F. VON MARTENS, *The Law of Nations*, 4th edn, London, 1829.

W. L. MATHIESON, *British Slavery and Its Abolition*, 2nd edn, Octagon, New York, 1967.

R. L. MEEK, *Social Science and the Ignoble Savage*, Cambridge University Press, 1976.

R. E. MEGARRY & H. W. R. WADE, *The Law of Real Property*, Stevens, London, 1957.

G. R. MELLOR, *The British Imperial Trusteeship, 1783–1850*, Faber, London, 1951.

N. H. MICKENBERG, 'Aboriginal rights in Canada and the United States', *Osgoode Hall Law Journal*, 9, 1971, pp. 119–55.

J. MILLAR, *The Origin of the Distinction of Ranks*, 3rd edn, London, 1781.

T. L MITCHELL, *Journal of an Expedition into the Interior of Tropical Australia*, London, 1848.

A. P. MOLLOY, 'The non-treaty of Waitangi', *New Zealand Law Journal*, 9, 1971, pp. 193–7.

G. F. MOORE, *A Descriptive Vocabulary of the Language in Common Use Amongst the Aborigines of Western Australia*, London, 1842.

B. MORSE, 'Canadian developments', *Aboriginal Law Bulletin*, 12, Feb. 1985, p. 8.

S. MOTTE, *Outline of a System of Legislation*, London, 1840.

R. H. MOTTRAM, *Buxton the Liberator*, Hutchinson, London, [1946].

D. J. MURRAY, *The West Indies and the Development of Colonial Government, 1801–1834*, Clarendon Press, Oxford, 1965.

C. J. NAPIER, *Colonization, Particularly in South Australia*, London, 1835.

P. W. NICHOLS, 'No clear title', *Quadrant*, Jan.–Feb. 1979.

S. NIND, 'Description of the native of King George's Sound', *Journal of the Royal Geographical Society*, 1, 1831.

D. P. O'CONNELL, *The Law of State Succession*, Cambridge University Press, 1956.

—— *International Law*, 2nd edn, 2 vols, Stevens, London, 1970.

W. OGILVIE, *An Essay on the Right of Property in Land*, London, 1781.

L. OPPENHEIM, *International Law*, 8th edn, Longmans, London, 1967.

N. PETERSON (ed.), *Aboriginal Land Rights: A Handbook*, AIAS, Canberra, 1981.

R. PHILLIMORE, *Commentaries upon International Law*, 4 vols, London, 1854.

D. PIKE, *Paradise of Dissent*, 2nd edn, Melbourne University Press, Melbourne, 1967.

N. J. B. PLOMLEY (ed.), *Friendly Mission: The Tasmanian Journals and Papers of George Augustus Robinson 1829–1834*, Tasmanian Historical Research Association, Hobart, 1966.

—— *The Aboriginal/Settler Clash in Van Diemen's Land, 1803–1831*, Queen Victoria Museum, Launceston, 1992.

F. POLLOCK, *The Land Laws*, London, 1896.

A. POLSON, *Principles of the Law of Nations*, London, 1848.

A. G. PRICE (ed.), *The Explorations of Captain James Cook in the Pacific*, Angus & Robertson, Sydney, 1958.

F. P. PRUCHA, *American Indian Policy in Formative Years*, 2nd edn, University of Nebraska, Lincoln, 1970.

S. PUFENDORF, *De Jure Naturae et Gentium*, 1688 facsimile edn, Clarendon Press, Oxford, 1934.

S. RACHEL, *De Jure Naturae et Gentium Dissertationes*, 2 vols, facsimile edn, Carnegie Institute, Washington DC, 1916.

J. REDDIE, *Inquiries in International Law*, Edinburgh, 1842.

H. REYNOLDS, *Frontier*, Allen & Unwin, Sydney, 1987.

—— *The Other Side of the Frontier*, Penguin, Ringwood, Vic., 1982.

H. RICHARD, *Memoirs of Joseph Sturge*, London, 1864.

K. ROBERTS-WRAY, *Commonwealth and Colonial Law*, Stevens, London, 1966.

J. L. ROBSON (ed.), *New Zealand: The Development of Its Laws and Constitution*, Stevens, London, 1954.

C. D. ROWLEY, *A Matter of Justice*, ANU Press, Canberra, 1978.

—— *Recovery, The Politics of Aboriginal Reform*, Penguin, Ringwood, Vic., 1986.

J. SALMOND, *Jurisprudence*, 10th edn, Sweet & Maxwell, London, 1947.

F. K. VON SAVIGNY, *Von Savigny's Treatise on Possession*, 6th edn, London, 1848.

R. L. SCHUYLER, *Parliament and the British Empire*, Columbia University Press, New York, 1929.

R. SCRUTON, F. BRENNAN & J. HYDE, *Land Rights and Legitimacy*, Australian Institute for Public Policy, Perth, 1985.

J. SELDEN, *Of the Dominion or Ownership of the Sea*, London, 1652.

Senate Standing Committee on Constitutional and Legal Affairs, *Two Hundred Years Later*, AGPS, Canberra, 1983.

N. SHARP, 'Following in the Seamarks? The Salt Water People of Tropical Australia', *Indigenous Law Bulletin*, Apr. 2000, p. 4.

M. SHAW, 'The Western Sahara case', *British Year Book of International Law*, Clarendon Press, Oxford, 1979.

T. SIMPSON, 'On the track to Geneva', *Aboriginal Law Bulletin*, 19, April 1986, p. 9.

J. SIMSARIAN, 'The acquisition of legal title to terra nullius', *Political Science Quarterly*, vol. 53, 1938, pp. 111–28.

B. SLATTERY, *Ancestral Lands: Alien Laws*, University of Saskatchewan, Saskatoon, 1983.

—— *Canadian Native Law Cases*, vol. 2, 1870–90, University of Saskatchewan, Saskatoon, 1981.

—— *French Claims in North America, 1500–59*, University of Saskatchewan, Saskatoon, 1980.

J. C. SMITH, 'The concept of native title', *University of Toronto Law Journal*, vol. 24, no. 1, 1974, pp. 1–16.

A. H. SNOW, *The Question of Aborigines*, Govt Printing Office, Washington DC, 1919.

South Australia in 1842, London, 1843.

C. E. STEPHEN (ed.), *Sir James Stephen: Letters*, privately printed, Gloucester, 1906.

G. STEPHEN, *Anti-slavery Recollections*, London, 1854.

J. STEPHEN, *Essays in Ecclesiastical Biography*, 4th edn, London, 1860.

J. STEPHEN (snr), *England Enslaved by Her Own Slave Colonies*, London, 1826.

J. K. STEPHEN, *International Law and International Relations*, London, 1884.

J. STEPHENS, *The Land of Promise*, 2nd edn, London, 1839.

J. STORY, *Commentaries on the Constitution of the United States*, 5th edn, Boston, 1891.

P. DE STRZELECKI, *Physical Description of New South Wales and Van Diemen's Land*, London, 1845.

F. C. STUART, A Critical Edition of the Correspondence of Sir Thomas Fowell Buxton, 2 vols, MA thesis, London University, 1957.

C. STURT, *Two Expeditions into the Interior of Southern Australia*, 2 vols, London, 1833.

R. J. SURTEES, 'The development of an Indian reserve policy in Canada', *Ontario Historical Society Journal*, 61, 1969, pp. 87–98.

C. J. TARRING, *Chapters on the Law Relating to the Colonies*, London, 1882.

H. TAYLOR, *A Treatise on International Public Law*, Callaghan, Chicago, 1901.

C. G. TEICHELMANN, *Aborigines of South Australia*, Adelaide, 1841.

H. TEMPERLEY, *British Antislavery, 1833–1870*, Longmans, London, 1972.

—— 'Capitalism, slavery and ideology', *Past and Present*, 75, May 1977, pp. 94–118.

W. TENCH, *Sydney's First Four Years*, Angus & Robertson, Sydney, 1961.

J. W. TEXTOR, *Synopsis of the Law of Nations*, 2 vols, facsimile edn, Carnegie Institute, Washington DC, 1916.

R. TORRENS, *Statement of the Origin and Progress of the Colony of South Australia*, London, 1849.

Tracts Relative to the Aborigines, London, 1843.

T. TWISS, *The Oregon Question Examined*, New York, 1846.

Uniting Church of Australia, *Aboriginal Land Rights*, UCA, Melbourne, 1983.

W. E. UNRAU, 'An international perspective on American Indian policy: the South Australian Protector and the Aborigines Protection Society', *Pacific Historical Review*, 45, 1976, pp. 519–38.

E. DE VATTEL, *The Law of Nations*, London, 1760; London, 1834; 3 vol. facsimile edn, Carnegie Institute, Washington DC, 1916.

F. DE VICTORIA, *De Indis*, Carnegie Institute, Washington DC, 1917.

T. A. WALKER, *The Science of International Law*, London, 1893.

—— *A Manual of Public International Law*, Cambridge, 1895.

R. WARD, *An Enquiry into the . . . Law of Nations in Europe*, 2 vols, London, 1795.

L. A. WARKOENIG, *Analysis of Savigny's Treatise on the Law of Possession*, Edinburgh, 1839.

J. WESTLAKE, *International Law*, Cambridge University Press, Cambridge, 1904.

F. WHARTON, *A Digest of the International Law of the United States*, 3 vols, Washington, 1886.

H. WHEATON, *Elements of International Law* (1836), Clarendon Press, Oxford, 1936.

G. G. WILSON & G. F. TUCKER, *International Law*, 5th edn, Harrap, London, 1936.

M. WILSON & L. THOMSON (eds), *The Oxford History of South Africa*, 2 vols, Clarendon Press, Oxford, 1909.

V. WINDEYER, 'A birthright and inheritance', *Tasmanian University Law Review*, 1, 5, Nov. 1962, pp. 635–69.

C. WOLFF, *Jus Gentium*, Clarendon Press, Oxford, 1934.

R. WOODESDON, *Elements of International Law*, London, 1779.

T. D. WOOLSEY, *Introduction to the Study of International Law*, Boston, 1860.

World Council of Churches, *Justice for Aboriginal Australians*, ACC, Sydney, 1981.

J. WRIGHT, *We Call for a Treaty*, Collins/Fontana, Sydney, 1985.

K. W. YATES, *Aboriginal Land Rights Explained*, Congregational Union of NSW, Sydney, 1972.

INDEX

Aborigines
  acquiescence and prescription
    46–7, 49, 54
  Banks on 37–8, 64–5, 68, 71, 209
  bushcraft 75
  early assumptions about 97
  and explorers 74–6, 83
  and feudal tenure 51–4
  identity with homeland 80–2
  as nomads 19, 20–3
  oral history of rights recognised
    201–3
  original proprietors 86–9
  population size 66–70, 75
  primeval simplicity 28–35
  proprietors of land 65, 72–4
  settlers' observations of 67–74
  society 70–2, 74, 80
  subjects of the Crown 48–9
  tenure, nature of 83–5
  trespass protocol 82–3
Aborigines Protection Society 75,
  92–3, 109, 113–14, 115,
  120
  Sydney branch 89, 106–7, 111
  see also British and Foreign
    Aborigines Protection Society
Adeyinka Oyekan v. Musendiku Adele
  238–9
Angas, George Fife 142–4
  proposes reserves 168–9
  questioned by Commons Select
    Committee 166–8
antislavery crusade
  Divine Displeasure arguments
    110–12
  equality as argument 112–15
  and land rights movement 97,
    99, 100–5
Arthur, Sir George 81
  on Batman Treaty 156–7
  on native title 121, 180
  and Port Phillip Protectors
    179–80
  and Tasmanian Aborigines 93–4,
    108, 114–15, 117, 180
Attorney General v. Brown [NSW]
  44–5
Australia
  area claimed by British 10,
    13–14, 15, 22–3, 45, 48,
    49–50, 51
  'uninhabited' 37–9, 40, 41–2, 74
Australind project 175–7

Banks, Sir Joseph
  questioned by Commons Select
    Committee 64–5
  reports on Aborigines 37–8,
    64–5, 68, 71, 209
Batman Treaty 153–4
  Colonial Office response 156–60
  implications of rejection 154–6,
    160, 161–2
Blackburn, Justice
  and Batman Treaty rejection 154,
    156
  and creation of reserves 170
  Gove Land Rights case (1971) 9,
    39, 52, 150–1, 152, 155–6
Blackstone's *Commentaries* 32,
  39–41, 52

Brennan, Justice 207, 210, 212, 213
British and Foreign Aborigines Protection Society 104–5
Burge, Pemberton and Follet legal opinion 159–60, 161
Buxton, Thomas Fowell 100–5, 106, 118, 119, 120, 122, 123, 128, 179

Canada
  application of English law 53
  compensation 239, 241–2
  native title 52, 59–60, 63, 246
  reserves 173–4
census of Aboriginal people 75
Chapman, Justice [NZ] 56–7
Coe v. The Commonwealth 39
Collins, David 72, 93
Colonial Office
  response to Batman Treaty 156–60
  and South Australian Colonization Commission 51, 121–5, 132–44
colonisation
  Blackstone's *Commentaries* on 39–41
  equated with slavery 106–7
  problem of land 115–18
colonists *see* settlers
common law
  applied to Aborigines 27–8
  and native title 57, 59–61, 180
  of possession 23–8
Commonwealth v. Yarmirr 223–6
compensation for acquired land 60–1, 170
  Adeyinka Oyekan v. Musendiku Adele 238–9
  Arthur on 114–15
  controlled by commissioners 133–4
  humanitarians on 117–18
  not mentioned to Phillip 50
  questioned by settlers 89
  use at Crown discretion 174–5
conflict
  Divine Displeasure argument 110–11
  equality arguments against 112–15
  land as source of 93–7
  settlers' concern over 109–10
  Tasmania 93–4, 107–8, 109, 117
conquest as rationale for tenure 43, 44–6, 48, 62
Cook, Captain James 11, 12, 62, 68, 69
Cooper v. Stuart 39
Croker Islanders' native title claim 223–6, 245–6
Crown prerogative and land acquisition 48–51

Das Voltas Bay penal settlement 62–3, 65
Deane, Justice 208–9
Denning, Lord 60, 61
desire for land, and possession 18
discovery as basis for possession 11–13, 17
Drummond, Justice 214–15

Edwardsen v. Morton [US] 234–5
equality arguments against slavery and conflict 112–15
explorers, contact with Aborigines 74–6, 83

Index

extinguishment of title 61, 160, 179, 226–7
Fejo v. The Northern Territory 230–2, 234
Eyre, Edward 74, 75–6, 94, 173

Fejo v. The Northern Territory 230–2, 234
feudal tenure and possession 51–4
first settlement, claims arising from 9–10, 13–14
fishing and hunting rights
  Croker Islanders' case 223–6, 245–6
  Yanner v. Eaton 221–3

Gaudron, Justice 208–9, 217, 218
Gawler, Lt-Col George 81, 88
  plan for reserves 162–5, 169, 172–3
Gipps, Sir George 58–9, 87, 196
Glenelg, Lord 51, 87
  and South Africa 119–20
  and South Australian colonists 121, 122, 123–5, 130
Gove Land Rights Case (1971) 9, 39, 52, 150–1, 154, 155–6
Great Reform Bill (1832) [UK] 99–100
Grey, Sir George 75, 82, 118, 123, 165
Gummer, Justice 217

Hunter, Captain John 68

Imperial Crown Land Sale Act (1842) 174–5
'inchoate' title to land 13
international law of possession 17–23

Jamaican slave rebellion 108
Johnson v. McIntosh 234

King, Philip Gidley 73–4
Kirby, Justice 217–18, 220, 225–6, 230–2, 233, 234

land
  area claimed by Britain 10, 13–14, 15, 22–3, 45, 48, 49–50, 51
  purchase and tenure 57, 61–2, 64–5
  as source of conflict 93–7
  see also compensation
land rights
  and antislavery movement 97, 99–105
  embodied in Letters Patent 132, 135–6, 150–1, 152, 162, 165
  extinguished 61, 160, 170, 226–7
  failure in South Australia 148–52
  reasons for not extinguishing 219–20
  settlers' understanding of 79–97
land rights movement
  in 1830s and 1840s 97, 99–125
  issue forgotten by 1848 192–203
land rights recognition
  compensation 153, 174–6, 192
  internationally 63
  reserves established 153, 162–74, 192
  right of use and occupancy 153–62, 192
Larrakia people 230–2
Letters Patent
  failure in South Australia 148–52

land rights embodied in 132,
  135–6, 150–1, 152, 162, 165
Lipan Apache Tribe v. The United States of America 240

Mabo, Eddie 205–6, 221, 245–7
Mabo and Others v. Queensland
  aftermath 221–43
  importance of 247–8
  jurisprudence in line with history 209–10
  overturns *terra nullius* 39, 206–7
Maconochie, Alexander 107
Marshall, Chief Justice (US) 55–6
missionaries 95
Murray Island land rights 207–11

Napier, Col. Charles 108, 114, 127–8
native title
  arguments against 89–93
  Chapman's definition 56–7
  extinguished 61, 160, 170, 226–7
  Marshall's principles of 555–6
  as part of common law 57, 59–61, 180
  pastoral leases 184–5
  Yorta Yorta claim 227–30
  see also fishing and hunting rights; land rights
New Zealand
  application of English law 52
  compensation 239, 242–3
  Land Claims Bill 161
  land purchase claim (1840) 161–2
  Maori native title 52, 56–7, 136, 152, 155, 162
  reserves 169, 174

nomadic people, possession of land 19–23, 40
Nootka Sound 63
Norman conquest as rationale for tenure 45
North America
  application of English law 52
  discovery as basis for possession 12–13
  land purchase 62
  meaning of *terra nullius* 15
North American Indians
  assumptions of primeval simplicity 28–9
  compensation 239–41
  extinguishment 234–5
  native title 42, 55–6, 58, 63, 155, 234–5
  reserves 171–2

occupation as basis for tenure 43–4, 46–7, 90
Olney, Justice 228–30

pastoral leases
  Aboriginal rights on 185
  exclude Aborigines 185–6
  implications of 188–90
  proposed by Grey 184–5
  protection of leaseholders 185–6
  and Wik case 187–90, 212–16
Phillip, Governor Arthur
  area of authority 49–50
  and numbers of Aborigines 68, 69, 75
  power to grant land 49, 50
Port Phillip Association 57
Port Phillip colony
  reserves 91–2, 95, 96, 145, 173
  see also Batman Treaty

Port Phillip Protectorate 179–83
possession of land
  Blackstone on 38–40
  in common law 23–8
  discovery as basis for 11–13
  in international law 17–23
  losing 18–19
  nomadic people 19–23, 40
  Roman law 11, 17, 32
  the seashore 26
prescription and tenure 46–7, 54
primeval simplicity view of
    Aborigines 28–35
Protectors of Aborigines 95–6
  to be appointed 123, 132–5
  on conflict 111
  Port Phillip Protectorate 179–83
  Robinson 180–3
  role of 141, 145–5, 180

res nullius 17
reserves
  and acceptance of land rights
    153, 162–74, 192
  Angas 168–9
  fate of initiatives 191–3
  Gawler in SA 162–5, 169, 172–3
  King 73–4
  meaning and purpose 171–3
  Robinson 168–9, 181–3
right of occupancy and tenure
    43–4, 46–7, 90
Robinson, George Augustus 88
  proposal for reserves 168–9,
    181–3
  in Tasmania 81, 95, 96
  in Victoria 91–2, 95, 96, 145,
    173
Roman law of possession 11, 23,
    40

settlers
  attitudes to reserves 170
  attitudes to own tenure 42–3,
    53–4
  concern at hostilities 109–10
  discuss land rights 1830s 146–8
  and forgetting of Aboriginal rights
    191–203
  knowledge of Aborigines 68,
    69–74
  understanding of Aboriginal
    tenure 79–97
slavery abolition and land rights 97,
    99, 100–5
South Africa
  Adeyinka Oyekan v. Musendiku Adele
    238–9
  conflict 119–20
  reserves 174
South Australian colony 125
  failure with land rights 148–52
  pastoral leases 186–7
  protector 132, 134, 135,
    141–4
  reserves 162–5, 169, 172–3
South Australian Colonization
    Commission
  and Colonial Office 51, 121–5,
    132–44
South Australian Constitution Act
  concerns with 127–9
  and Letters Patent 133, 135–6,
    150–2, 162
  'waste and uninhabited land'
    38–9
Stephen, George 110
Stephen, James
  acknowledges native title 85, 86,
    87–8
  on antislavery 100, 199, 118

on Batman venture 157–8,
159–60
Stirling, Governor 75
Sturt, Charles 83, 88, 162, 169
Symonds v. The Crown [NZ] 56–7

Tasmania
Arthur 93–4, 108, 114–15, 117,
180
conflict 93–4, 107–8, 109, 117
land rights 103–4, 107–8
Robinson 81, 95, 96
settlers' knowledge of Aborigines
81–2
Tench, Watkin 68, 69, 70
tenure, basis for 19
Aborigines were savages 42–3,
48
conquest 43, 44–6, 48, 62
Crown prerogative 48–51
expropriating under-used land
89–93
feudal tenure 51–4
native title 54–61
prescription and acquiescence
46–7, 54
purchase 57, 61–2, 64–5
right of occupancy 43–4, 46–7,
90
settlers' attitudes to own 42–3,
53–4
settlers' understanding of
Aboriginal 79–97
see also possession of land
terra nullius
Aboriginal attitude to 65
Coe v. The Commonwealth 39
Cooper v. Stuart 39
early assumptions about 67

justification for claim 16–17,
34–5, 38–9
meaning of 14–15, 34–5
overturned by Mabo 39, 206–7
and rejection of Batman Treaty
154–6, 160, 161–2
see also possession of land
Toohey, Justice 208, 210–11, 213,
217–19
Torrens, Sir Robert Richard 129,
131
Treaty of Waitangi 155, 242

United States
U.S. v. Santa Fe Railway Co. 234
see also North America; North
American Indians

Victoria
Robinson 91–2, 95, 96, 145, 173
*Yorta Yorta Aboriginal Community v.
The State of Victoria* 227–8
see also Port Phillip colony

Waitangi, Treaty of 155, 242
Waitangi Tribunal 242, 247
Wakefield, E.G. 175
Western Australia
Australind venture 175–7
Wik Peoples v. The State of Queensland
aftermath of decision 215–16,
220
and pastoral leases 187–90,
212–16, 217–19

Yanner v. Eaton 221–3
*Yorta Yorta Aboriginal Community v. The
State of Victoria* 227–8